T0328257

SCIENCE FOR POLICY HANDBOOK

Editorial Board

Emanuele Ciriolo

Anne-Mette Jensen-Foreman

Koen Jonkers

David Mair

Daniel Neicu

Jens Otto

Laura Smillie

European Commission, Joint Research Centre (JRC), Brussels, Belgium

Nicola Magnani

European Commission, Joint Research Centre (JRC), Petten, Netherlands

Jolanta Zubrickaite

European Commission, Joint Research Centre (JRC), Ispra, Italy

SCIENCE FOR POLICY HANDBOOK

Edited by

Vladimír Šucha

Marta Sienkiewicz

European Commission, Joint Research Centre (JRC),
Brussels/Belgium

ELSEVIER

Elsevier
Radarweg 29, PO Box 211, 1000 AE Amsterdam, Netherlands
The Boulevard, Langford Lane, Kidlington, Oxford OX5 1GB, United Kingdom
50 Hampshire Street, 5th Floor, Cambridge, MA 02139, United States

Copyright © 2020 European Union, Published by Elsevier Limited.
This is an open access publication under the CC-BY license (http://creativecommons.org/licenses/BY/4.0/).
Illustrations: © Adobe Stock, all rights reserved.
Icons in page corners: from thenounproject.com, under CC-BY license.

Notices

Practitioners and researchers must always rely on their own experience and knowledge in evaluating and using any information, methods, compounds or experiments described herein. Because of rapid advances in the medical sciences, in particular, independent verification of diagnoses and drug dosages should be made. To the fullest extent of the law, no responsibility is assumed by the publisher for any injury and/or damage to persons or property as a matter of products liability, negligence or otherwise, or from any use or operation of any methods, products, instructions or ideas contained in the material herein. Although all advertising material is expected to conform to ethical (medical) standards, inclusion in this publication does not constitute a guarantee or endorsement of the quality or value of such product or of the claims made of it by its manufacturer.

Library of Congress Cataloging-in-Publication Data
A catalog record for this book is available from the Library of Congress

British Library Cataloguing-in-Publication Data
A catalogue record for this book is available from the British Library

ISBN: 978-0-12-822596-7

For information on all Elsevier publications visit our website at
https://www.elsevier.com/books-and-journals

Publisher: Glyn Jones
Editorial Project Manager: Ali Afzal-Khan
Production Project Manager: Paul Prasad Chandramohan
Cover Designer: Alan Studholme

Typeset by TNQ Technologies

Working together
to grow libraries in
developing countries

www.elsevier.com • www.bookaid.org

Table of Contents

List of Contributors

Daniel Albrecht
European Commission
Joint Research Centre (JRC)
Ispra, Italy

William Becker
European Commission
Joint Research Centre (JRC)
Ispra, Italy

Anne-Katrin Bock
European Commission
Joint Research Centre (JRC)
Brussels, Belgium

Laurent Bontoux
European Commission
Joint Research Centre (JRC)
Brussels, Belgium

Pernille Brandt
European Commission
Joint Research Centre (JRC)
Brussels, Belgium

Paul Cairney
University of Stirling
Stirling, United Kingdom

Vera Calenbuhr
European Commission
Joint Research Centre (JRC)
Brussels, Belgium

Coralia Catana
European Commission
Joint Research Centre (JRC)
Brussels, Belgium

Jonathan Cauchi
European Commission
Joint Research Centre (JRC)
Brussels, Belgium

Massimo Craglia
European Commission
Joint Research Centre (JRC)
Ispra, Italy

Jorge Costa Dantas Faria
European Commission
Joint Research Centre (JRC)
Brussels, Belgium

Tom De Groeve
European Commission
Joint Research Centre (JRC)
Ispra, Italy

Marie-Agnes Deleglise
European Commission
Joint Research Centre (JRC)
Brussels, Belgium

Albane Demblans
European Commission
Joint Research Centre (JRC)
Brussels, Belgium

Marion Dewar
European Commission
Joint Research Centre (JRC)
Brussels, Belgium

Marcos-Dominguez-Torreiro
European Commission
Joint Research Centre (JRC)
Ispra, Italy

Leandro Elia
European Commission
Joint Research Centre (JRC)
Ispra, Italy

Elisabeta Florescu
European Commission
Joint Research Centre (JRC)
Brussels, Belgium

Silvio Funtowicz
Centre for the Study of the Sciences & the
Humanities (SVT)
University of Bergen
Bergen, Norway

Marton Hajdu
European Commission
Joint Research Centre (JRC)
Brussels, Belgium

Enkelejda Havari
European Commission
Joint Research Centre (JRC)
Ispra, Italy

Jiri Hradec
European Commission
Joint Research Centre (JRC)
Ispra, Italy

Ivan Kalburov
European Commission
Joint Research Centre (JRC)
Brussels, Belgium

d'Artis Kancs
European Commission
Joint Research Centre (JRC)
Brussels, Belgium

Maciej Krzysztofowicz
European Commission
Joint Research Centre (JRC)
Brussels, Belgium

Sven Langedijk
European Commission
Joint Research Centre (JRC)
Ispra, Italy

Carlo Lavalle
European Commission
Joint Research Centre (JRC)
Ispra, Italy

Sari Lehto
European Commission
Joint Research Centre (JRC)
Brussels, Belgium

Giulia Listorti
European Commission
Joint Research Centre (JRC)
Ispra, Italy

David Mair
European Commission
Joint Research Centre (JRC)
Brussels, Belgium

Manuel Palazuelos Martínez
European Commission
Joint Research Centre (JRC)
Seville, Spain

Giuseppe Munda
European Commission
Joint Research Centre (JRC)
Ispra, Italy

Sharon Munn
European Commission
Joint Research Centre (JRC)
Ispra, Italy

Daniel Neicu
European Commission
Joint Research Centre (JRC)
Brussels, Belgium

Jens Otto
European Commission
Joint Research Centre (JRC)
Brussels, Belgium

Nicole Ostlaender
European Commission
Joint Research Centre (JRC)
Ispra, Italy

Paolo Paruolo
European Commission
Joint Research Centre (JRC)
Ispra, Italy

Ângela Guimarães Pereira
European Commission
Joint Research Centre (JRC)
Ispra, Italy

Alexandre Pólvora
European Commission
Joint Research Centre (JRC)
Brussels, Belgium

Alessandro Rancati
European Commission
Joint Research Centre (JRC)
Brussels, Belgium

Jerry Ravetz
Institute for Science
Innovation and Society
Oxford University
United Kingdom

Adrien Rorive
European Commission
Joint Research Centre (JRC)
Brussels, Belgium

Paulo Rosa
European Commission
Joint Research Centre (JRC)
Ispra, Italy

Rossana Rosati
European Commission
Joint Research Centre (JRC)
Ispra, Italy

Eckehard Rosenbaum
European Commission
Joint Research Centre (JRC)
Ispra, Italy

Serge Roudier
European Commission
Joint Research Centre (JRC)
Seville, Spain

Jennifer-Ellen Rudkin
European Commission
Joint Research Centre (JRC)
Brussels, Belgium

Michaela Saisana
European Commission
Joint Research Centre (JRC)
Ispra, Italy

Fabiana Scapolo
European Commission
Joint Research Centre (JRC)
Brussels, Belgium

Sven Schade
European Commission
Joint Research Centre (JRC)
Ispra, Italy

Marta Sienkiewicz
European Commission
Joint Research Centre (JRC)
Brussels, Belgium

Catherine Simoneau
European Commission
Joint Research Centre (JRC)
Ispra, Italy

Laura Smillie
European Commission
Joint Research Centre (JRC)
Brussels, Belgium

Paul Smits
European Commission
Joint Research Centre (JRC)
Ispra, Italy

Eckhard Störmer
European Commission
Joint Research Centre (JRC)
Brussels, Belgium

Vladimír Šucha
European Commission
Joint Research Centre (JRC)
Brussels, Belgium

Lene Topp
European Commission
Joint Research Centre (JRC)
Brussels, Belgium

Xavier Troussard
European Commission
Joint Research Centre (JRC)
Brussels, Belgium

René van Bavel
European Commission
Joint Research Centre (JRC)
Seville, Spain

Maurits van den Berg
European Commission
Joint Research Centre (JRC)
Ispra, Italy

Pieter van Nes
European Commission
Joint Research Centre (JRC)
Brussels, Belgium

Stijn Verleyen
European Commission
Joint Research Centre (JRC)
Brussels, Belgium

Daniel Vertesy
European Commission
Joint Research Centre (JRC)
Ispra, Italy

Ian Vollbracht
European Commission
Joint Research Centre (JRC)
Ispra, Italy

Thomas Völker
Centre for the Study of the Sciences and the Humanities (SVT)
University of Bergen
Bergen, Norway

Marion Westra van Holthe
European Commission
Joint Research Centre (JRC)
Ispra, Italy

Foreword

The world is moving at unprecedented speed. Four fundamental changes are unfolding: the change in technology, which is triggering a societal transformation; climate change, which is increasingly urgent and the geopolitical shift from West to East. As is always the case, these changes are accompanied by wicked problems and unexpected effects, as well as potential benefits. It all represents a huge pressure on policy and politics to deliver fast and resolve complex problems. The time is short and stakes are high. Evidence, and in particular sound scientific evidence, is badly needed to inform policymaking. Science is however not fully ready. It is struggling to cope with the change. It is too entrenched in thematic silos, challenged by its own integrity problems, and very often alienated from society. All this, together with the explosion of data, in particular fake data, has created a toxic mix, which sometimes results in post-fact policy decisions and distrust of experts.

We, in the European Commission's science service (JRC), were in the middle of this storm. Although we undoubtedly delivered many important pieces of evidence in the fields of nuclear, food safety and security, environment, climate, energy, transport, resource efficiency, etc., we were often left at the fringe of the policymaking process. Struggling to deliver transversal knowledge, failing to foresee the foreseeable, unable to establish and communicate societal trends, we were increasingly ill at ease in our role.

It was time for a change. Our linear, deficit model of science for policy was in many respects exhausted. It was clear that we were going to face more and more difficulties in fulfilling our mission of 'putting science into the heart of EU policymaking'. So, we started to experiment with and develop a new model which we call Science for Policy 2.0.

First, we focussed on better understanding the ever-changing policy world by interacting more closely with policymakers. We introduced placements of scientists into policy departments and created safe places for mutual exchanges. A specific training programme for all scientific staff was designed to breed a new type of professionals, fully embracing both science and policy. The old science–policy demarcation model is no longer effective. Nor is it necessary. We believe that, with the right arrangements, we can provide objective advice to policymakers, while working alongside them.

Breaking the scientific silos was our second priority. The basic principle was to put science at the service of complex, transversal policy issues, rather than keeping it in comfortable, well-defined, scientific boxes. This entailed a dramatic change in our internal organisational structure and our work programme.

Thirdly, we entered into the new field of knowledge management, helping our colleagues in policymaking departments to deal with the deluge of data, information and knowledge which is now available. We have developed several tools, products and processes enabling effective vertical and horizontal knowledge management. Our aspiration is to deliver cutting edge knowledge when and where it is needed by policymakers.

Finally, we introduced a series of measures to improve our future-oriented competences and tools, like horizon scanning, foresight, trend analysis, quantitative modelling and complex science.

Our new approach was met with an unexpectedly fast, enthusiastic and positive response from our policy colleagues. Expressions like 'finally we can use your science', 'now we understand what you are doing' and 'we did not expect that science can be so useful' were frequently used at different meetings and bilateral encounters. It was very encouraging and motivated our staff to do more.

In this handbook, we set out 'what works' in the context of European policymaking in our experience but do not claim that this works everywhere. Still, we hope very much that it can be useful and inspire others. At the same time, we also raise a large number of questions, with further reflections to come as we learn from the responses to COVID-19. We know that we are only just beginning to get grips with this big, new field of Science for Policy 2.0 and that we need contributions from other players. That is why, as well as sharing our experiences, we want to trigger a discussion and collaboration with all who are interested in joining us in this endeavour.

Vladimír Šucha,
Director General of the Joint Research Centre of the European Commission (2014–2019)

How to Use the Handbook

Scientists and policymakers need to work closer together to deliver progress for our societies, economies and our planet. For the last 60 years, the Joint Research Centre (JRC) has been working at this interface for the European Union. This handbook collects what we have learnt about the science–policy environment and shares our vision, best practice and innovative ideas to deliver impact for our societies.

This short section gives readers some background on the JRC. Together with an overview of this book contents, this will provide the necessary context for understanding how you could apply our advice in your organisation.

Institutional Context of the JRC

The Joint Research Centre is part of a system of scientific support to the European Union. We are an integral part of the European Commission, which means we interact primarily with the Commission's policy departments. The Commission also receives independent scientific advice through the Scientific Advice Mechanism.[1] We work both with policymaking staff at all levels and their Commissioners and also with MEPs and national governments as well as other EU bodies such as the Committee of the Regions. We are independent from any national, commercial or civil society interests. We are publicly funded from the EU Framework Programme for Research & Innovation and the EURATOM research and training programme.

The JRC supports policymakers in all formal phases of the policy cycle: problem definition and agenda setting, policy formulation, implementation and evaluation. Policy development and decisions taken on the EU level are diverse: they cover broad thematic areas and have various forms (different legislative acts, recommendations, support mechanisms and programmes). Therefore, JRC's support to policymaking is quite diverse, and not all advice from this book will be 100% applicable to all cases. Still, main principles apply to most contexts in which we engage.

Our institutional setup gives us more direct access to policymakers than it is the case of research bodies (although the majority of our scientists work in campuses away from Brussels: in Italy, Spain, the Netherlands, Germany and Belgium). However, the institutional access does not itself guarantee a seamless relationship. Trust, good communication, innovations in processes and other aspects covered in this handbook determine the quality of collaboration and results. As any organisation, the Commission has its silos, which sometimes hinder collaboration and mean that we are familiar with many of the challenges other scientists experience when working outside government.

---

[1] https://ec.europa.eu/research/sam/index.cfm, accessed 05.05.2020

Differences Between Science for Policy and Academic Science

The fact that we are an organisation working not only in a policy context but also inside a policymaking institution is an important lens through which the advice in this book has to be interpreted. We support policymaking at all stages of the policy cycle and often in direct collaboration with policy departments. While we take a policy-neutral stance, our mandate is to produce science relevant for policy and generating insights needed to create policy options. Our values of integrity, openness, innovation, accountability and inclusiveness are aligned with those of a broader scientific community, but we have partially different drivers and incentives.

Many scientists in academia work driven purely by curiosity. Our areas of research priorities are strongly influenced by the policy agenda, with some room for exploratory research. We fully believe that all types of research are valuable, blue-sky and applied, including in arts and humanities. At the same time, this book may not be of so much use for researchers who do not have an ambition to have an impact on policy.

The following typology describes the differences between regulatory and academic science as developed by Ruggles (2004)[2], adapted for the EU context. Science and knowledge management for policy, though broader than regulatory science, encounter very similar challenges. In the majority of cases, we situate ourselves closer to the regulatory side of Ruggles' spectrum, and our advice in this book should be viewed as coming from that realm.

	REGULATORY SCIENCE	ACADEMIC SCIENCE
INSTITUTIONS	Government/industry	Universities
GOALS	Information needed to meet regulatory requirements and to provide reliable information for decision-makers. Research 'questions' are framed by legislators and regulators and have immediate social and economic implications.	Original research framed by scientists and driven by rational analysis, curiosity and expert judgement. To expand the understanding and knowledge of the natural world through an ongoing process of questioning, hypothesising, validation and refutation.
ROLE OF UNCERTAINTY	Predictive certainty is required by the political process and the legal system. Knowledge is frequently and necessarily generalised to situations very different from those in which the original data were collected. Uncertainty is unwelcome by the public, legislators and the courts.	Uncertainty is expected and 'embraced'.

---

[2] Ruggles, A., 2004. Regulatory vs. Academic Science. CIRES Center for Science and Technology Policy Research. http://sciencepolicy.colorado.edu/ogmius/archives/issue_9/research_highlight.html, accessed 05.05.2020

	REGULATORY SCIENCE	ACADEMIC SCIENCE
INSTITUTIONS	Government/industry	Universities
COMPLETENESS OF INFORMATION	Must frequently act before all the necessary information is developed.	Publish when a body of information has been developed, tested and validated.
STATISTICAL SIGNIFICANCE/ ACCEPTABLE ERROR/BURDEN OF PROOF	Often work with a legal mandate to minimise Type II error with the result that Type I error is increased.	Strive to minimise Type I error.
ROLE OF VALUES	Regulatory scientists are required to consider and work with the values of many including the public, politicians, the scientific community and the regulatory community.	Academic scientists work primarily with their own and their collaborators' values; seldom have to incorporate public or political values.
PRODUCTS	'Grey literature' baseline data, monitoring data and regulatory documents.	Published, peer-reviewed papers and books, presentations at professional meetings.
TIMEFRAME	Determined and driven by statute, regulation and the political process; finite and often quite short. Resolution of problems being reacted to is often crisis driven or driven by court-mandated timelines.	Open-ended; usually carried out relatively free of an urgent need for the information generated.
POLITICAL INFLUENCE	Directly exposed to political priorities.	Indirectly influenced by the researcher's own political philosophy and by their perception of the preferences of grant and tenure review committees.
ACCOUNTABILITY	Legislatures, courts and the public.	Professional peers.
INCENTIVES	Compliance with legal requirements, working for the public good.	Professional recognition, advancement in tenure system; university administration.

Collective versus Individual Reading of the Handbook

When writing about a transformation of science for policy practices, it is difficult to separate advice for individuals and organisations. Scientists need to adapt their ways to achieve more meaningful contributions to policy (and so do policymakers). Equally, a successful adaptation is not possible without a culture change in teams, collective new capacities, structural innovations, new priorities, incentives and mechanisms approved top-down, and broader organisational transformations (see Chapter 3).

Equally, not each and every person working in a science for policy context will have a direct contact with policymakers. However, science for policy is about teamwork and collaboration of multiple actors. Even if close interactions with policymakers are a task of a narrow group, the input they provide comes from a chain of reactions in the broader organisation. Having an understanding of what policymaking requires and how the science–policy interface operates (and differs from pure science) is helpful for everyone and helps increase the relevance of scientific support.

Some of the advice can seem overwhelming for one individual to implement. However, this book is not intended as a one-to-one recipe that can be realised by superhuman scientists. We hope that individual readers get inspired, incorporate what is possible in their personal behaviour and become the advocates for a broader change in areas beyond their immediate control. We want people to experiment and adapt our advice to their reality.

Finally, we need to acknowledge that it takes two to tango. The burden of improving the science–policy relationship does not fall on the scientists alone. We engage in transformative activities with policymakers, too, and are currently developing work targeting skills, capacities and understandings of science and evidence for policymakers. However, this book is written for scientists and knowledge organisations, as this is the essence of our practice.

What This Handbook Offers

The scope of this book focuses on *science for policy*: not on all science, nor on the details of the scientific process. The main ingredient which underpins all discussions about the effectiveness of science–policy interaction is good science. Writing this book, we consciously omit discussing tips for being a better scientist. We assume that every reader has the standards of excellence and integrity of their discipline well-internalised. Where we see a need to debate and learn more is the *science for policy*, the area which adds new questions to the scientific practice, bringing it closer to a political process, value-laden trade-offs and different timeframes.

We see a twofold urgency now: to increase the understanding of how science for policy is different from academic science and to bring science closer to policymaking. Throughout this book, we discuss the need for a transition from Science for Policy 1.0, where the two are separated and cross occasionally, to Science for Policy 2.0, where they are integrated. This change is a difficult one to navigate, but necessary if science is to bring meaningful input to solutions for our societies.

We are not expecting all science to change, but we see a need to keep experimenting with how working in a policy context changes the role of scientists. Aiming to achieve policy impact requires new tools and skills, rethinking norms and practices and figuring out ethical codes.

The vision and practices presented in this book are a work in progress that will continue to be updated. As such, it is crucial to note that the book was written before the global COVID-19 outbreak. This crisis has highlighted the importance of much of the advice given here and it has played a part in the JRC's response.

At the same time, such a significant crisis inevitably calls for deep reflection. We are committed to learning from this crisis, together with the wider science for policy community. It is necessary both to be prepared for any future crises, but also to constantly develop more and more effective and democratically legitimate science for policy mechanisms.

Section I of the book sets the scene and describes the current challenges with the deficit model of scientific advice to policy: Science for Policy 1.0. Section II presents the turn towards Science for Policy 2.0. There, co-creation and close, permanent collaboration between scientists and policymakers, as well as other policy actors – experts, stakeholders, citizens – is at the core of the model. We present the building blocks and its different facets: from institutional setup and individual skills, working through communities and engaging citizens, preparing for policy impact and defining relevant research questions, towards co-creating new policy processes with big data and AI. Section III describes cross-cutting approaches necessary to implement co-creation: anticipatory thinking with foresight, design for policy, learning from monitoring one's impact and knowing how to communicate strategically. Finally, Section IV takes the readers through the principles of Science for Policy 2.0 in selected specific areas, which are particularly crucial for robust evidence-informed policies.

The list below offers an overview of different topics covered in this book.

For Starters...

1. Check Foreword and Chapter 1 for a rationale why science and policymaking need a new relationship.
2. Check Chapter 2 to learn about Post-Normal Science and how it underpins Science for Policy 2.0.

Organisational and Institutional Setup

If you want to know...

1. ...how the JRC transformed itself in recent years to be a more agile knowledge for policy organisation, check Chapter 3.
2. ...about our Knowledge Centres, organised around multidisciplinary policy areas and stimulating cross-boundary conversations on what knowledge is needed, check Chapter 6, 16 and 19 for specific examples.
3. ...about our Competence Centres of policy-relevant methodologies, helping policymakers apply them to generate relevant evidence, check Chapter 3 and 12 for specific example.
4. ...how we systematically help scientists and policymakers get to know each other better, check Chapter 6.
5. ...how we support the interaction of science and policy through the work of in-between facilitators, check Chapter 6.
6. ...how we plan and coordinate the work of the entire organisation so that it is both scientifically excellent and useful for policy, check Chapter 6 and 3.

New Skills, Competencies and Behaviour for Moving Towards Science for Policy 2.0

If you want to know...

1. ...what collective skills of staff are needed to be an effective science for policy organisation, check Chapter 4.
2. ...how to strategically plan for impact of scientific evidence, check Chapter 5.
3. ...how to monitor the uptake and impact of evidence on policy and society, and later collectively learn from that monitoring, check Chapter 14.
4. ...what mechanisms to use to translate policy problems into research questions, check Chapter 6.

5. …how to navigate interests which interfere into Science for Policy 2.0 and evidence-informed policymaking, check Chapter 10.

Adapting to Complexity

If you want to know…
1. …how to mobilise collective intelligence of staff, partners and stakeholders through communities of practice, check Chapter 7.
2. …what a Policy Lab approach - creating a space for exploration, experimentation, openness and understanding - can offer, check Chapter 13.
3. …how to promote an anticipatory culture in policymaking and knowledge generation, e.g., through horizon scanning, megatrends monitoring, scenario building, speculative design and serious games, check Chapter 12.
4. …how to explore problems systemically, gain a better understanding of complexity of given issues and contribute to more holistic problem definitions or solutions, check Chapter 11 and Chapter 13.
5. …how big data can transform the landscape of evidence for policy, and policymaking itself, check Chapter 9.

Science for Policy 2.0 in Specific Areas

If you want to know…
1. …what the principles for evidence-informed advice in a crisis are and which tools are appropriate for such context, check Chapter 16.
2. …which quantitative modelling approaches prove useful in the policy cycle, including uncertainty and sensitivity analysis, multicriteria decision analysis, composite indicators and ex-post impact evaluation, check Chapter 18.
3. …how to support regional development and innovation strategies with tailored solutions involving multiple stakeholders in the process, check Chapter 19.
4. …how to better understand human behaviour and use this knowledge to design more effective policies, including using randomised controlled trials, experiments or qualitative research, check Chapter 17.

Outreach, Partnerships and Collaboration

If you want to know…
1. how to include citizens both in scientific projects and in broader deliberation on policy objectives, values and solutions, check Chapter 8.
2. …how we run institutional science for policy communications, including insights on key principles, target groups, as well as increasing clear writing and effective visualisation skills, check Chapter 15.
3. …how to mobilise collective intelligence of staff, partners and stakeholders through communities of practice, check Chapter 7.
4. …how we promote evidence-informed policymaking with national and regional parliaments, check Chapter 6.

Science for Policy 1.0: Deficit Model

Image: Vaclav - https://stock.adobe.com/be_en/images/green-frog/164733972?prev_url=detail
Icon in page corners: Bridge icon by Phạm Thanh Lộc, from the Noun Project (https://thenounproject.com/search/?q=bridge&i=2303977)

Against the Science-Policy Binary Separation: Science for Policy 1.0

Authors: Marta Sienkiewicz, David Mair

Key takeaways:

- Science and policy are often seen as different worlds, 'two communities' which operate under different regimes.

- Their relationship requires more contact, cooperation and co-creation: science and policy separation prevents us from solving complex problems.

- Policymaking is not, as often assumed, a regular and linear cycle. Knowledge and evidence enter the process at many stages and in dispersed ways. With information overload, interests and even deliberate disinformation, it is unclear where to place trust. Closer links of scientists and policymakers build relationships necessary for sense-making.

- However, technocracy is not the answer. Policy is not made by science, or at least not science alone. It includes values, political concerns and a need to build majority coalitions. Evidence needs to be useful for developing policy solutions, but it will not replace politics.

- Co-creation, understood as interlinked collaborative approaches aimed to increase dialogue, trust, understanding of needs and diversity of input, can increase the importance and impact of evidence for the benefit of public policies.

Science for Policy Handbook
http://dx.doi.org/10.1016/B978-0-12-822596-7.00001-7

Copyright © 2020 European Union,
Published by Elsevier Limited.

A traditional view of the science–policy interface portrays two separate communities, each with their own principles, cultures and ways of working. Science and policy differ on multiple grounds: in the way they define and approach problems and solutions, the nature of their questions, timeframes and time horizons, attention spans and breadth of perspectives, attitudes to uncertainty. These contradictions are further heightened by the challenging environment in which they meet: messy multilateral political processes, floods of information, a changing media landscape and the growing importance of social media, both for content dissemination and identity building for voters.

Science has been involved in policy for many years, so the calls advocating for its prominent role are not revolutionary. However, 60 years since the inception of the JRC, we acknowledge that the times have changed. Supporting policy at arms length is not enough. The urgency of complex societal problems relies on the right combination of the best knowledge and a collective dialogue about values, to define directions for the future. This requires a new, more effective model of science–policy co-creation, in which not only scientists but policymakers should be involved.

Policy Is Not All (or Even Mainly) About Science

At the JRC, a scientific organisation with a mandate to inform policy, we are by definition convinced about the value of scientific evidence for public policy. However, this value should not blind scientists to the limits of scientific evidence in addressing policy issues.

The ideal of 'evidence-informed policy' is of a system of government where all pertinent evidence is considered (provided by a value-free scientific process), the full range of opinions listened to and a decision taken that optimises the values preferences of the citizens. The debate about the facts ('analytical') is ideally clearly delineated from the debate about values ('normative'), with a linear policy cycle which establishes the evidence base, agrees the normative objectives of the policy before proceeding to identify options and then weighs their costs and benefits in order to make a choice. For various reasons, this model does not represent the reality of evidence-informed policymaking.

As Jerome Ravetz (1999) claimed, scientists often live with a flawed assumption about the nature of the policy environment, as if it welcomed routine puzzle solving by experts as an adequate knowledge source for decisions. In reality, the fundamental reason why evidence-informed policymaking is a difficult process is the fact that policy problems are of a different category to scientific problems because they not only have an analytical, scientific dimension but also a normative, values-related one. Policymaking needs to simultaneously find the necessary trade-off between the different values at stake and to find practical solutions to policy problems. Policy problems are 'wicked' (Rittel and Webber, 1973), which means that they cannot be unambiguously and neutrally defined, nor ever really solved. Their resolution, which has to be repeated over time, depends on political assessments (see more in Chapter 6).

Policymaking is a complex process that includes both an analytical and a normative dimension. This leads to a twofold problem. On the one hand, scientists and policymakers will define problems differently: one as something to solve technically, the other as a much more social process of negotiating solutions that have majority support. Therefore, their thinking and

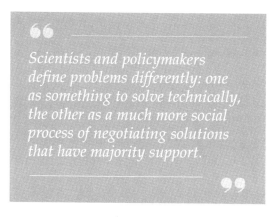

> *Scientists and policymakers define problems differently: one as something to solve technically, the other as a much more social process of negotiating solutions that have majority support.*

problem-solving strategies will be different, given that policymakers need to find the best knowledge and make sure it leads to a consensus or at least a majority on values, i.e., is both technically and politically feasible. This parallel normative track interferes in the analytical one, as the norms and values must determine what evidence is commissioned, selected and how it is framed. Moreover, these ways of working form the culture of these groups, which shapes what they expect from their interlocutors. Unsurprisingly, they are sometimes puzzled why the other side is not playing by the same rules.

This duality does not make it impossible to include science in a policy process, but it is not an easy task, nor one to be taken for granted. The quality of the solutions notwithstanding, policy decisions can certainly be taken without science. Scientists and policymakers do not recognise sufficiently that the desire to inform public policy through scientific knowledge and evidence is not a law of nature but a value proposition that needs to be argued for. The case for informing policy through evidence needs to be made more explicitly by those who support it in a way that resonates with the values of citizens, not only of fellow scientists.

There are different types and definitions of evidence, but the assessment of them is also affected by these different standpoints of science and policy. Scientists can reject some of them as 'unscientific'. Policymakers, due to the nature of their problems, need to take into account different types of evidence as legitimate (Schultz, 2013) such as their judgement of the trade-off between competing values, political ideologies, religious principles, their moral sense of right, anecdotes and a word of mouth, and so on. These concerns are all valid and must be incorporated in the decision-making, and the right mix of them is not scientifically quantifiable. After all, public debate in a democracy by definition must contain factual arguments and moral reasoning, the latter of which cannot be solved scientifically. Decisions in a democracy are therefore not cost–benefit optimisation equations. The values bases for policymaking may also be a better guide to public and political reactions, and thus the level of support for and success in the implementation of a policy.

A political process limited to claims based only on *scientific* consensus would therefore amount to a form of scientism and an alienating technocracy. Antiintellectualism and antiscience views are already becoming troublesome for scientists (albeit more nuanced that could be perceived, see Rutjens et al., 2018), and any claims to higher *moral* ground could heighten that trend. Therefore, with all good will to see their science influence policy, scientists need to understand that designing public interventions is a delicate balancing act between societal values, political priorities, competing interests and scientific knowledge making up evidence. The fact that scientists produce empirical data does not follow that they as a group should have a more privileged voice for their values in public decision-making than any other group.

Whether a solution to a question falls more under the realm of science or that of policymaking depends on two factors: how technical an issue is and at what point of policy intervention it is considered. For instance, moral questions, such as abortion regulation, leave almost no room for scientific input, which cannot become the basis of a solution. Pielke (2007) used the cases of tornado response, ecstasy regulation and abortion to illustrate how a general principle of balancing between the science and political realm depends on how technical an issue is (see also an interesting discussion in Craig, 2019). Equally, science can play a more leading role at the level of policy implementation, as most often the crucial debates on values are resolved before a policy is adopted.

Not All Science Becomes Evidence Useable in Policy

In a digital world filled with unfiltered, decentralised information, everyone can claim to have some kind of 'evidence' backing their position. How should we define *legitimate* evidence to be systematically incorporated into the policy processes?

The terms 'science' and 'evidence' are often used interchangeably, but since evidence is a broad and ambiguous category with connotations beyond the realm of science, it is essential to clarify its meaning. In the context of public policy 'knowledge based in science is presented as evidence to support reasons used in a policy argument (…) [it] is broadly taken to mean data, information, concepts, research findings, and theories that are generally accepted by the relevant scientific discipline' (Prewitt et al., 2012, pp. 7–8). Hence, evidence in the policy process provides a basis to help identify policy options and reach a decision, even if ultimately it happens by balancing knowledge with values and political priorities. However, as opposed to the justice system, judgements made using scientific evidence do not carry claims to absolute moral right or wrong.

Not all science automatically becomes evidence *for policy*. The road from science to evidence leads through an interpretative process and there is an inherent inferential gap between scientific findings and the 'real-world' conclusions (Douglas, 2009). Evidence always means *science contextualised*. Justin Parkhurst (2016) offered a useful framework for defining good evidence and good *use* of evidence in policymaking. It implies that while the overall scientific production is rich and potentially relevant for policy, only a fraction of it will become evidence useable for a particular policy decision. According to Parkhurst, good evidence for policy needs to fulfil three criteria to be appropriate for a specific policy in question:

- address policy concern at hand, instead of any loosely related topic;
- be constructed in ways useful to address policy concern, methodologically able to answer the questions at hand;
- be applicable to a local policy context.

Therefore, assessing whether the arguments made in a policy context are backed not just by any science but by proper scientific evidence relevant to the issue should be a concern in the policy process. It should be a task for scientists and scientific advisors.

Such contextualisation cannot happen without strong collaboration and sound mutual understanding between science and policy. For this, the science for policy field must move away from 1.0 model of parachuted, ad hoc advice delivered either unsolicited when it suits scientists, or in rush when policymakers suddenly need it. Instead, it should embrace the continuous, long-term relationships with policy stakeholders, throughout the policy processes. To be relevant and incorporated into policy and societal debates, scientists cannot avoid engaging with the world outside of science (more on how to reconcile it with traditional norms of science in Chapters 5 and 10).

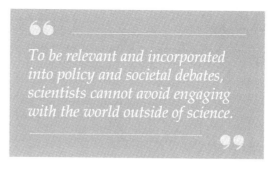

> To be relevant and incorporated into policy and societal debates, scientists cannot avoid engaging with the world outside of science.

At the JRC, both in our conceptual thinking and in our daily practice as a scientific organisation, 'evidence' is inevitably understood as the result of a scientific process. It extends beyond impact evaluations or formal and informal data related to intervention programmes, as it is often framed (Ball, 2018). We link the definition of evidence with the values and standards of robust, systematic scientific methods, their objectivity, transparency and openness for scrutiny. Democracy may not be all about science, but science remains the most reliable and systematic way of gathering knowledge about the world, even if not perfect. Simple opinions and anecdotes are not evidence, although we all, as citizens, have the right to them. They form an indispensable part of the policy ecosystem, give crucial context to final decisions and affect the success of a policy. If evidence is to be appreciated and incorporated in the process, they cannot be neglected (Oliver et al., 2014), and often can be incorporated into the evidence generation (see, for instance, Chapter 8). Still, they do not *constitute* evidence.

In View of Trade-offs, Why Care About Evidence?

While almost all politicians and civil servants say that they appreciate how useful evidence is in building policy solutions (Andrews, 2017; Talbot and Talbot, 2014) and are often ready to support 'evidence-based policy', the perception often remains that the uptake of research knowledge in government is low (Head et al., 2014). The recent 'post-fact' debate also appears to have devalued the place of science in policymaking, with some politicians pointing to the alleged citizens' fatigue with expertise, although others saying this is exaggerated (Institute for Government, 2016; Jasanoff and Simmet, 2017).

There is no growing trend in the high incidence of policy being uninformed, and the insufficient use or misuse of science is nothing new (Oreskes and Conway, 2010). Nonetheless, our democratic system, underpinned by the values of the rule of law and enlightened decision-making, assumes that the policy process is at least to a large degree rational. Politicians have at least paid lip-service to the value of expertise and rationality. In more and more countries, more radical views on the role of facts in policymaking appear to gain acceptance. There is also some evidence of acute disinformation on politically salient (or politicised) questions, like migration or vaccines. Hence, there is some urgency to strengthen the thinking and capacities of advocates for evidence-informed policy. Scientists and their organisations are natural contenders for that title.

Using evidence in policymaking clearly is a choice, given multiple other bases for policy interventions and decisions (Newman, 2017). But if we acknowledge that the policy decisions are legitimately influenced by a mix of factors and result from a political trade-off, why should we care about a strong role of evidence in this process? In our view, two arguments make a pragmatic case for evidence-informed policymaking, not reducible to values and simple preferences: 1) the complexity of global policy problems and the interconnectedness of global policymaking/governance systems and 2) the challenging environment that they create for development of robust, successful policies. The object and environment of policymaking are so complex that without evidence, we are at high risk of unintended consequences (Chalmers, 2003).

In the era of the 'wicked problems' (Rittel and Webber, 1973), the solutions developed without sufficient expertise and evidence are likely to fall short of success. The scale and inevitability of unintended consequences are too large to risk a nonevidence-informed decision. Costly regulatory or investment errors would likely follow. Equally, the interconnectedness of the global governing systems means that the spill-over effects of one policy action often bring consequences for other actors, on a global scale. Real responsibility can rarely be assumed only for the area directly under one's formal jurisdiction, and the price of action extends beyond direct consequences in a local context. Complex governance also brings with it many actors with particular interests and often unequal power, which create ground for 'proxy wars': situations in which facts – and 'alternative facts' – are then exploited to back up value-based positions.

Using knowledge in a structured way can help distinguish values and power dynamics from facts in these debates. Even though science will not resolve the underlying value conflicts, it can help disentangle facts and values and refocus the debate. This can be achieved when science moves from periodical advising to participating on equal terms throughout the entire process. Advocating for the incorporation of scientific knowledge in the policy process is a value choice, even if it often seems like an *obvious* choice to scientists. There are no guarantees that an evidence-informed solution will inevitably be successful, but given the complexities, it may be the best bet.

Mismatches in Supply and Demand: What Separates Science and Policy?

Global science provides a cornucopia of knowledge of robust quality and relevance to nonscientific audiences. If policymakers and politicians want to arrive at working solutions, they have more than enough material to consult in their decision-making. Thus, this supply–demand equation should give a good basis for collaboration. Then why is engaging in evidence-informed policymaking an extremely difficult process, more of an art than pure science (Gluckman, 2014)? We offer two major explanations: one related to the differences between science and policy and their resulting separation. A 'Two-Communities Theory', stating that science and policy form distinct worlds, was formulated already in the 1970s (Caplan, 1979), and despite obvious evolutions (Newman et al., 2016), it remains relevant in some aspects. The other relates to broader factors which operate around the science–policy interface and limit the possibilities of even well-meaning actors on both sides.

What Divides Science and Policy?

The current separation between science and policy can be partly explained by large differences in institutional and organisational setups. Science advisory structures are often separated from the policymaking process, while universities and research institutes often do not have easy channels of access to policymaking. However, institutional setups are not all to blame.

Cultural divisions between science and policy are perhaps more pertinent. The two are so distinct that any fruitful collaboration between them requires major adaptations from both sides. Their practical modes of operation, as outlined earlier in this chapter, are difficult to align. The lack of flexibility to move beyond them poses a threat to successful evidence-informed policymaking, even despite plentiful supply and demand of knowledge. Mutual adjusting of norms and expectations can only be achieved through dialogue, relationships and mutual learning. Detached science, 'injected' without proper context, can only be half effective at best.

- *Timeframes*

A common cartoon image of a policymaker as someone facing urgent deadlines and demanding all inputs for yesterday is not so far from reality. With increasing pressures on governments to deliver, the life of policymakers is extremely fast-paced, with even tighter schedules for decision-makers (Andrews, 2017). This gives rise to spontaneous requests for knowledge and evidence, with high expectations and difficult timelines for scientists. Policy develops fast and expects answers to problems almost immediately, while creation of scientific knowledge, especially through new research, can take years. In such an environment, especially when scientists are not systematically kept in the policymaking loop, the effectiveness of scientific support is limited.

- *Attention Span*

Policymakers lack the time necessary to digest complex information and expect simple, clear messages. Given the typical scientific standards of methodological transparency and objectivity, researchers (with good intention!) often present material which is far too detailed and thus inadequate for the reality of decision-makers. The situation is less extreme for more operational, junior policymakers, but the mismatch often still exists. This gives little time for deeper reflection and making optimal use of evidence, and may result in ignoring scientists' message entirely, if it fails to capture the attention or loses the competition with a more gripping policy brief or communication. For more on how to adapt to this reality in your communications efforts, turn to Chapter 15.

It is also true that researchers, especially academics with additional teaching responsibilities, are extremely busy as well. Their tight schedules affect their willingness to engage with policymakers in the first place. Especially in situations where science is separated from and not solely mandated to contribute to policy, researchers have to juggle competing priorities, as a result often excluding policy engagement. Their current incentive structure for career progression puts it low on the priority list. However, once they include it within their activities, they tend to overestimate the amount of detail policymakers can process, simply because in their working culture, there is much more room for slower reflection.

- *What Counts as Future?*

Scientists and policymakers also differ in their usual definitions for what constitutes long-term and short-term visions and solutions. Purely scientific questions do not have strict deadlines. While research efforts are structured through funding cycles and specific projects, the production of knowledge is never finite. The horizons of scientific enquiry do not need to be limited to short-term timelines. Policymakers, on the other hand, most often prioritise short-term goals over long-term objectives. As Andrews (2017, p. 4) points out, ministers – as an example of particularly high-level decision-makers – have limited time to achieve their impact. Their typical mandates do not necessarily correspond to election calendars: ministers rotate much more often, which instils a mode of constant campaigning. On top of pressure for delivering, it also has a negative impact on the state of institutional memory. Both have important consequences for the science for policy relationship: loss of analyses already delivered, reinventing the wheel, and lack of incentive to think about the cycles ahead. In such a climate, policymakers rarely have comprehensive knowledge strategies which could strengthen the anticipatory culture and lessen the burden of unexpected urgent requests dictated by the fast pace of policymaking.

Scientists will not easily change this pattern of behaviour. Nonetheless, they may prepare themselves better by understanding the drivers of their policy areas, state of the debates, and anticipating knowledge needs on the policymakers' agendas. Chapter 12 explores the techniques for building this anticipatory culture.

- *Attitudes Towards Uncertainty*

Science by definition incorporates uncertainty in its pursuit. Scientists are therefore more aware of its inevitability and perhaps more able to accept it as part of the interpretative process. Policymakers are less comfortable with scientific uncertainty and expect scientific knowledge to be 'more certain' than other sources. They also know that uncertainty in a policy proposal can undermine its success or even put an end to it (Oreskes and Conway, 2010). Therefore, communicating inherent uncertainty of scientific findings or policy projections in a constructive way is a difficult but also extremely important aspect of the science–policy interaction, which can have a decisive impact.

All these differences become even more heightened when an issue enters an openly political debate. The stakes are then usually even higher, with a debate that is less technical and less attentive to detail and nuance.

What Are the Challenges in the Science–Policy Environment?

- *Myth of a Mechanistic Linear Policy Cycle*

To understand the difficult reality of informing policy through evidence, one must also realise how misleading the metaphors describing policymaking really are (Cairney, 2016; Cairney et al., 2019). The famous policy cycle is far from a logical and structured sequence of events, especially once an issue enters a political debate. The debates move in different directions and sources of knowledge influencing it are both numerous and difficult to scrupulously map. The ambiguity and complexity of policy problems, the inherent uncertainty of evidence (whether from knowledge gaps, poor communication of knowledge, conflicting evidence or information overload) and the growing plurality of values preferences and difficulties in organising effective debates about values (including distinctly from analytical debates) mean that the policy process is very far from the ideal linear discussion.

The picture is even messier when one realises that the policy cycle would not repeat itself without people, who bring their values, inherent human biases and mental shortcuts into the process. Add to it multiple political interests and considerations and policymaking becomes more of a drama (Greenhalgh and Russell, 2006) than a calculated machine. While this chaos does not by default predetermine wrong decisions, often a perfectly rational course of action in the eyes of a scientist may be unacceptable due to the complexities of this process (Rittel and Webber, 1973).

There are no convenient, predetermined slots in the policy cycle where evidence can be mechanically injected and followed by a direct reaction. Timing is of course vital as policy processes are not random, but engagement happens not through one-off contributions in a defined stage of the cycle, but rather through continuous interactions with multiple actors. And even if evidence manages to reach the policy- and decision-makers at the right time, its final role in the debate and the decision is far from predictable.

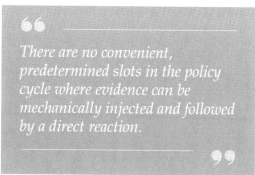

> *There are no convenient, predetermined slots in the policy cycle where evidence can be mechanically injected and followed by a direct reaction.*

- *Information Overload*

Evidence-informed policymaking is highly difficult simply because we are flooded with too much knowledge and information. Sounds paradoxical? Although at first glance, we may appreciate a large supply of easily available facts, with this abundance of knowledge come issues of quality, robustness, choice and trust.

The amount of information available at our fingertips has skyrocketed throughout the years. We dispose of more and more sources of information, but do not necessarily have more consensus or clarity on *knowledge* that emerges out of it. Navigating this ocean of sources is almost physically draining and may pose further threats to rationality in decision-making (see Part 3 of Hallsworth et al., 2018). First and foremost, however, it creates several structural difficulties for using scientific evidence for policymaking, such as

- the challenge of properly assessing the quality of information, for the policymakers, decision-makers and the public, and ensuring that it is right and relevant for a given context;
- the competition between science and other sources of knowledge;
- the issues of legitimacy of using one piece over the other;
- the possibility to find 'evidence' backing any position;
- the lack of a universal canon and a broad community of knowledge (manifested in echo chambers and filter bubbles), where a real debate would be possible, leading to more consensus and clarity on the issues at stake.

All these structural challenges mean that making sense of knowledge is increasingly difficult, especially under time pressure in complex policy environments.

- *Media Landscape and Internet*

Too often the media misrepresent the scientific consensus and treat new or dissenting pieces of information with equal weight, for the sake of a 'balanced approach' or by attracting attention to novelty (Boykoff and Boykoff, 2007; Cook et al., 2018). Deliberate disinformation campaigns which target the public with false and carefully crafted messages further complicate this landscape. This ecosystem creates a dangerous playing field where different types of information compete for the scarce attention of the public and policymakers, especially in crucial public debates. At the same time, despite the sense of overload, the access to *high quality* information is substantially hindered, with many academic publications residing behind paywalls. Scientists' traditional ways of communicating need to evolve and adapt to better fit the public and political discourse. More on this can be found in Chapter 15.

The separation of science and policy hinders the creation of trustworthy relationships, which are extremely important in sensitive and dynamic policy environments.

Science for Policy: From 1.0 to 2.0

The challenges seem even more insurmountable when science and policy keep to their distinct cultures. Currently, in what we call a Science for Policy 1.0 mode, science and policy are too far apart. They cannot fully deliver on their promise of robust solutions in the era of complexity. Instead of a tight partnership across all stages of policy development and debate, they too often base their interaction on one-off interventions and detached, even unsolicited recommendations. This divide does not help with finding a more cooperative middle ground between the worlds of science and policy.

The separation of science and policy also hinders the creation of trustworthy relationships, which is of extreme importance in sensitive and dynamic policy environments. Trust is a direct function of the understanding of needs, relevance of support, reliability and quality of human relationships. Given the complexity of the challenges, policymakers need reliable partners able to objectively and confidently guide them through the state of knowledge on their given subjects. Honesty is required, but it will not come without trust.

Bringing science and policy closer together can be achieved by engaging them in co-creation at all stages of policymaking, as well as in evidence-making (Chapter 10 discusses the ethics and dilemmas of such a proposal). Co-creation manifests itself in different aspects of the development of science for policy (e.g., co-creation *of* research questions, *of* evidence base, *of* anticipatory knowledge strategies, co-creation *through* collaboration with stakeholders or citizens, *through* participation of scientists in the whole of policymaking). It involves people in different roles on a spectrum between science and policy. For some it means moving closer towards the middle, developing distinct skills, facilitating mutual understanding, leaving the traditional expectations of their professional environments. Trust is vital and truly possible only if science and policy come genuinely closer together.

Does it mean we should primarily focus on institutional design in order to implement the 'merger' of science and policy? On the one hand, the onus for the effectiveness in science–policy collaboration lies in the quality of the relationships, trust, timing, form and format of the interaction and the scientific products used in the policy process. Blaming institutional arrangements is certainly too simplistic. However, eventually the results of a philosophical reflection on the relationship between science and policy inevitably need to be translated into some institutional changes. Closing the gap between science and policy through co-creation requires new principles for institutional practices. This handbook further explains how to experiment with co-creation at different stages of science and policy development.

Image: Dero2084 - https://stock.adobe.com/be_en/images/death-cap-in-the-forest-it-is-poisonous-mushroom-commonly-known-as-the-amanita-phalloides/270284647?prev_url=detail
Icon in page corners: Fungus icon by sumhi_icon from the Noun Project (https://thenounproject.com/search/?q=toadstool&i=1326641)

Post-Normal Science: How Does It Resonate With the World of Today?

Authors: Silvio Funtowicz, Jerry Ravetz

Key takeaways:

- Post-Normal Science approach operates in a reality that can be summarised by a fourfold statement:

  - Facts are uncertain,
  - values in dispute,
  - stakes high,
  - and decisions urgent.

- That initial insight expressed in Post-Normal Science is still important for helping in the diffusion of the lessons of this handbook.

- Post-Normal Science amounted to an existence theorem: there exists a class of policy-related scientific issues for which straightforward research studies, and even professional consultancy, are incomplete, inadequate or inappropriate. A plurality of new methods and new participants is required.

Copyright © 2020 European Union,
Published by Elsevier Limited.

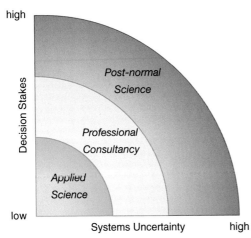

FIGURE 1 Post-Normal Science diagram.

The motto and diagram that define Post-Normal Science (PNS) are now quite familiar to those engaged in science for policy. With a small set of words and graphics, they express the essential features of the challenges of that field. We have the fourfold statement:

(1) Facts uncertain, (2) values in dispute, (3) stakes high and (4) decisions urgent. With this comes the triple-zone quadrant diagram (Fig. 1).

One critical feature of the diagram is the intermediate case, 'professional consultancy'. This enriches the structure so that it avoids conveying the message of a simple transition from a trouble-free past to a problematic present.

There is a close historic connection between PNS and the Joint Research Centre. One of the authors, Silvio Funtowicz, arrived at the JRC when the idea was just taking shape, and the tolerant ambiance enabled him to engage in dialogue and thereby to develop and enrich the initial insight. He also built a base of understanding among colleagues, so that in many ways the present handbook embodies the approach of PNS. The JRC may therefore take credit for its role in nurturing PNS on its way to maturity.

Although it is rapidly gaining support in the policy science community, this approach is still far from universally understood. That initial insight, expressed in PNS, is therefore still important for helping in the diffusion of the lessons of this handbook. It is also useful to recall the context in which it emerged, since that inherited way of looking at science is still very much with us. For generations up to the very recent past, it was universally assumed that science simply provides us with truth, expressed in that ever-increasing body of facts that increase our knowledge and control of the world around us. Then policy advice, based on policy-related science, has a simple task, which is to speak truth to power.

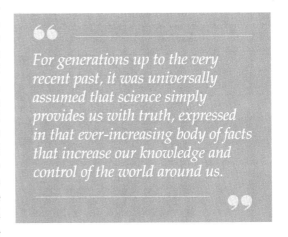

For generations up to the very recent past, it was universally assumed that science simply provides us with truth, expressed in that ever-increasing body of facts that increase our knowledge and control of the world around us.

Starting with the use of atomic weapons in WWII, followed by the development of the destructive H-bombs, it became clear that something had to change. But what? There was a succession of dramatic events, starting with *Silent Spring* (Carson, 1962), the Three Mile Island disaster (1979), then Chernobyl (1986) and afterwards the BSE ('mad cow') crisis in the United Kingdom (1986–2001). In the background was a series of drastic reversals of advice in health and nutrition, notably cholesterol and heart disease. The initial response of risk analysts to the new challenges was to make computer models of the hazardous situation with probabilities assigned to the unwanted events, so that policymakers would have precise numbers to guide their decisions. But when uncertainties were incorporated into the calculation, all too often the risk would be characterised as 'zero-infinity', a vivid way of expressing a situation where the probability is unmeasurably small, but the possible damage is unmeasurably large. Such dilemmas were captured by the concept of 'trans-science' developed by Alvin Weinberg (1972), but he saw the problem as a simply quantitative one, to be resolved by the development of improved measurement methods.

The authors of PNS were well prepared to engage in a creative partnership to enhance this understanding. Jerry Ravetz had already published his seminal work *Scientific Knowledge and its Social Problems* (1971) and had drafted *The Acceptability of Risks* (1977) for the Council for Science and Society. He had also begun reflections on quantitative reasoning and its pathologies. Silvio Funtowicz had a background in mathematics and logic and had already worked on risk analysis at the practical and theoretical levels. Their first joint effort focused on quantification; its product was *Uncertainty and Quality in Science for Policy* (1990), where they developed the NUSAP notation. Their introduction of the idea of quality of scientific information (expressed in the Pedigree category) suggested an extension of their analysis beyond the field of risk assessment, to policy-related science in general. By then, it was clear to them that in policy debates involving science, it was unwise to assume either that uncertainty could be tamed, as with error bars, or that quality could be taken for granted.

In the early days, the sympathetic editor of *Futures* journal, Zia Sardar, facilitated the publication of papers on and around the PNS theme. Contacts were made with the ecological economics community and through that to scholars developing new ideas of complexity. From its scientific origins in risk analysis, PNS has evolved to encompass complexity and governance, although the original formulation has still seemed to serve well. Interest and support have grown gradually, as always in the early phase of an exponential process. Zia's confidence has been repaid. In a recent survey, the 1993 essay *Science for the Post-Normal Age* received the highest number of citations by all publications, which deal with futures, anticipation and prediction.

One additional feature of the PNS analysis gradually came to prominence. Viewed abstractly, PNS amounted to an existence theorem: there exists a class of policy-related scientific issues for which straightforward research studies, and even professional consultancy, are incomplete, inadequate or inappropriate. The corollary is that if such problems are to be resolved, a plurality of new methods and new participants will be required. Thus was born the 'extended peer community'. Precedents existed, as in 'popular epidemiology', the community scientists at the polluted Love Canal, New York, and the concerned parents at Lyme, Connecticut. Although agreed on the need of

> " There exists a class of policy-related scientific issues for which straightforward research studies, and even professional consultancy, are incomplete, inadequate or inappropriate. "

such an extension, many scholars sensed that this was one radical innovation too far, and in their interpretation of PNS, they have substituted the 'extension of peer review' for the more challenging 'extension of the peer community'. Now that the concepts of 'engagement' and 'cocreation' are commonplace, it is useful to be reminded that this transformation of the politics of policy science did require some deep reflection.

The full public maturing of PNS arrived about two decades after the original defining paper (1993). In 2014, the leading scientific journal *Nature* published a paper by a well-respected policy scientist, in which 'Post-Normal' appeared in the title. He is Sir Peter Gluckman, then Chief Scientific Advisor in New Zealand and now President-Elect of the prestigious International Science Council. In his article, and in numerous essays since then, he has shown how his experience led him to incorporate the insights of PNS as the way to understand the challenges of his work.

The JRC has already promoted activities that support the development of PNS, and the extension of its critical insights to other areas. Among them is the organisation of the second PNS symposium, New Currents in Science: The Challenges of Quality (PNS Symposium, 2016 https://ec.europa.eu/jrc/en/event/work shop/challenges-quality). We can now expect more initiatives here and elsewhere, as the lessons of this handbook become understood and diffused.

The contribution of PNS to our understanding of science in society can be summed up quite simply: In the social process of science, quality is achieved, not by a delusory pursuit of certainty, but by the skilled management of its uncertainties, involving all who have a concern for the issue. It is very encouraging indeed that this handbook articulates this insight so effectively.

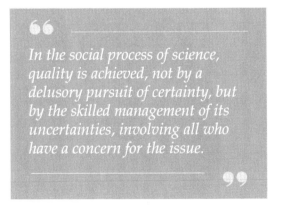

In the social process of science, quality is achieved, not by a delusory pursuit of certainty, but by the skilled management of its uncertainties, involving all who have a concern for the issue.

Science for Policy 2.0: Co-creation

Image: Mathisa - https://stock.adobe.com/be_en/images/life-cycle-of-male-blue-pansy-butterfly-junonia-orithya-linnae-us-on-twig/170699962?prev_url=detail
Icon in page corners: Butterfly icon by Atif Arshad, from the Noun Project (https://thenounproject.com/search/?q=Butterfly&i=2700661)

Institutional Framework for the Science–Policy Interaction

Authors: Vladimír Šucha, Marion Dewar

Key takeaways:

- With many issues hotly contested, 'boundary organisations' sitting at the intersection of the knowledge and policy spheres are more important than ever and should be fully integrated into policymaking structures. They may take a form of the embedded or affiliated institution or platform.

- Along with producing new knowledge themselves, these boundary organisations must act as lighthouses, helping policymakers to navigate their way through today's vast sea – or even ocean – of knowledge. To solve 'wicked' challenges, these boundary organisations must bridge the gap between scientific disciplines and policy fields.

- A new type of 'scientists for policy' with a capacity to understand and value the challenges of the policymaking should be nurtured. Constant interaction and cooperation between science and policy should be the main working method.

- The trust between scientists and policymakers is the most important ingredient allowing science to be fully used in policy cycle.

- To produce solutions that have traction in the real world, all relevant perspectives, including values and perceptions, must be taken into account. In the digital age, people will no longer tolerate being excluded from the debate.

Science for Policy Handbook
http://dx.doi.org/10.1016/B978-0-12-822596-7.00003-6

Copyright © 2020 European Union,
Published by Elsevier Limited.

Most of the chapters of this handbook advise on the practices of individual scientists and policymakers. By contrast, this chapter tackles institutional issues. It has been included because it is impossible to separate the practices of individual scientists and policymakers from the institutional setting in which they are working. This chapter is inspired by the reform of the Joint Research Centre (JRC), initiated in 2016. The JRC employed more than 2000 scientists and is a department (or Directorate General) of the European Commission. This was the first comprehensive reform of the organisation for many years. It was designed to place the JRC ahead of the curve – to put it in a stronger position to tackle the challenges of the coming decades. Although it is still in the early stages of its implementation, lessons can already be learnt. Equally, while the JRC is unique, many of these lessons are more generally applicable. That is why we think the chapter will be of interest to people in leadership or management positions who are able to shape or influence institutional structures. However, it should also be of more general interest, since everyone has a stake in, and should think critically about, the setting in which they work.

The Changing Relationship Between Policy, Science and Society

It is clear that any organisation wishing to translate knowledge into policy advice must reflect on the profound recent changes observed in the science, society and policy nexus. These changes, many of which have been discussed in other parts of this book, could be summarised as follows:

First, *the world of policy is changing*. In today's highly interconnected societies and economies, policymakers have to deal with hugely complex systems and systems of systems. As a result, many of the policy challenges they face are 'wicked'. In other words, they bleed into each other, so that their scale and scope is difficult to

> *It is clear that any organisation wishing to translate knowledge into policy advice must reflect on the profound recent changes observed in the science, society and policy nexus.*

define. They do not have clearly identifiable 'one-off' solutions. Success cannot be easily measured.

Second, the *knowledge landscape is also becoming very fluid and incredibly rich*. In the past, knowledge was produced by universities, mainly in North America and parts of Europe. Now, there are excellent universities in many parts of the world. Moreover, a whole host of other entities are also producing knowledge, including digital platforms, industries, fab labs, etc. It is not just those with recognised qualifications, e.g., PhDs, producing knowledge, it is citizen scientists and young entrepreneurs.

This creates huge opportunities and also challenges. It can be difficult for us to know which data, information or knowledge we can trust (see more in Chapter 10). At the same time, the old, trusted, established knowledge outlets have lost or risk losing – at least part of their authority. Just as in the media landscape, the old reference points are dissolving. This makes it harder and harder to get our bearings. It is as though we are sailing on a sea of knowledge and finding it difficult to navigate. There is an urgent need for organisations that can help policymakers and others to make sense of the deluge.

Equally, some of the knowledge being generated is not strictly speaking 'scientific' but it is nevertheless valid and useful. For example, new methods of discovery are emerging, driven by the availability of 'big data' (see Chapter 9 for possible evolutions that can result from that). Unlike the scientific method, which is based on the formation of hypotheses, these methods are inductive, based on picking out patterns and correlations in the data. Much of this work may not be reproducible, as the scientific method requires, because the data on which it is based are constantly evolving.

This creates a new role for science and scientists: to help to distinguish between poor/false knowledge and relevant, verifiable, authoritative knowledge. The border line should not be made between 'scientific' and 'nonscientific' knowledge but between false and real facts. If science was able to embrace a role of a verifier of quality of arguments, it would strengthen its legitimacy to hold a privileged position in the policymaking process.

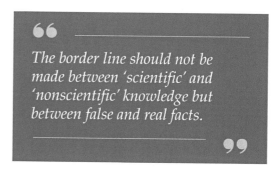

The border line should not be made between 'scientific' and 'nonscientific' knowledge but between false and real facts.

Third, the *social context is changing*. Trust in policy elites has diminished following the crisis. The picture as regards trust in scientists is more nuanced, but there are causes for concern. For the moment, surveys show that scientists are held in high esteem (Special Eurobarometer 401, 2013), but this could change given the current very low levels of trust generally. The media has picked up on science's reproducibility crisis, and this may filter through to public opinion in time. People are inspired by breakthroughs in fundamental science, such as the confirmation of the existence of the Higgs Boson. However, when science is used for policy, it is becoming more hotly contested.

This may be because the stakes are higher and the issues facing regulators are more important. New technologies have a profound effect on almost every aspect of people's lives. There has been longstanding concern about the use of technology in nutrition, but this now extends to other issues, such as algorithms, which can be used for recruitment and many other purposes, including policy decision-making. Many people have the feeling that the issues are too complex for specialised scientists to understand them (Special Eurobarometer 340, 2010). On the top of everything, the speed of the change is accelerating enormously. Penetration of technologies that took in the past a few decades is now taking less than 5 years. Moreover, because the stakes are so high, people may feel that business and other interests may seek to influence scientists and that scientists may not be immune to these pressures (Special Eurobarometer 401, 2013). These fears may be exaggerated, though there are documented cases of this happening.

Finally, the *Internet changes everything*. Everyone can express a view. This is immensely positive, but it carries risks. The authority of scientists and other experts is being challenged. A certain degree of scepticism about 'expertise' is warranted; it may be a sign of maturity not barbarism (Saltelli, 2017). However, if people do not defer to experts, they face tough challenges in deciding which evidence or other material they should trust.

One thing is certain: whether one views this as a positive development or not, it is no longer possible for political or technocratic elites to decide, on their own, which issues to tackle, which perspective to view them from and which knowledge to use as a basis for decisions. These issues have to be decided more collectively.

The Importance of Boundary Organisations and Skills

Based on our experience, the following sections will look at (i) the way in which science advice should be organised to cope with today's rapidly changing environment and (ii) the functions that science advisory organisations should fulfil.

The way in which science advice is traditionally 'institutionalised' naturally differs between countries and entities, depending on culture, context and history. However, there are two points which are worth making:

First, in some (mainly Anglo-Saxon) countries, a single individual performs the role of Government Science Adviser. The Commission itself experimented with this model in 2012.

Unfortunately, although it works well in some cases, this model has significant drawbacks. It depends too much on the calibre of the single individual appointed to the post. It concentrates a lot of influence in the hands of that one individual. This means that, when advice is given, it can be perceived as representing the subjective views of that person. It is clearly a disadvantage, and also a common feature built in the Science for Policy 1.0 model.

Due to the growing complexity and importance of decisions, it seems to be wiser to put in place advisory groups or structures, where the constant interactions between scientists and policymakers are allowed.

Second, while a wide range of different organisations and institutions should be involved in providing advice to policymakers, one type of organisation has a particularly important role to play, that is, 'boundary organisations', i.e., those which sit at the intersection of science or knowledge and policy.

In the past, science advice might have been seen as an ordinary service, like those provided by consultants. A specific client, a policymaker, might request a piece of research relating to a particular issue. The scientist would carry out the research, hand over it at the beginning of the policymaking process and then have no further involvement.

> " *Due to the complexity and importance of the decisions, it seems wiser to put in place advisory groups or structures, rather than relying on single individuals acting as a Government Science Adviser.* "

This approach worked well when policy challenges, though difficult, were discrete, fairly easy to define and had clearly identifiable one-off solutions. However, with today's 'wicked' challenges, this simple, linear 1.0 approach no longer works, as explained in Chapter 1.

'Wicked challenges' rarely have definitive solutions, so scientists and policymakers have to stay in constant and ongoing dialogue with one another. This constant interaction is a key to mutual understanding, building trust and overcoming of the differences between scientific and policymaking cycles. This is the essence of Science for Policy 2.0, built on cocreation throughout the entire process of policymaking.

Equally, science itself does not necessarily provide clear-cut answers. Indeed, it has become less linear and more probabilistic. Scientists have to keep talking to policymakers to sensitise them to these limits and uncertainties.

Science advice should therefore be fully integrated into the policymaking process. It should be like xenoliths in the rocks. They are of a different origin to the surrounding rock but fully embedded in it.

The JRC is part of the structure it is advising and it brings a huge advantage in science–policy interactions. However, this is not essential. Other alternatives and more innovative solutions can achieve the same result, if they adopt a cocreative philosophy and practices, for example, science for policy institutes at universities or academies with a direct link to the governments (shared employment). Another solution would be thematic policy platforms established across different research organisations nationally or internationally regrouping the best experts in the given policy area and cooperating with a relevant ministry (for example, a platform on the agriculture research may provide a space for the researchers from the relevant fields and be in contact with the policymakers at different levels of government or regulatory agencies).

What really matters is the attitude of those involved and the relationships that they have with each other. That is why, as part of its reform, the JRC sought to change the way it works with other parts of the European Commission. The aim is to work together with them closely and iteratively and, crucially, in a relationship of equals. The institutional setup helps, but it is the cultural change that helps forging better collaboration.

Just over 3 years into the implementation of the reform, it is clear that the attitude of policymakers in the Commission towards the JRC is much more positive. They see it as a strategic partner, not a consultant. They are also more ready to acknowledge the scientific contribution and accept the scientists at the very early stages of their policy reflections.

In fact, they have perhaps been more open to this change than JRC scientists themselves. This may be because policymakers have more incentive to strengthen their relationship with scientists. It is they, after all, who are directly responsible for solving ever more complex policy problems. It is they who are in the firing line.

On the other hand, some of the scientists remain, perhaps, driven more by their intellectual curiosity than by policy concerns. They may be motivated primarily by the esteem of the scientific or academic community, rather than by the impact they have on policy. This behaviour is a serious impediment to the full use of science in policy. We think that we need a new type of scientist driven by the scientific curiosity, academic reputation as well as by a policy impact.

A New Type of Scientist for Policy Impact

To find a balance between policy impact and academic curiosity is not easy. We are seeking to promote the emergence of this new profession by developing and testing different approaches:

- We developed a special competence framework for scientists and policymakers engaged in the use of science in policy (see Chapter 4). We are providing both groups with a specialised training, and at the same time, we developed joint sessions to allow mutual understanding to grow.

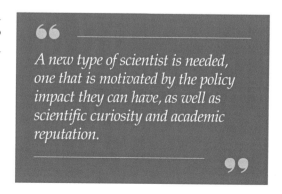

> A new type of scientist is needed, one that is motivated by the policy impact they can have, as well as scientific curiosity and academic reputation.

- Different forms of detachments, short- to mid-term mobility schemes for the scientists towards the policy departments and vice versa were introduced (see Chapter 6).
- The thematic communities of practice were established and they play an immensely important role in mutual understanding between scientists and policymakers (see Chapter 7).
- At the same time, we have launched a 'Collaborative Doctoral Partnership' programme, which allows PhD students from around the EU to spend time working in the JRC, so giving them experience of working in a European 'science for policy' environment.

While this entire handbook helps scientists with a transition to this new role, Chapters 4, 5 and 10 in particular are a good starting point to learn how to manage the change.

Which Functions Should Boundary Organisations Fulfil?

If the current rapidly changing situation cements the importance of boundary organisations, it also calls for changes in the functions that those organisations fulfil. We clearly see three major functions that are key for the boundary organisations to embark on:

Lighthouses in the Sea of Knowledge

The knowledge organisation's focus had always been to create new scientific knowledge by carrying out its own research work. This needs to change. Managing the existing knowledge, verifying it and making sense for different purposes should become an additional dimension of every knowledge organisation. In 2016, we, in the JRC, decided to do this and add a new function, that of 'managing' knowledge from other sources – i.e., collating and analysing it and presenting it to policymakers in a coherent and digestible form. It did not mean to abandon the knowledge creation but to complement it.

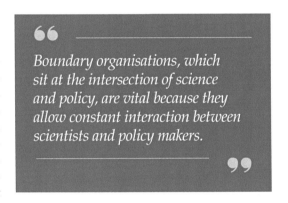

> Boundary organisations, which sit at the intersection of science and policy, are vital because they allow constant interaction between scientists and policy makers.

Achieving the shift required a culture change across the whole JRC, a change in the mindset of almost everyone working there. Although this change is not yet complete, good progress has been made, thanks to a number of factors:

- A strong impulse from the head of the organisation
- An openness to ideas and insights from staff at all levels
- Staff 'ambassadors' whose role was to inform colleagues about the new approach and encourage them to buy into it
- The creation of a new 'Knowledge Management Directorate' charged with identifying or developing knowledge management methodologies and delivering specific training to staff in core knowledge management skills, e.g., systematic reviews and metaanalyses, data analytics, data visualisation, info graphics and management of communities of practice

- The creation of a special 'knowledge management unit' in all the other Directorates of the JRC. Their mission is to spearhead the drive towards knowledge management in their Directorates. They report to the head of their Directorates (their Directors) but are also connected to the Knowledge Management Directorate in a flexible matrix structure
- Producing a set of flagship knowledge management products (reports) showing in concrete terms what could be the policy impact of a well-chosen topic.

We decided also to create specific tools for the vertical and horizontal knowledge management. Vertical knowledge management instruments – 'Knowledge Centres' – are the thematic virtual hubs collecting the most relevant pieces of knowledge in certain vertically defined areas (like disaster risk management, food security, food authenticity, migration and demography, etc.). These bring together expertise and knowledge from different locations inside and outside the Commission. Their job is to inform policymakers in a tailored, concise and independent manner about the status and findings of the latest scientific research. They clearly present any legitimate disagreements within the scientific community and seek to quantify the level of uncertainty associated with the available knowledge. Horizontal knowledge management is represented by our 'Competence Centres' that are pulling together all scientific competences of the JRC in certain field (creation of composite indicator and dashboards, modelling, text mining, impact evaluation, etc.). For an example, see Chapters 6, 12, 16 and 19.

The shift towards knowledge management – or sensemaking – could be emulated by other organisations working with other parts of society, e.g., business – not just those who work with policymakers, as the JRC does. Making sense of knowledge is a challenge for the whole society. If almost all players are now producing large amounts of data and knowledge, they are also all struggling to cope with the deluge that is being created.

There is therefore room for many organisations to take on the role of 'lighthouses', including administrations at all levels, regulatory organisations and even central banks. Indeed, one could argue that it is only their ability to make sense of knowledge that gives these nonelected bodies their legitimacy. If knowledge-based organisations do not embrace the role of the lighthouses of authoritative knowledge, they will leave more space for false or fake facts and ultimately contribute to the creation of the postfact society where the space for the scientific knowledge creation will be limited or none.

Breaking Boundaries Between Disciplines and Policies

Today's wicked problems need to be viewed from different angles, if we are to have any chance of comprehending them.

Along with breaking boundaries between knowledge and policy, it is therefore increasingly necessary to span the boundaries between scientific disciplines and policies.

The JRC starts with an advantage; it works across the full range of EU policy fields and it also employs scientists from a huge range of disciplines.

However, working across disciplines is notoriously difficult. The structure of many academic institutions discourages multidisciplinary collaboration. It may be difficult to obtain funding and opportunities for publication may be limited.

While the situation is improving is some countries, many of these barriers remain. Most scientists employed by the JRC work there for a limited period before returning to their universities. They are therefore not immune to these concerns.

At the same time, the European Commission, like all public administrations, is a hierarchical organisation divided into different departments (Directorates General). This has benefits (efficient allocation of resources, clear lines of accountability), but it can also create silos.

Moreover, the JRC has its own hierarchy and divisions (it is made up of 10 Directorates, each one comprising 6–8 units).

Overcoming silos therefore means transcending the organisational structure, without abandoning or undermining it. To achieve this, the JRC has taken the following steps:

- It has chosen to organise its work, not around individual areas but around 'priority nexus' which link different issues, e.g., migration and territorial development or food, nutrition and health. This ensures that linkages are made.
- It prioritises projects involving many different parts of the Commission. At an early stage in policy development, different departments may have different points of view. It is important that they frame the research questions together, so that they can all accept the results of the research.
- A creation of an internal communication platform, which is now being rolled out across the European Commission, was a crucial step in making different parts of the organisation connected and to unzip the people's tacit knowledge. The platform allows information to be shared and groups to be created by colleagues at any level in the organisation. Take up by staff has been very rapid, thanks to a concerted campaign and training available to all. It has proved a very powerful tool for cross-unit and cross-Directorate collaboration.
- A digital platform was complemented by different physical 'Collaborative Spaces' to allow scientists from different sites, directorates and units to spend some time working together in the same physical space.
- The launch of new generation of JRC 'transversal projects' has proved to be a spur for collaboration. Tangible outcomes of the traversal projects are multidiscilinary reports that would never occur within the traditional settings (e.g., on Resilience (Campolongo, 2018), What makes the society fair? (Al Khudhairy et al., 2017), Artificial Intelligence (Craglia et al., 2018), Blockchain (Nascimento et al., 2018), etc). Staff members are keen to be involved in them, and this encouraged them to come forward with interesting, crosscutting proposals (Future of work and education, Connected and automated transport, Future of Cities, Geography of Discontent).

Cross-disciplinary cooperation has helped to close the gap between natural and social sciences. This is important in all societal challenges we face. Separation of social sciences and humanities from natural, medical and technical sciences is hugely counterproductive and may lead to many mistakes in policy decisions.

Breaking Boundaries Between the Academic and Nonacademic Realms

Along with breaking barriers between academic disciplines, it is often necessary for boundary organisation to bridge the gap between policymakers and academics, on the one hand, and practitioners or stakeholders, on the other. This is because, when tackling complex policy problems, it is important to take all relevant perspectives into account.

Saltelli and Giampietro (2017) advocate, inter alia, direct interaction with social actors carrying legitimate but contrasting normative values to avoid a compressed framing of issues which then forms the basis for quantitative analysis. The result is a restricted understanding of the issues, given a spurious impression of precision by that quantification.

In fact, the European Commission makes strenuous efforts to take account of all relevant points of view when framing policy options. This is a key part of its impact assessment methodology. It is done using a number of mechanisms, such as the 'Your Voice in Europe' portal.[1] However, the JRC has also built in some safeguards. Since it has developed a relationship of equals with its policymaking counterparts in the Commission, it is able to jointly frame research questions with them (see more in the Chapter 6). There is no question of policymakers framing these questions on their own in response to the pressures they are under.

The engagement (of different science disciplines, stakeholders, regional/local representations, civil society organisations and citizens) is a key feature of the success for policymaking. We need to invent more efficient and more genuine forms of engagement. We did a few first steps in this direction and invented a 'Policy Lab'[2] (see more details in Chapter 13), which facilitates participatory processes, using sophisticated tools and methodologies. The processes allow policymakers, scientists and stakeholders to frame policy and research questions together and to decide on the type of knowledge which should be produced or mobilised.

A Stronger Culture of Anticipation and Thinking out the Box

In 1993, Funtowicz and Ravetz coined the term 'Post-Normal Science' to describe situations where 'facts are uncertain, values in dispute, stakes high and decisions urgent' (Funtowicz, S. Ravetz, J.R., 1993) (see Chapter 2). This formulation has proved to be very prescient. It was true when it was coined but perhaps even Funtowicz and Ravetz themselves could not have imagined how much truer it would be today.

The unprecedented pace of technological development has indeed created myriad interconnections which result in 'wicked' challenges for policymakers. It has created high stakes policy issues that frequently give rise to clashes in values. It has created an explosion of data, information and knowledge, resulting in complex epistemological challenges for policymakers and indeed society at large.

However, it is the last part of Funtowicz and Ravetz's formulation, which refers to decisions being urgent, that is the most important. Decisions are often taken hastily without time for mature reflection. With today's unprecedented and ever increasing pace of change, it is becoming harder and harder for policymakers to stay ahead of the curve.

Where options are narrowly framed, it is not necessarily in response to pressure from particular interest groups; it may just be due to time pressure. The public is demanding more inclusive policy processes, but there is often no time to organise them. Expectations are growing, but time is increasingly short.

The only way to square this circle is to spot issues early so that work can begin on them as soon as possible. For this reason, the JRC is strengthening its anticipatory capacity. It already has many of the necessary capacities and tools, including horizon scanning,

---

[1] https://ec.europa.eu/info/law/contribute-law-making_en, accessed 05.05.2020.
[2] https://blogs.ec.europa.eu/eupolicylab/, accessed 05.05.2020.

technology watch activities, foresight processes, modelling and media monitoring. It is building expertise in the use of these tools and developing new ones (for more, see Chapter 12).

All new JRC projects must take account of possible or likely future scientific, technological and other developments that can impact on or be relevant to the matter in hand. It is embedding an anticipation culture across the organisation. It is an important cultural change from backward looking approach to forward looking. It is the only way how to shape the collective mind of the organisation in order to cope with the fast changing reality.

Nurturing creativity and 'out-of-the-box' thinking is an important ingredient of the anticipatory culture. In this respect, nothing more than active engagement with art is helping to look at things from unconventional angle. This was the main driver of our Science and Art programme where artists are invited to join JRC scientists to discuss, reflect and innovate and to place JRC research into a wider context of science–art–policy–politics. It started very low profile back in 2015 and is growing almost exponentially since. So far, it has tackled issues such as food, fairness, artificial intelligence or 'big data' and has provided some unexpected insights.[3]

---

[3]See more at http://publications.jrc.ec.europa.eu/repository/bitstream/JRC107774/kjna28727enn.pdf, accessed 05.05.2020.

Image: Azraelmaster777 - https://stock.adobe.com/be_en/images/working-bees-in-honey-hive/206459101?prev_url=detail
Icon in page corners: Bee icon by Icon Solid, from the Noun Project (https://thenounproject.com/search/?q=Bees&i=1054089)

Skills for Co-creation*

Authors: Lene Topp, David Mair, Laura Smillie, Paul Cairney

Key takeaways:

- Although the JRC is at the centre of the 'science–policy interface', it faces the same problem experienced by academic researchers: there is often a major gap between the supply of, and the demand for, policy-relevant research.

- This gap relates primarily to key differences in the practices, expectations, incentives and rules of researchers and policymakers. To address it, JRC synthesised interdisciplinary work on the 'science–policy interface' to promote a skill and training agenda.

- Our skills framework identifies the ways in which *organisations* (as opposed to individuals) containing researchers, policymakers, communicators and knowledge brokers can adopt pragmatic ways to connect the demand and supply of policy-relevant knowledge by having teams of people with complementary skills.

- The skills framework contains eight skills that, in an ideal-type organisation, contribute to an overall vision for effective science for policy. Policymakers justify action with reference to the best available evidence, high scientific consensus and citizen and stakeholder 'ownership'. Researchers earn respect, build effective networks, tailor evidence to key audiences, provide evidence-informed policy advice (without simply becoming advocates for their own cause) and learn from their success.

---

*This chapter is a revised, shortened and updated version of Topp et al. (2018), Knowledge management for policy impact: the case of the European Commission's Joint Research Centre, Palgrave Communications vol 4(87), published originally under CC BY 4.0 [https://creativecommons.org/licenses/by/4.0/]. For the original version, please see https://doi.org/10.1057/s41599-018-0143-3.

 Copyright © 2020 European Union,
Published by Elsevier Limited. 33

Table 1 Eight skills to support evidence-informed policymaking

1. *Synthesising research:* There is an oversupply of information to policymakers, compared to the limited 'bandwidth' of policymakers, producing the need to synthesise and prioritise the most robust and relevant knowledge.

2. *Managing expert communities:* Policy problems are complex and interdependent, calling for cooperation between disciplines and 'joining up' a wide range of policies.

3. *Understanding policy and science:* The policy process is better understood as an ecosystem than a policy cycle with linear stages, prompting new ways to understand the link between evidence and policy.

4. *Interpersonal skills:* We need to overcome a lack of mutual respect, understanding and empathy between scientists and policymakers and reflect on our behavioural biases that produce hubristic behaviour.

5. *Engaging with citizens and stakeholders:* Evidence-informed policy should be more informed by citizen and stakeholder views. Scientists should not exacerbate stakeholder exclusion by presenting issues as only technical.

6. *Communicating scientific knowledge:* Policymakers often do not pay attention to evidence on problems or have enough awareness of evidence-informed solutions.

7. *Monitoring and evaluation:* We need to ensure the routine monitoring of policy, partly to use evidence to evaluate success and hold policymakers to account (and monitor the success of evidence for policy initiatives).

8. *Achieving policy impact:* We should close the gap in expected behaviour between policymakers seeking evidence-informed recommendations and researchers trying to draw the line between the 'honest broker' and 'issue advocate' (Pielke, 2007; Cairney and Oliver, 2017; Smith and Stewart, 2017).

The JRC is at the centre of the 'science–policy interface', embedded inside the European Commission, and drawing on over 2000 research staff to produce knowledge supporting most policy fields. Yet, it faces the same problem experienced by academic researchers (Oliver et al., 2014): there is often a major gap between the supply of, and demand for, policy-relevant research. This problem is not solved simply by employing researchers and policymakers in the same organisation or locating them in the same building. Rather, the gap relates primarily to key differences in the practices, expectations, incentives, language and rules of researchers and policymakers (see Chapter 1).

To address this gap, a JRC team synthesised the insights of a large amount of interdisciplinary work on the 'science–policy interface' – drawing on published research and extensive discussions with experts – to promote a new skills and training agenda. The training initially developed for the Commission has many insights that are relevant to organisations that try to combine research, management, policymaking and communication skills to improve the value and use of research in policy. We recommend that such organisations should develop teams of researchers, policymakers and 'knowledge brokers' to produce eight key skills to support evidence-informed policies (see Table 1).

FIGURE 1 Eight skills to support evidence-informed policies.

As opposed to approaches promoting efforts of individual researchers, our skills framework identifies the ways in which *organisations* containing researchers, policymakers, communicators and knowledge brokers can adopt pragmatic ways to connect the demand and supply of policy-relevant knowledge by having teams of people with different background, perspectives and complementary skills. None of the individual staff is expected to possess all these skills (Fig. 1).

Each of them is discussed in more detail below, with several expanded as separate chapters of this handbook.

Synthesising Research

Skill 1: Employ methods to make better sense of the wealth of knowledge available on a given topic, particularly when driven by a research question 'coproduced' with policymakers.

Policymakers seek reliable 'shortcuts' to consider enough high-quality evidence to make good decisions quickly (Cairney and Kwiatkowski, 2017). The sheer amount of available evidence is beyond the capacity of the human mind without the assistance of research synthesis.

'Synthesis' describes many methods – including systematic review and metaanalysis – to make better sense of knowledge. 'Evidence gap maps' are particularly useful to bring together supply and demand. Their aim is to make sense of scientific debate or an enormous volume of scientific literature of variable quality, employing methods to filter information so that policymakers have access to robust scientific evidence. Synthesis helps identify, critically appraise and summarise the balance of evidence on a policy problem from multiple sources (Davies, 2006).

Increasing the *supply* of synthesised research is only the first step. We need to recognise the *demand* for evidence. There is a poor fit between researcher-led syntheses and policymaker needs (with exceptions, such as regulated markets which depend upon risk analysis models). Researchers are often not conscious of the synthesis needed for policymaking, and policymakers do not always recognise the potential contribution that synthesis can make (Fox and Bero, 2014; Greenhalgh; Malterud, 2016; Davies, 2006).

Therefore, the second step is to increase policy relevance by making sure that the research question is responsive to the needs of policymakers. We emphasise the need to understand how policymakers *phrase a research question* when making difficult trade-offs between competing interests and values (see Chapter 6).

Managing Expert Communities

Skill 2: Communities of experts, sharing a common language or understanding, are fundamental to applying knowledge to complex problems. Effective teams develop facilitation skills to reduce disciplinary and policy divides.

The JRC draws on psychological insights to promote collaboration across a 'community of knowledge' to harness the 'wisdom of crowds' (Sloman and Fernbach, 2017). To achieve the wisdom of crowds requires community management skills. Crowdsourcing is dependent on convening power, and communities cannot operate effectively without well-managed mapping strategies to combine the expertise of individuals and groups. The aim is to develop interdisciplinary and interpolicy networks committed to adapting expertise to the needs and reality of policymaking, making closer science–policy ties the norm. Success depends on generating a common sense of purpose, followed by a greater sense of trust and connection between members. As members share ideas and experience, they develop a common way of doing things that can lead to a shared understanding of the problem. Chapter 7 explains in detail our approach and advice in this area.

Understanding Policy and Science

Skill 3: Seek to better understand the policy process, which can never be as simple as a 'policy cycle' with linear stages. Effective teams adapt their strategies to a 'messier' context.

As discussed in Chapter 1, policymaking is far from an orderly linear process described by a cycle metaphor.

The nature of policymaking has profound implications for researchers seeking to maximise the impact of their evidence. First, it magnifies the 'two communities' problem, covered in more detail in Chapter 1. In this (simplified) scenario, science and politics have fundamentally different goals, rhythms and expectations of data and of each other. See Chapter 1 for an elaboration of these contradictions.

These problems would be acute even if the policy process were easy to understand. In reality, one must overcome the two communities problem *and* decipher the many rules of policymaking. A general strategy is to engage for the long term to learn the 'rules of the game', understand how best to 'frame' the implications of evidence, build up trust with policymakers through personal interaction and becoming a reliable source of information and form coalitions with people who share your outlook (Cairney et al., 2016; Weible et al., 2012; Stoker, 2010, pp. 55–57).

More collaborative work with policymakers requires contextual awareness. Researchers need to understand the political context and its drivers, identify and understand the target audience, including the policymaking organisations and individual stakeholders who are influential on the issue, and understand their motives and how they respond to their policy environment. Although *effective policymakers* anticipate what evidence will be needed in the future, *effective researchers* do not wait for such demand for evidence to become routine and predictable.

Chapter 5 shares our detailed advice on how to gather policy intelligence in a science for policy institution.

Interpersonal Skills

Skill 4: Effective actors are able to interact well with others in teams to help solve problems.

Successful policy is built on interaction: policy-relevant knowledge transpires from a myriad of interactions between scientists, policymakers and stakeholders. Skills for social interaction – sending and receiving verbal and nonverbal cues – are central to policymaking success (Klein et al., 2006, pp. 79; Reiss, 2015). They allow us to get along with peers, exchange ideas, information and skills, establish mutual respect and encourage input from multiple disciplines and professions (Larrick, 2016). They are easier to describe in the abstract than in practice, but we can identify key categories:

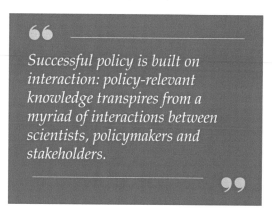

> Successful policy is built on interaction: policy-relevant knowledge transpires from a myriad of interactions between scientists, policymakers and stakeholders.

1. *'Emotional intelligence'*: The personality traits, social graces, personal habits, friendliness and optimism that characterise relationships.

2. *Collaboration and team building:* Scientists and policymakers who are able to navigate complex interpersonal environments are held in high esteem. Boundary-spanning organisations are characterised by a dynamic working environment full of individuals with different personalities and experiences. Self-directed collaborative working

environments are replacing many traditional hierarchical structures, which makes it critical to have actors able to communicate and collaborate effectively and show new forms of leadership (Bedwell et al., 2014).

3. *The ability to manoeuvre:* Scientists and policymakers are constrained by their environments but can also make decisions to change them (Damon, Lewis, 2015; Chabal, 2003). Effective actors understand how and why people make decisions, to identify which rules are structures and which rules can be changed.

4. *Adaptability:* Interpersonal skills are situation specific; what may be appropriate in one situation is inappropriate in another (Klein et al., 2006).

Such skills seem difficult to teach, but we can combine the primary aim of training workshops, to raise awareness among scientists and stakeholders about how their behaviour may be perceived and how it influences their interaction with others, with the initiatives of individual organisations, such as '360 degrees' reviews of managers to help them reflect on their interaction with colleagues.

Chapter 5 addresses in part elements related to interpersonal skills for effective scientific support.

Engaging with Citizens and Stakeholders

Skill 5: Well-planned engagement with stakeholders, including citizens, can help combine scientific expertise with other types of knowledge to increase their relevance and impact.

Bodies such as the European Commission identify stakeholder engagement as a key part of their processes (Nascimento et al., 2014; European Commission, 2015, 2017). However, engagement comes in many forms, with the potential for confusion, tokenism and ineffective participation (Cook et al., 2013; Cairney and Oliver, 2017; Cairney, 2016a, pp. 100–102).

Modern policymaking institutions foster civic engagement skills and empowerment, increase awareness of the cultural relevance of science and recognise the importance of multiple perspectives and domains of knowledge. They treat engagement as an ethical issue, pursuing solidarity through collective enterprise to produce values that are collective decided upon and align policymaking with societal needs (European Commission, 2015). Skills for citizen and stakeholder engagement are crucial to policy legitimacy. Engagement is a policy aim as well as a process, prompting open, reflective and accessible discussion about desirable futures.

In that context, the JRC aims to help researchers and policymakers develop skills, including

- *Policy deliberation:* Focus on long-range planning perspectives, continuous public consultation and institutional self-reflection and course correction.
- *Knowledge coproduction:* Focus on intentional collaborations in which citizens engage in the research process to generate new knowledge.
- *Citizen science:* Engage citizens in data gathering to incorporate multiple types of knowledge.
- *Informality:* Encourage less structured one-on-one interactions in daily life between researchers and publics.

Chapter 8 discusses related tools and approaches in detail. Chapter 7 sheds some light on the principles of working with stakeholders and Chapter 10 on how to navigate interests while collaborating and sourcing external knowledge.

Communicating Scientific Knowledge

Skill 6: Research impact requires effective communication skills, from content-related tools like infographic design and data visualisation to listening and understanding your audience.

Poor scientific communication is a key feature of the 'barriers' between evidence and policy (Oliver et al., 2014; Stone et al., 2001). Research results are often behind 'paywalls' or 'coded' for the academic community in jargon that excludes policymakers (Bastow et al., 2013). If policymakers do not have access to research, they are not able to make evidence-informed decisions. Policymakers use the best *available* information. If scientists want policymakers to choose the best evidence, they need to communicate more clearly, strategically and frequently with policymakers (Warira et al., 2017).

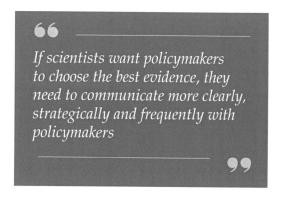

If scientists want policymakers to choose the best evidence, they need to communicate more clearly, strategically and frequently with policymakers

Evidence-based ideas have the best chance of spreading if they are *expressed well*. Effective researchers recognise that the evidence does not speak for itself and that a 'deficit model' approach – transmit evidence from experts to nonspecialists to change their understanding and perception of a problem – is ineffective (Hart and Nisbet, 2012). Rather, to communicate well is to know your audience (Cairney and Kwiatkowski, 2017).

'Communication' encompasses skills to share and receive information, in written and oral form, via digital and physical interaction, using techniques like infographic design and data visualisation, succinct writing, blogs, public speaking and social media engagement (Estrada and Davis, 2015; Wilcox, 2012). Some go further than a focus on succinct and visually appealing messages, to identify the role of 'storytelling' as a potent device (see skill 8 and Davidson, 2017; Jones and Crow, 2017).

Chapter 15 shares our approach and advice in this area.

Monitoring and Evaluation

Skill 7: Monitoring and evaluating the impact of research evidence on policymaking helps improve the influence of evidence on policymaking.

Senior policymakers in the European Commission have worked hard to embed better regulation into the DNA of the European Commission, installing a priority driven, evidence-based and transparent policy process.

However, there are nascent metrics to gauge the ways in which, for example, government reports cite academic research, which could be supplemented by qualitative case studies of evidence use among policymakers. There remains a tendency for studies to define impact imprecisely (Alla et al., 2017). Therefore, at this moment, we describe evidence impact evaluation as a key skill for researchers seeking to monitor their effectiveness, but we recognise that each research organisation needs to develop its own methodology, which can be based on principles that must be adapted to specific objectives and institutional contexts.

Chapter 14 presents the approach of the JRC in that area.

Achieving Policy Impact

Skill 8: Effective evidence-informed support to policymaking goes beyond simply communicating research evidence, towards identifying options, helping policymakers understand the likely impact of choices, distinguishing facts and values in the debates and providing policy advice from a scientific viewpoint.

A key feature of the JRC annual conferences (Cairney, 2016b, 2017a) is the desire by many scientists and scientific advisors to remain as 'honest brokers' rather than 'issue advocates'; they draw on Pielke's (2007) distinction between (a) explaining the evidence-informed options and (b) expressing a preference for one. However, the idea of an 'honest broker' is often at odds with the demand by policymakers for evidence-informed recommendation or, at least, the demand that knowledge brokers consider the political context in which they are presenting evidence, or even adapt to it.

Nonetheless, we need to develop skills that scientists are willing to use. For many researchers, an appeal to objectivity – or, at least, the systematic means to reduce the role of cognitive bias on evidence production – is part of a scientific identify. A too-strong call for persuasive policy advice may cause many experts to retreat from politics. They may feel that the use of persuasion in policy advocacy is crossing an ethical line between honest brokerage and manipulation. Many scientists do not accept the argument that an appeal to scientific objectivity is a way to exercise political power (Jasanoff and Simmet, 2017). Nor would all scientists accept the argument by Cairney and Weible (2017, pp. 5) that 'policy analysis is inherently political, not an objective relay of the evidence … The choice is not whether or not to focus on skilful persuasion which appeals to emotion, but how to do it most effectively while adhering to key ethical principles'.

Consequently, the development of skills to achieve policy impact must be pragmatic, to incorporate a scientist identity and commitment to ethical principles that emphasise impartial policy advice. We accept that our encouragement of scientists to become better-trained storytellers will be a hard sell unless we link this training strongly to a meaningful discussion of the ethics for participating in policymaking. Indeed, the current pursuit of policy-relevant scientific advice is quite modest, about making sure that scientists are 'in the room' to ensure that inferences are correctly drawn from the evidence and that politicians are clear when they are moving beyond the evidence. The skills of scientists in explaining and applying scientific methods, and articulating a 'scientific way of thinking' (if such a general way of thinking exists), helps ensure that decisions are well-founded and that policymakers can consider how they combine facts and values to make decisions.

Chapters 5 and 10 share our detailed advice on how to deal with the expectations about scientists' conduct when working in a policy context and navigate the science–policy interface.

Conclusion

Better evidence-informed policies require eight skills that can help address the science–policy gap. If we initially think of these skills in the abstract, as key elements of an ideal-type organisation, we can describe how they contribute to an overall vision for effective science for policy: policymakers justify action with reference to the best available evidence, high scientific consensus and citizen and stakeholder 'ownership', and researchers earn respect, build effective networks, tailor evidence to key audiences, provide evidence-informed policy advice (without simply becoming advocates for their own cause) and learn from their success. Table 2 highlights the proposed impact of each skill in an ideal-type organisation, compared with less effective practices that provide a cautionary tale.

In recommending eight skills, we argue that 'pure scientists' and 'professional politicians' cannot do this job alone. Scientists need 'knowledge brokers' and science advisors with the skills to increase policymakers' demand for evidence. Policymakers need help to understand and explain the evidence and its implications. Brokers are essential: scientists with a feel for policy and policymakers understanding how to manage science and scientists. In Chapter 6, we describe how our internal facilitators in-between the two realms strengthen the collaboration between individual scientists and policymakers.

At the outset, the aim of the skills framework was to map the complementary skills desired for scientists working at the science–policy interface and develop corresponding training modules. At the JRC, we took a conscious decision to use the training not only for upskilling of staff but also to support the mindset change underpinning the sensemaking part of the JRC vision, i.e., ' … *making sense of collective scientific knowledge for better EU policies*'. The individual needs of organisations will determine to what extend each of eight skills are required in their specific work context. At the JRC, a review of existing training modules helped us to identify the gaps in our training offering as we want to offer staff trainings covering the full range of skills framework primarily though in-house training or alternatively point them to external training providers. Along the same lines, we have integrated the complementary skills into our job profiles, hence ensuring that future recruits possess skills to support evidence-informed policies.

Table 2 Eight skills and their potential impact

Skill	The ideal type	The cautionary tale
Synthesising research	Researchers will present a concise, timely and policy-relevant synthesis. Policymakers will be able to justify action with reference to the best available evidence.	Researchers will provide too much information, too late, and with unclear relevance. Policymakers will be engulfed by information, unable to learn before they act or too able to cherry-pick evidence.
Managing expert communities	Researchers will speak with a coherent and authoritative voice. Policymakers will act with confidence, built on scientific consensus.	Researchers will speak over and undermine each other. Policymakers will lack confidence, or play experts off each other.
Understanding policy and science	Researchers will know how and when to present evidence. Policymakers will have access to the most relevant and useful researchers.	Researchers will become ineffective and dispirited. Policymakers will not know who the most relevant and useful researchers are.
Interpersonal	Researchers will form effective networks and earn respect. Policymakers will know and trust researchers.	Researchers will become marginalised. Policymakers will not trust the researchers who claim to 'speak truth to power'.
Engaging citizens and stakeholders	Researchers will help enhance the substance, credibility and legitimacy of knowledge. Policymakers can combine key evidence and public views to make sustainable political choices.	Researchers remain in silos. Citizens and stakeholders are excluded and any evidence-based policy on which policymakers could rely lacks credibility and legitimacy.
Communicating scientific knowledge	Researchers tailor messages to their audience, generating emotional interest and memorable presentations. Policymakers understand the evidence on policy problems and effectiveness of solutions.	Researcher evidence gets lost and receives no attention. Policymakers do not understand or pay attention to the evidence on policy problems and have limited awareness of effective solutions.
Monitoring and evaluation	Researchers and policymakers learn, partly through trial and error, which of their strategies work.	Researchers and policymakers stick to the same strategy without knowing if their evidence makes an impact.
Achieving policy impact	Researchers combined evidence advocacy and political awareness to achieve policy impact. Policymakers receive policy-relevant advice on which they can act with greater confidence.	Researchers become marginalised and rarely trusted in day-to-day politics. Policymakers receive evidence but remain unsure about its relevance and risk of inaction.

Image: Jonnysek - https://stock.adobe.com/be_en/images/ammonites-fossil-texture/157397067?prev_url=detail
Icon in page corners: Nautilus icon by Oleg and Polly, from the adobe (https://stock.adobe.com/be_en/images/nautilus-copy/255875136?prev_url=detail)

Achieving Policy Impact

Main authors: Marta Sienkiewicz, Pieter van Nes, Marie-Agnes Deleglise

Contributor: Adrien Rorive

Key takeaways:

- Policy impact does not happen by itself. It requires strategic planning for engaging relevant audiences with the science, including active participation in policymaking environment.

- Presenting research to broad audiences in a variety of nonscientific fora allows to gain allies carrying the message forward.

- In order to plan a robust strategy, scientific organisations need to focus on building relationships and gathering policy intelligence: understanding drivers, actors and their different roles, the importance of timing and appropriate language, and the ways to increase visibility in policy and stakeholder circles.

- Policy impact planning fits already at the project design stage and can be adapted as circumstances change. It is useful to take into account societal and political contexts, as well as connections to other disciplines and policy areas, as the projects develop.

- Gathering policy intelligence and building skills for increased impact is a collective exercise. It is therefore wise to promote institutional instruments for systematic organisational learning and exchanges of peer tacit knowledge.

Copyright © 2020 European Union,
Published by Elsevier Limited.

Scientists working in a policy context are not mere advisors, called up to answer an isolated question only when specific knowledge is needed. Parachuting detached knowledge into the policymaking process without proper cocreation is likely to be inefficient or even misunderstood (see Chapter 1). Instead, we believe science can only bring meaningful insights to policy if researchers and policymakers work closely together. Thus, scientists should actively participate in the policymaking process, even if they do not hold a policy

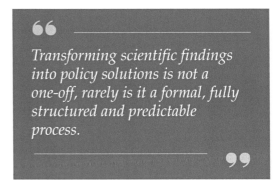

> *Transforming scientific findings into policy solutions is not a one-off, rarely is it a formal, fully structured and predictable process.*

position. They need to be engaged and understand the societal and political context of their work, in order to achieve policy impact. They need to be mindful of how to communicate, with whom to engage and be deliberate about planning their interventions.

This does not come naturally to many scientists. Conventional academic training does not emphasise policy engagement as a central expectation in the scientific profession. Therefore, scientists who start working in a science for policy context need to learn the policy world and its norms, and consider how to navigate an environment full of pressures different from academic life. This chapter aims to help: it sheds light on key principles to which scientists (and their organisations) need to adapt to achieve impact. For advice on how to become engaged without jeopardising scientific integrity, see Chapter 10.

New Practices Helpful to Increase Impact on Policy

Transforming scientific findings into policy solutions is not a one-off, rarely is it a formal, fully structured and predictable process. Scientists and scientific organisations need to develop strategies and be aware of the importance of roles, communication, relationships and overall visibility in order to be able to better operate in the policy environment. Here are a few principles.

Scientists Should Know About Different Policy Actors and Their Role in the Process

Policymaking is a complex ecosystem with many actors involved, who vary in their priorities, interests, attention spans and knowledge needs. It is therefore crucial for scientists to understand the whole policymaking arena, for two reasons:

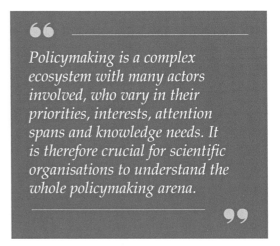

> *Policymaking is a complex ecosystem with many actors involved, who vary in their priorities, interests, attention spans and knowledge needs. It is therefore crucial for scientific organisations to understand the whole policymaking arena.*

- To be able to distinguish the roles and be clear with which hat on one speaks, with related norms and expectations.
- To understand the diversity of actors in the policymaking system.

As with all models of policymaking, the list below is a simplification of the picture, but a useful one to help researchers understand the key players:

- *The decision-maker*: the person or the body empowered to take the policy decision. Most often politicians.
- *The policymaker*: the person or the body assisting the decision-maker in reaching a decision by providing policy analysis and generating policy options.
- *The scientific expert*: the person or the body providing scientific support and advice to the policymaker and the decision-maker, giving the best evidence on which to base the solutions. This evidence and advice also involve reviewing or identifying policy options from a scientific point of view and highlighting new implications for policy consideration from research results. This is an active role covering the full policy cycle from a problem definition to policy implementation and, where needed, the anticipation of future questions.
- *The stakeholders*: people or organisations that affect or are affected by a decision and have an interest in its outcome. They exert influence on the policymaker and decision-maker and lobby for a preferred outcome of the decision. They can be consulted in the formulation of the questions on which scientific advice is sought and they may also have scientific knowledge relevant for the advice.
- *The citizens*: all of us that ultimately are affected or also can affect the implementation of the decisions and the outcomes. Citizens can be involved not only for their matters of concern, for insights and knowledge about the particular policy issue but also because their expectations, values and imaginations matter.

In practice, people or organisations may find that they fulfil more than one of these roles in the decision-making process. Proper governance demands that everyone in the decision-making process understands which role they are playing at all times and avoid combining different roles to avoid conflicts of interest (see more in Chapter 10). Scientists are not always only the scientific experts: they can also act as issue advocates or as stakeholders (Pielke, 2007), or even play a more direct policy drafting or decision-making role. The art of scientific support also lies in *making clear* which role one occupies when and remaining impartial where possible. When advising, it is vital to clearly state to which values or objectives a piece of advice responds, if it comes from a clear value-based point of view and includes an opinion on top of research results.

Moreover, these different policy actors form distinct audiences with different communication needs. There is no such thing as the general public, also not in the policymaking process (see Chapter 15). Achieving impact means adapting a message and framing to each of them, without misrepresenting the data and results or delivering contradictory messages.

The immediate audience, predetermined by a project or topic, is not always the only one worth targeting. Engaging with more actors who may be interested amplifies the message. Stakeholders and other scientific experts in particular can raise visibility of a project, as third-party endorsement of one's expertise can boost its credibility. Particularly valuable is such endorsement when granted by stakeholders with different perspectives. Other influential experts can vouch for one's credibility vis-à-vis policymakers, if the work is respected by trustworthy scientists and prestigious journals (more how to reach various audiences in Chapter 15).

Scientists Working in Policymaking Should Speak the Language Policymakers Understand and Pay Attention to

The policymaking world is one in which bandwidth is limited, attention is scarce and solutions are often needed urgently. Faced with an overflow of information, human brains have developed coping mechanisms to manage, evaluate and prioritise it (Hallsworth et al., 2018; Banuri et al., 2017), often called cognitive biases. They increase our effectiveness in processing information and are also a proof that humans do not behave entirely rationally all the time. Such cognitive shortcuts can, for example, make us put more trust in information that confirms already held beliefs (confirmation bias), consider something important or useful just because it easily comes to mind (availability bias), make us unable to accurately judge how much we or the others know, how much we agree or disagree with each other or reinforce each other's views in homogenous groups. There are many more of these shortcuts, and while they do not doom us to failure,[1] they need to be reckoned with by anyone aiming to introduce new ideas and knowledge in an environment competitive for attention.

The policy world is full of competing providers of information, with different interests (see Chapter 10). Given the tempo and cognitive shortcuts of policymaking even in noticing new information (Hallsworth et al., 2018), scientific facts need ambassadors, willing to make their work visible, understandable and communicated effectively (Cook and Lewandowsky, 2011). Trust matters in how knowledge is validated, spread and accepted (O'Connor and Weatherall, 2019).

The quality of science is indisputably a key precondition for impact (although what quality means is a subject of ongoing debate, see Sarewitz, 2011, as well as Chapters 2 and 8 of this handbook). However, there is no iron law that excellent science will by itself attract attention. Therefore, any information and knowledge provider, scientists included, has to be purposeful about their communication, outreach and engagement. There is no way of reporting one's data that would be 100% neutral – there is no 'view from nowhere' and every presentation decision is a value-based choice. Ignoring this communication aspect does not guarantee impartiality. Thinking strategically about communication is not by definition lacking in scientific integrity.

Communication choices about which framing and narratives to use shape perceptions and decisions. People are more likely to support public health interventions when the predictive data present how many deaths can be avoided, instead of how many lives saved (Tversky and Kahneman, 1981). A choice of a frame matters even if the underlying data remain the same and has to do with people's interpretation and underlying values. Such a choice can carry important political consequences (Lakoff, 2004) and is not neutral - not paying attention to it does not mean one is a more objective scientist.

As the intake of evidence into policy processes does not happen without researchers' conscious efforts and strategies for attaining impact, being heard when engaging with policymakers requires also attention to language, both in its form and tone.

To be understood by a nonscientific audience, clear writing and balancing simplification and complexity are crucial (see Chapter 15 for our approaches to clear writing and visual

---

[1] Hallsworth et al. (2018) detail techniques that counter the detrimental effects of these unconscious biases on noticing information, deliberating on decisions and executing them.

communication). Double meanings and connotations of some scientific terms in a nonspecialist context[2] represent pitfalls that hinder communication.

The tone of language is just as crucial in ensuring trust and effective relationships: being constructive but not offensive is indispensable. Within scientific communities, researchers often pay little attention to the sensitivities of other researchers if they think they are wrong. 'Reviewer 2' always seems particularly hostile. However, when scientists review policy documents or exchange arguments in policy debates, the purpose of their involvement is to help improve the outcome. This requires that policymakers are convinced it is worth listening to researchers' arguments. Scientists and policymakers are partners in the process, not competitors, which requires mutual respect and a constructive tone.

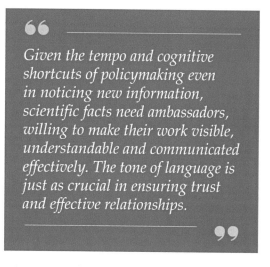

> *Given the tempo and cognitive shortcuts of policymaking even in noticing new information, scientific facts need ambassadors, willing to make their work visible, understandable and communicated effectively. The tone of language is just as crucial in ensuring trust and effective relationships.*

Of course, scientific integrity comes first and scientists must not turn a blind eye to wrong or inaccurate arguments or self-censor in pointing out necessary changes in policy-related documents. This is how scientists add value in the process, but they are more likely to succeed if they convey their points constructively. Writing with denigratory language affects trust, which can eventually damage the relationships and close off opportunities for dialogue. This applies not only to reviewing and commenting on policy documents but also to publishing policy-relevant papers (see Chapter 10 for advice on quality checks for publications).

There may be situations when blunter language is needed to warn against certain decisions. Scientists should not hesitate to speak more forcefully when justified but should recognise when bridges are being burned and weigh this judgement carefully. In that context, it is also vital to communicate uncertainty in ways that will be understandable for policymakers, without stifling their decision-making.

Scientists Should Look for Windows of Opportunity, Build Relationships and Gather Intelligence About Policy Actors and Drivers

Irrespective of the context, planning for policy engagement and impact must happen from the beginning of a research project, and adapted if necessary. Anticipation is an ally of impact. Relationships and policy intelligence can help researchers to know when they could have valuable input and time it strategically. This way one can volunteer new perspectives, instead of waiting for a request that may not come. Two aspects are necessary to plan impact realistically: understanding the policy drivers and building relationships in the policy arena.

Policy problems are interconnected and complex and require joint initiatives in response. Interdisciplinarity and systemic thinking are an important part of a more agile scientific support

---

[2]A video produced by Wellcome Trust shows some very relevant examples: 'Beware double meanings when you talk science': https://www.youtube.com/watch?v=Mscn8QBu2Ws, acc. 02.05.2020.

(see Chapter 11). Modern science for policy organisations should strive for it but this requires gathering 'policy intelligence', understanding of the different facets of the policy debates and drivers (Oliver and Cairney, 2019).

Scientists usually work on a narrow subject in detail, but the repercussions of their knowledge may be relevant for multiple policy fields and contexts. Equally, it is unlikely that one single piece of research will be decisive. Often connecting different pieces of research is crucial: it is not always that the latest study is most useful for policy. A well-known phenomenon from several years back may not have penetrated the policy sphere and may be more significant. Scientific novelty is not always a virtue in science for policy.

Navigating that reality is difficult. Some findings raise the interest of different actors (e.g., in different policy areas), who do not always approach it with the same reasons and attitudes. One set of results may be useful for one area and complicate the plans in the other. For that reason, science for policy organisations must work towards understanding multiple sides of policy processes and not work in silos.

> " Irrespective of the context, planning for policy engagement and impact must happen from the beginning of a research project - anticipation is an ally of impact. Science for policy organisations must work towards understanding multiple sides of policy processes and not work in silos. "

One way of trying to get this understanding is networking beyond scientific circles (Badgett, 2015). It also helps to win legitimacy and brings multipliers of work, beneficial for visibility and trust. Both online and offline networking, being visible in not only scientific events, but also policy-relevant ones, help to understand where important conversations are happening, who is involved in them and how they drive policies. These affect the context of one's research and policy support. Policy influencers can also be prominent scientists or analysts with an active policy role. Chapter 10 sheds more light on how to avoid undue influence of interests when engaging nonscientific partners in science for policy work.

The right understanding of policy drivers and developments helps to proactively arrange and plan cooperation ahead of time (Badgett, 2015). By understanding this complex puzzle and investing in a strong network of policy actors at various levels, researchers can strategically build long-term relationships with policymakers, which are vital for impact. Policy support is very much a face-to-face, peer-to-peer endeavour, in which interpersonal relations can be the catalyst or downfall to a functioning collaboration. However, these relationships can pose some danger to integrity, or be abused for undue influence. For more on this, consult Chapter 10.

Understanding the drivers and forging relationships with policymakers helps to identify windows of opportunity for engagement, in terms of timing, scope of support and agency. Policy intelligence helps to understand interests and developments among different groups that may all have interest in one's research, but with different intentions. This can help to adapt to various interlocutors – to their individual goals and state of the relationship – and avoid conflicts and misunderstandings.

Timing is a crucial driver of policymaking. Being on time and respecting the deadlines is key if one wants to receive any place in the policymaking process. However, figuring out the right timing and the expectations is not always easy or in control of the scientists. When policymakers are under time pressure to gather evidence, the strength of the existing relationship plays a role in whether scientists will have a window of opportunity.

Understanding the policy process also helps researchers to interpret what type of support they can provide at a given moment. For instance, at a later stage of policy development, only concise and easy to integrate data are welcome. Any detailed and nuanced input can be useful earlier, at the framing or drafting stages. Mixing these up will deter policymakers from using such evidence.

Of course, gathering 'policy intelligence' is not always possible for individual scientists, but there are institutional processes that can help:

- Horizon scanning (see more in Chapter 12): early capturing of even weak signals about topics gaining traction and likely to influence the policymaking agenda;
- Media monitoring: keeping track of the news and debates in relevant policy fields;
- Political briefs/dedicated policy officers: specific analysis on what is on the agenda, topics under formal debates, key policy events and developments in a field;
- Following policy influencers via social media: it helps to catch the pulse of a debate and recent developments and understand where the relevant conversations are happening.

It is not to suggest that one person should try to build up this entire picture alone. Science for policy is a team sport. Institutionally, there must be ways to gather intelligence on multidimensional policy drivers.

Image: Alex Stemmer - https://stock.adobe.com/be_en/images/amphiprion-ocellaris-clownfish-in-the-anemon-natural-marine-enriromnent/241766337?prev_url=detail
Icon in page corners: Clownfish icon by Ho Ching, from the Noun Project (https://thenounproject.com/search/?q=clownfish&i=475669)

From a Policy Problem to a Research Question: Getting It Right Together

Main author: Marta Sienkiewicz

Contributors: Pernille Brandt, Marion Westra van Holthe, Adrien Rorive, Ivan Kalburov, Stijn Verleyen

Key takeaways:

- The mismatch between what is studied and what policymakers need to know (or think they need to know) is a crucial reason behind the challenges of increasing the uptake of evidence in policymaking.

- Instead of attempting to 'translate' research results at the end of a project, systemic cocreation of research questions early in the process helps mitigate that problem.

- Knowledge organisations, and sometimes individual researchers, can try to bridge this gap by organising systemic linkages between scientists and policymakers, focused on translating policy problems to a set of researchable questions.

- Individuals should not shy away from 'questioning the questions' and attempting to understand policymakers' underlying goals to better define the type of knowledge that is missing. Early involvement of scientists also helps to refine the framing of a problem, bringing more clarity to what a perceived policy problem really is about.

- The JRC experimented with some institutional setups that can be adapted by other institutions. They include dedicated knowledge centres, coordinated work programming focused on policy relevance, exchanges between scientific and policy departments and employing dedicated facilitators between departments. The national and regional activities through Science meets Parliaments/Science meets Regions programme mainstream our philosophy across Europe.

Science for Policy Handbook
http://dx.doi.org/10.1016/B978-0-12-822596-7.00006-1

Copyright © 2020 European Union,
Published by Elsevier Limited.

Collaboration and relationships are reported as a key facilitator to evidence uptake (Oliver et al., 2014). Yet, the 'two communities' (see Chapter 1) often work in isolation. Science too often tries to bring new issues to the attention of policymakers and place it on their already full agendas as items to resolve (Cairney, 2016). Policymakers often realise after receiving scientific evidence that the information does not respond to the questions they need answering. It is symptomatic of Science for Policy 1.0, where the mismatch between the supply and demand sides of evidence leaves both frustrated and disappointed.

An obvious moment when the two can and should cooperate more is in discussing what knowledge is missing. Listening, engaging and iterating are fundamentals in Science for Policy 2.0, where a real partnership between scientists and policymakers is the driving force. Through such interactions, they can arrive at a mutual understanding about what needs to be answered and therefore what needs to be studied.

Using cocreation in deciding what to study brings two main advantages. It improves the relevance of the science, both through microlevel discussions on specific questions and macrolevel strategic planning of broader research topics. Moreover, dialogue early in the process creates a clear scope for a task, with clear expectations, which itself strengthens the relationship between science and policy, with increasing likelihood of a productive use of research. Over time, it is likely to create trust, and while collaboration should not be limited to defining what to study, it is a perfect moment to start forging these trusting working relationships.

This chapter presents some reasons why rethinking how we decide what to study for policy is important and how cocreation improves the process of scientific support and the implications for scientists. We also present some examples through which we promote dialogue around deciding what to study, and thereby strengthen relationships between science and policy.

Why Rethink How We Define Research Questions for a Policy Context?

The debate surrounding the evidence for policy field has long been focused on a need for translation of scientific results for nonscientific audiences. It implies that the scientific process happens apart from the policy process and that results only need to be better 'translated', because scientists and policymakers speak 'different languages'. However, the responsibility for creating useful science for policy lies not only on the side of scientists: policymakers also need to clearly articulate their needs, knowledge gaps and expectations. In science for policy, the detailed discussion of

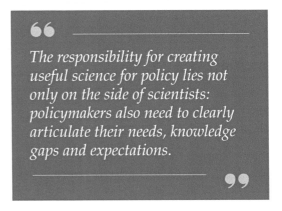

> The responsibility for creating useful science for policy lies not only on the side of scientists: policymakers also need to clearly articulate their needs, knowledge gaps and expectations.

what needs to be researched should predate the 'translation' process as this decision has fundamental consequences for the subsequent policy and research process. Involving scientists already in framing the problem can increase the effectiveness of scientific support and overall legitimacy of policies, provided that a diversity of research perspectives (of and within disciplines) is ensured and complemented by a broader discussion with citizens and stakeholders.

A lack, perceived or actual, of relevant and clear research is reportedly one of the key factors preventing effective use of evidence in policymaking. Policymakers' limited knowledge of research methods may not help either: it discourages them from using scientific evidence and distorts their expectations of what research can deliver (Oliver et al., 2014). Exchanging only dry assignments and working in isolation without a proper debate on what to study will not help either side achieve their goals.

Following their extensive systematic review of the science of using evidence, Langer et al. (2016) recommended that the processes of 'building consensus on fit-for-purpose evidence and policy-relevant questions [should be made] explicit and more formalised'. They also found that user engagement through building an agreement on what to study tends to be effective in increasing the likelihood of using evidence, next to Delphi panels and journal clubs (Langer et al., 2016, pp. 24–27).

We believe that innovating in the area of defining research needs and questions for policy processes is an extremely important step to increase the chances of policy impact from the use of evidence. It strengthens relationships, increases relevance of research and ensures that policymakers have more accurate expectations for what can be provided by researchers (Oliver and Cairney, 2019).

However, a better alignment of expectations is not always straightforward due to an underestimated difference between the nature of questions posed by researchers and policymakers, respectively. Moreover, the choices about what research to commission or what evidence to include in the decision-making process are not neutral and cannot be decided only on the basis of technical considerations. In fact, these choices are highly political. A decision not to ask or answer certain research questions can have important downstream effects on the policy process. Thus, researchers need to understand that their interlocutors approach problems differently. Policymakers need to include values and political considerations even in the seemingly technical aspects of evidence generation.

Tame Problems Versus Wicked Problems

It is a common claim that researchers and policymakers 'live in different worlds' (Chapter 1). However, a major reason is often unnoticed: namely that their respective problems and the nature of their inquiries are strikingly different. A lack of sufficient understanding of the other lies at the root of common frustrations. Rittel and Webber (1973) explained this tension by comparing the types of inquiries pursued by scientists and policymakers. They contrasted them as 'tame problems' of science versus 'wicked problems' of policy.

In science, the process of *solving* a problem is identical with the process of *understanding* the nature of that problem (Rittel and Webber, 1973, p. 162). Scientific questions, especially those tackled by individual research projects, are typically narrow in scope. Science has a collective responsibility to collect, verify and synthesise these results, in pursuit of more and more coherent knowledge. However, the scientific method cannot answer political or normative questions like 'what should be done about x'. Therefore, the process of interpreting science involves an inferential and philosophical gap between what is described and what conclusions can be drawn on that basis (Douglas, 2009).

Meanwhile, wicked problems of policy are not 'solvable' by technical knowledge. Such problems are defined as discrepancies between the state of affairs as it is and the state as it ought to be (Rittel and Webber, 1973, p. 165). They are complex, interconnected, infinite and need a multidisciplinary consideration, which makes it difficult to even determine a definitive formulation. It is also impossible to objectively verify whether the solution to them is 'true' or 'false', as in the case of science (where a hypothesis can be objectively verified). Defining a problem dictates the realm of solutions, and as such is a nonneutral exercise. Moreover, there are no criteria that enable one to prove that all solutions to a wicked problem have been identified and considered (p. 164), which makes the process imperfect by nature.

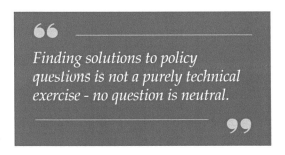

Finding solutions to policy questions is not a purely technical exercise - no question is neutral.

While questions posed to science are of an analytical nature, policymakers also must deal with normative issues. A classical approach of science cannot attempt to *solve* open societal issues of a wicked kind. Policymakers still need to answer the analytical parts – to figure out what the technical possibilities to reach an objective are – but they simultaneously need to reconcile conflicting values and objectives and also ensure that the course of action is approved by a majority, including of the public. Their best solution is one which best reconciles all these imperatives. Scientists help with the technical part, but the rest falls to the policymakers and decision-makers.

Sometimes research is commissioned to determine whether a policy action is even required. Such assessments should be asked of researchers only in their technical capacity, as they cannot judge the threshold for considering something worthy of a political or policy response. The frame for interpretation comes from policymakers or even politicians and the public. More on the division of roles in the policy context can be found in Chapter 5.

Scientists' Role in Framing of Policy Problems

Finding solutions to policy questions is not a purely technical exercise and no question is neutral. The way it is defined, some of its key aspects highlighted at the expense of others, bears consequences for what research can be useful and what solutions can be designed. Framing a policy problem is a political decision and an expression of power. However, it is not always a fully conscious choice. Particular definitions of a problem can seem obvious due to unconscious cognitive shortcuts, such as availability bias, confirmation bias and group reinforcement, among others (Hallsworth et al., 2018).

It is here that scientific experts, impartial as they should be, can propose reframings[1] and lead the discussions on possible alternative definitions of problems, questions, variables, indicators and methods to capture the relevant type of information. This is also the right moment to understand and explore the values behind a policy direction from the facts sought to inform the decision, distinguish the solutions from the diagnosis (Hallsworth et al., 2018, p. 31). Engaging in reframing and other self-critical reflections increases the chances that the

---

[1] More on the concrete strategies can be found in Dewulf and Bouwen (2012). Hallsworth et al. (2018) also cover solutions to mitigate the other abovementioned biases.

right knowledge is employed in the process and that a more nuanced definition of the problem could be adopted. Techniques for widening the frames are discussed by Dewulf and Bouwen (2012), as well as Hallsworth et al. (2018). Some of the design approaches (Chapter 13) can also be useful in that endeavour.

This can only work if done together with policymakers. Scientists' role is then a supporting one, almost one of a facilitator, monitoring if the evidence is not abused, incorrect conclusions drawn and facts weaponised. Scientists have the right to point out some logical fallacies or inappropriate use of evidence in the process of problem definitions (although in a constructive tone, see more in Chapter 5). Due to their political nature and a need for legitimacy of such a process, reframing activities also benefit from citizen engagement, either through their direct involvement in the process or by using insights generated through previous participatory activities. Given the uncertain and highly contested area of science for policy, citizens should be able to influence what needs to be researched by the experts hired to provide the evidence and to increase the quality and legitimacy of the process. For more details, see Chapter 8.

Implications for Science for Policy Researchers

Acknowledging the difference in respective questions of science and policy and the politically constructed nature of questions has consequences for researchers.

Firstly, they cannot expect the same analytical-only approach from their policy interlocutors. Given how many factors influence finding a solution on the policymaking side, the mindset of policymakers will be far from purely analytical (Oliver and Cairney, 2017). Hence, it is very important to speak of evidence-informed, rather than evidence-based, policymaking. To properly understand what needs to be researched, scientists need to know the ultimate policy goals and major unknowns among policymaking actors (including citizens and stakeholders). This helps them design research questions more likely to provide answers relevant for drafting policy responses to advance these goals. It is not about cherry-picking data, but understanding where knowledge is lacking. Sometimes it means that the questions initially posed change radically because only through dialogue both sides realise the true extent of the knowledge gaps and evidence needed to bridge them.

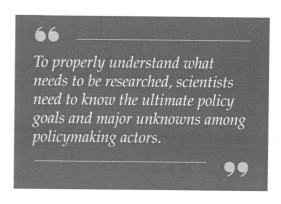

To properly understand what needs to be researched, scientists need to know the ultimate policy goals and major unknowns among policymaking actors.

As policy questions and research questions are not interchangeable, there is a need for an iterative process of translation from policy questions to research questions. This implies active engagement, openness and attention to detail. It has to be done in a cocreative way, including opening up and 'questioning the question'.

Researchers should not take policy questions at face value. The questions posed in 'dry' assignments do *not* specify such levels of detail, so they require actual in-depth conversations. Equally, the questions *not* being asked by policymakers are worthy of consideration.

The decisions about several aspects of a research design have to made: population, indicators, measurements, definitions, scope, etc. It means debating whether the questions expressed are really the ones to be answered. It is an analytical inquiry, a systematic analysis of knowns and unknowns to finally propose better alternatives in order to produce the most relevant knowledge to fill the gaps identified by policymakers. Given how little one side knows about the other, and how differently they conceptualise answerable questions in their 'bubbles', scientists should not fear probing for more information to make sure their research is relevant.

In the policy context, scientific research is used with sociopolitical concerns in the background. This means that research findings may become politically inconvenient or touch upon issues which are politically sensitive. A dialogue on the questions and expectations allows to fully assess the sensitivity of an issue and adapt a communication strategy accordingly, early in the process. It includes both a plan on how to communicate sensitivities to policymakers, and to external audiences, with the right framing and appropriate degree of confidentiality.

Our Best Practice

We have established that the nature of questions that policymakers deal with and ones that scientists respond to makes it necessary to work together on deciding what knowledge to collect, to avoid misunderstandings. Here are a few strategic activities that the JRC has implemented in order to foster the relationships with policymakers and the collaboration around research needs for policy.

We Experiment With Novel and Interdisciplinary Approaches to Governance of Knowledge

In order to increase the relevance and uptake of our research for policymaking, we have set up special entities focused on knowledge for policy in several priority areas (e.g., migration and demography, disaster risk management, territorial policies, among others). These so-called Knowledge Centres (managing knowledge around a certain area) help to collect policy-relevant knowledge and questions around a given field in one place.

The joint governance of the Knowledge Centres by research and multiple policymaking departments ensures that the research questions in their action plans are truly driven by the knowledge needs of policymakers. The diversity of participants helps to make sure that the cross-cutting 'wicked problems' meet a policy response as comprehensive and as coherent as it can be, accompanied by relevant knowledge to answer appropriate questions. They are, however, just as important in managing the policy questions as in managing knowledge. Often comparing questions from different policy actors reveals the deeper knowledge needs behind the questions or alternative framings.

The Knowledge Centre on Migration and Demography (KCMD) is one example of this approach. It is steered by eight Commission departments and the European External Action Service, who regularly meet in the KCMD Steering Group at middle management level, including inter alia departments responsible for migration and home affairs, international development, civil protection and humanitarian aid, foreign policy, EU political strategy, research and statistics.

Recent work of the KCMD on improving EU migration data is a good example of our cocreation when it comes to knowledge gaps. Data on migration are known to be patchy and not always timely. Instead of trying to improve the situation alone only on the research supply side, the KCMD organised a regular series of workshops to discuss EU migration data with relevant Commission departments and EU agencies who are either users or publishers of migration data. Together, they focused on identifying uncertainties and gaps in data, reviewing analytical tools and policy needs, and on the most relevant concrete actions to improve the data. KCMD efforts are also strengthened by multiple internal and external partnerships and collaborations of data scientists, economists, policymakers and operational authorities.

Sustained close relationships with groups of policymakers allow to provide tailored support to Commission departments for priority ad hoc analysis requests. Parallel to the Knowledge Centres, we also run Competence Centres, which facilitate the use of specific tools in policymaking (e.g., foresight (see Chapter 12), modelling (see Chapter 18), text mining, evaluation, among others).

Our Work Programme Is Tuned in to the Policy Priorities

Ensuring that what scientists study remains close to policy needs can be achieved through various ways. Face-to-face interpersonal interactions represent an important channel for cocreation. In the JRC, this approach is complemented by a top-down process, the Work Programme. Designed to provide an overview of the JRC's annual research activity, its coordination process provides additional benefits. Indeed, the Work Programme goes through a set of formal processes throughout its yearly production cycle, which allows policy considerations to input into research planning.

For instance, the Work Programme undergoes ex ante and ex post evaluations, whereby independent panels scrutinise respectively planned work and delivered outcome to check their policy relevance. At the ex ante stage, panels deliver opinions to senior staff on such relevance. These opinions trigger strategic discussion at the top level of the organisation and can lead to significant modifications.

The Work Programme is also submitted to all policy departments (Directorates-General, DGs) for consultation. This process is yet another check of policy relevance where DGs are formally invited to share views on ongoing cooperation. This consultation allows policymakers to flag new priorities and represents an opportunity to discuss new cooperation.

It is important to note that not all research organisations enjoy such proximity to policy-making processes. Equally, this formal macrolevel planning does not replace the importance of interactions between individual researchers and policymakers on lower levels (sometimes strengthened by facilitators and knowledge managers), to ensure alignment of details or fulfilling the needs emerging ad hoc beyond the planned activities. The JRC Work Programme may not be directly replicable in other organisations, but it highlights how a top-down approach can complement lower-level interactions to ensure policy relevance. The principles behind our system – debate, consultation, evaluation – can be incorporated in other forms, with equivalent policy audiences. Chapters 13 and 7 provide some inspiration for the cocreative processes.

Our Scientists Join Policy Departments through Short-term Exchanges

With a growing complexity of policy problems, the JRC staff must become more agile, be able to quickly grasp the orientations of priorities in policy support while maintaining scientific excellence. Close relationships with policymakers help orient in such an environment

(Chapter 5 elaborates on that further, with more information on managing related risks in Chapter 10). To that aim, we set up the JRC Exchange Programme, which gives a possibility to participate in a short-term stay (2–4 weeks) in policy departments relevant to one's scientific work. The visits are most frequently based on already existing collaborations with policymakers and help deepen the relationships.

The exchange is meant to help scientists

- Gain better insights in policy development processes;
- Foster working relations and strategic collaborations;
- Provide feedback on key policy issues requiring scientific input;
- Give ad hoc support to the host in helping them understanding specific scientific issues in policy debates.

While the exchanges are not designed solely to focus on defining research questions, it is one of the crucial tasks they can accomplish. The exchanges happen throughout the whole year, which means that researchers and their managers can propose a stay at a moment most suitable, e.g., for defining the scope of a new project or for best understanding the needs of policymakers for an upcoming big collaboration.

The exchange also helps forge stronger relationships through systematic, face-to-face contact. Trust and better contextual awareness of each other's realities develop. This principle is in some areas extended in efforts to create 'mirrored units' in the JRC and policy departments, whose work is complementary and where staff often has experience of working on the other side.

We Empower Facilitators Between Science and Policy

The science–policy interface is a broad field with many roles on the spectrum from pure scientists to politicians. We believe all researchers working in organisations aiming to impact policy should be aware of how science for policy differs from pure science. However, not all of them will be in direct contact with policymakers and will not have to acquire all the knowledge about the policy context.

The culture of Science for Policy 2.0 relies heavily on teamwork. Different parts of scientific organisations count on each other for knowledge and skills relevant to effective policy support (Chapter 4 explains these in detail), contributing to joint impact. In the JRC, we have a team of desk officers and knowledge managers with knowledge of specific policy fields that facilitate collaboration between our scientists and policy departments. Researchers are still encouraged to engage with policymakers bilaterally, but the transversal perspective and expertise provided by these desk officers offers an additional advantage, both to scientists and to policymakers. Literature names them knowledge brokers, but we consider the entire JRC as a knowledge broker. Therefore, we rely on other terms to refer to these actors.

- Our facilitators strive to establish or complement connections and interactions between policymakers and scientists and facilitate the exchange of ideas regarding what and how to study to address a policy problem. Far from replacing existing relationships between the two communities, they act as a catalyst to increase cooperation and craft new ones.
- Our facilitators help increase context sensitivity. They can provide insights on policy developments and advise on ongoing or future processes to identify windows of opportunity for input. Reporting on political events can also help translate their significance to researchers, thereby making them aware of the nuances of a policy field.

- Our facilitators help instil interdisciplinarity in the organisation. With the emergence of increasingly more complex policy questions, the required expertise needs to come from multiple fields. These multifaceted issues highlight the need to draw knowledge from various areas and bring experts together. By being in-between policy and science, facilitators benefit from an understanding of a policy issue and of an institutional setup in the research community. They can utilise this transversal view point to identify synergies, introducing experts from additional fields to the mix.

We Stimulate Dialogue and Stronger Relationships Between Scientists and Policymakers in the National and Regional Contexts

Our way of working is not limited to the European Commission or the EU level. We want to promote the culture of cocreation in evidence-informed policymaking throughout Europe. One way we go about it is by organising the 'Science meets Parliaments' series of events with the European Parliament since 2015, later extended to 'Science meets Regions' events across Europe. These events bring together scientists and policymakers at EU, national and regional levels and engage them in a regular dialogue to find the right approach to how science can best support the local challenges at hand.

We tested the concept in Brussels and in some other EU regions on a smaller scale before we rolled out an EU-wide pilot project 'Science meets Parliaments/Science meets Regions', approved by the European Parliament, in 2018–19. Our events are now present in 26 member states, regions and cities, supporting scientists and policymakers in finding local solutions together while stressing the importance of evidence in policymaking. While we facilitate these events and lend scientific support where relevant, the ownership ultimately lies with the local organisers themselves, who define with local scientists the issue they want to tackle and the expertise they need.

To this end, we fund events accompanied by scientific studies, with the local organising authorities taking full ownership of the event and its follow-up. We are also preparing an educational package for policymakers to help them effectively collaborate with researchers and make use of scientific evidence in their own decisions.

Conclusion

Despite seeming like technical debates, honest discussions about knowledge needs and defining the policy-relevant research questions are a process of political negotiation. They mix power relations, expert advice, values, cognitive shortcuts and time pressures. They require trust and strong relationships, as well as mutual understanding of each other's potential and expectations.

Done well, through an interaction and with the inclusion of citizens' and stakeholders' perspectives, these processes bring an increase in quality of science for policy in a complex world. A broader consensus, as opposed to singular decision of either scientists or policymakers, increases the legitimacy and relevance of the knowledge being produced. Moreover, the collaborative approach strengthens the trust and relationships in the science–policy interface, clarifies expectations and increases the chances for the research to be productively used.

Image: Julia - https://stock.adobe.com/be_en/images/leafcutter-ants-carrying-leaves-on-a-branch/276006169?prev_url=detail
Icon in page corners: Ant icon by Royyan Wijaya, from the Noun Project (https://thenounproject.com/search/?q=ant&i=1089857)

Working Through Communities

Author: Coralia Catana

Key takeaways:

- Knowledge for policy emerges from connections between different actors, inside and outside policy or scientific institutions. One of the ways to channel their tacit as well as explicit knowledge is to work through communities of practice (CoPs).

- Communities focus on specific knowledge or competences needed, facilitating learning and exchanges which improve performance.

- The chapter focuses on the benefits and different ways organisations, researchers and policymakers can mobilise a vast array of internal and external stakeholders around common issues, topics and practices and with specific goals, in the form of communities.

- Effective collaboration through communities reduces duplication, allows exchange and broader inputs from various parts of an organisation as well as its relevant circles and leads to greater strategic alignment while increasing efficiency and quality of work.

- The chapter offers a self-assessment tool for a community – the CoP Success Wheel – encompassing eight success factors. For a community to succeed, it is important to create the right environment which includes setting strategic goals and objectives, real governance and support from senior management, empowered community leaders, investment in the community management role and sound and user-friendly digital environments to host conversations, exchanges and repositories of knowledge.

Science for Policy Handbook
http://dx.doi.org/10.1016/B978-0-12-822596-7.00007-5

Copyright © 2020 European Union,
Published by Elsevier Limited.

Communities – A Form of Collective Intelligence

Mobilising knowledge, i.e., people and resources, is vital nowadays for the co-creation of policies. Therefore this chapter focuses on the benefits and the different ways organisations, researchers and policymakers can mobilise a vast array of internal and external stakeholders around common issues, and with specific goals, in the form of communities. Such pooling of knowledge from many

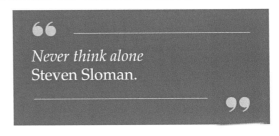

Never think alone
Steven Sloman.

places and people is vital for modern scientific organisations producing relevant input in a policy context.

One new way of working is with **communities**, sometimes referred to as knowledge communities, communities of practice (CoPs) or of interest (see the next section for some terminological clarifications). What binds them all is the social interaction at their core: they naturally take advantage of social learning and exchange between members. Such interaction can take physical or virtual forms, or both. Communities give people opportunities to experiment with what they have learnt, in safe environments and with the support of other people.

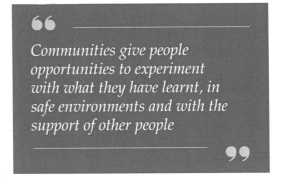

Communities give people opportunities to experiment with what they have learnt, in safe environments and with the support of other people

In *The Knowledge Illusion*, cognitive scientists Sloman and Fernbach (2017) show that our intelligence resides not in individual brains but in the collective mind. We think in groups and no individual knows everything. Sloman puts forward the importance of communities of knowledge as collaborative processes, built on trust between the community members, that house expertise in the right way and that know how to take advantage of it. Communities help to see blind spots and opportunities in our current knowledge and promote knowledge sharing as a default basis for policies based on the collective intelligence of the organisation's people and external partners (Wenger-Trayner and Wenger-Trayner, 2015).

A growing number of web-based applications have proven that a group of diverse, independent and informed people might well outperform even the best individual estimate or decision (Bonabeau, 2009). To unlock the potential of collective intelligence, we need to understand how collective intelligence systems and tools work. 'They need not magic, but the science from which the magic comes' (Malone et al., 2010).

To tap into a crowd's wisdom and avoid tapping into a crowd's madness (Bonabeau, 2009), it is important to get the mechanisms for harnessing the power of collective intelligence right. When the MIT Centre for Collective Intelligence looked into hundreds of examples of web-enabled collective intelligence, researchers identified a small set of building blocks as the 'genes' of collective intelligence systems (see Fig. 1).

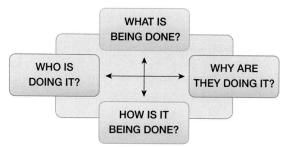

FIGURE 1 The design questions behind collective intelligence. (After Malone et al. (2010).)

In our individual brain, linking observation, analysis, creativity, memory, judgement and wisdom makes the whole much more than the sum of its parts. Mulgan argues that assemblies or communities work the same way: the ones 'that bring together many elements will be vital if the world is to navigate some of its biggest challenges, from health and climate change to migration. Their role will be to orchestrate knowledge and also apply much more systematic methods to knowledge about that knowledge – including metadata, verification tools and tags, and careful attention to how knowledge is used in practice' (Mulgan, 2017).

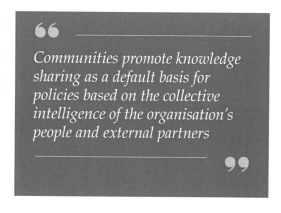

> *Communities promote knowledge sharing as a default basis for policies based on the collective intelligence of the organisation's people and external partners*

For public institutions, collective intelligence at work challenges structures, roles and boundaries; therefore it is important for organisations to be aware of how they observe their environments and how they harvest the know-how of their employees, external partners and other audiences. Sometimes it may require developing entirely new ways of thinking and working (Mulgan, 2017).

Communities of Practice – Definitions, Typology, Success Factors and Benefits

Definitions

Based on our experience at the European Commission, the concept of communities of knowledge or knowledge communities, as labelled by Sloman, is narrowed down to communities of practice (CoPs). Our working definition of a CoP is *a group of individuals who share their interests and problems within a specific topic and gain a greater degree of knowledge and expertise through regular interaction.* In a CoP people share and develop their knowledge within a domain, as well as use and develop the community's body of knowledge which includes practices, methods, guidelines and other resources. Communities of practice go beyond just sharing information as practitioners have a desire to build and improve their practice (Ingham, 2017).

Three main elements define a CoP: the shared **domain** of interest, the **community** where members engage in joint activities and discussions and the **practice** itself, as members are practitioners who share a repertoire of resources such as experience, stories, tools, etc. (Wenger-Trayner and Wenger-Trayner, 2015).

Unlike independent and loosely governed bodies of years ago, today's communities require real structure. Recent research also shows that communities work best if they have clear accountability and management oversight (McDermott and Archibald, 2013).

To become effective, a community operates best according to the following drivers: **acquiring** (user-centric information provision), connecting (networking and exchange) or **co-creating** (results oriented co-work, creation of new knowledge, learning process).

Typology

A JRC assessment study of about 20 internal (JRC and the Commission) CoPs identifies three basic community types:

- Hub – CoPs that connect people with knowledge content; the primary value is to *inform* the organisation around the topic of practice.
- Platform – CoPs where members collaborate to produce new knowledge; the primary value is *discussion* and *collaboration* around the topic of practice.
- Service – CoPs that provide a service; the primary value is to *deliver* value and *cooperate* with the rest of the organisation in the achievement of its goals.

This typology represents a progression of CoP types (Fig. 2). CoPs typically begin life as Hubs, then progress to Platforms and then mature into Services. This can be seen as an evolution of value over time, though it should be noted that Hubs and Platforms offer value in their own right; they are not necessarily destined to evolve into the higher value types, though the potential for this could always be explored. This reinforces Sloman's theory that in a community of knowledge, what matters more than having knowledge is having access to knowledge (Sloman and Fernbach, 2017).

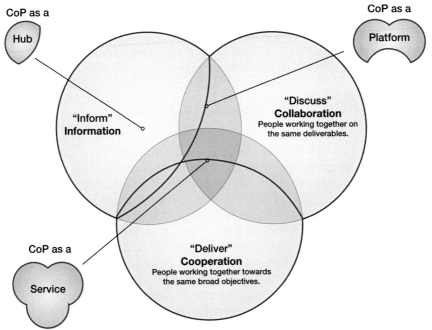

FIGURE 2 Typology of communities of practice.

Benefits and Motivation

Effective collaboration reduces duplication, allows discussion and broader inputs earlier in the policy cycle and leads to greater strategic alignment in the organisation, while increasing the efficiency and quality of our work.

The added value and benefits of a CoP are in sharing of three components of knowledge: *data*, *information* and *tacit knowledge* (= experience). The CoP's specific added value is the access to tacit knowledge by means of networking people. Communities of practice ensure direct link between learning and performance, as the same people participate in project teams.

Capturing and retaining tacit knowledge is difficult; however, this is often shared within and between communities. Bringing together a diverse group of people that share the same challenges, but have different experiences, creates a wider pool of knowledge to draw from to address shared problems.

Success Factors for Communities to Thrive

Most of the success factors described here are linked to the framework for designing collective intelligence endeavours proposed by MIT Centre for Collective Intelligence and mentioned in the first section of this chapter. Within the JRC, we performed thorough research assessing the state of our communities and identified several factors which contribute to the development of thriving communities. We incorporated them in a 'success wheel', which contains eight aspects necessary to create and maintain well-functioning CoPs. The success wheel can also be a framework for designing, assessing and continuously improving a community (Fig. 3).

For a community to succeed, it is important to create the right environment which includes the following:

Setting Strategic Objectives

Formal goals and deliverables energize communities and provide a reason and a focus to meet and participate. They are worked out by the community members and should be steered by a core group of individuals that hold the potential of becoming more connected. The goal has to originate from the community owners and members. They have to convince themselves of the value of the community by uncovering their own goals and objectives. Once the goal is there, it needs to be translated into specific behaviours we want members to perform. Behaviours will change from group to group, but their common denominator is that they all feed towards the goals.

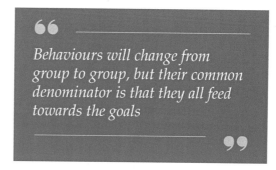

> *Behaviours will change from group to group, but their common denominator is that they all feed towards the goals*

For co-creating community goals and strategic objectives, Collison proposes very good helpers in the form of questions which can guide productive conversations around three CoP drivers: collect–connect–create (Collison, 2014):

- 'What knowledge can we **collect** – what can we each bring to the table?'

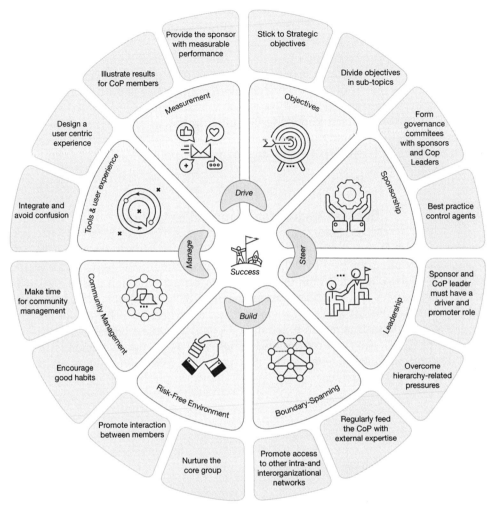

FIGURE 3 Communities of practice success wheel.

- 'Which subtopics and specific questions can we **connect** together to discuss, where a conversation is more appropriate than formal information sharing?'
- 'What are the areas and challenges where we could collaborate and **create** new knowledge (products, guides, recommendations, processes) together?'

When setting up the CoP on mapping (related to geospatial science) in the European Commission (EC), the community owners in the JRC identified the goals and their related behaviours which were validated by the community members. Here is an example of goals and behaviours identified by community owners.

Goal 1	Ensure coherent and coordinated mapping activities across JRC and EC
Behaviour 1	When working on a new map, members consult the CoP reference space to check for geographical correctness, mapping conventions and links to key resources (e.g., GISCO, ESTAT, etc.).
Behaviour 2	Members share/point to their maps in the community.
Behaviour 3	Facilitator creates reference library in the community, which covers geographical correctness, mapping conventions and links to key resources.
Behaviour 4	Geographic information system users from policy departments join the community.
Goal 2	Improved efficiency and effectiveness of mapping
Behaviour 1	Members post their questions and challenges. Facilitator responds to questions on geographical correctness by pointing to key resources and by inviting other members to respond.
Behaviour 2	Members inform peers about their upcoming mapping activities and projects.
Behaviour 3	Members attend regular face-to-face meetings to discuss topics of their interest.
Behaviour 4	Members identify shared training needs.

Sponsorship: Support From Your Organisation

Two decades ago, communities were thought to be self-organising and self-sustaining, operating independently of hierarchy. Recent research shows that communities need strong endorsement from the organisation's top leadership to make a difference in the long term. In the case of internal CoPs in an organisation, research shows that the vitality of communities and their results depend a lot on the extent to which senior managers acknowledge, support and invest in them. For example, in the JRC, the Deputy Director-General sponsors several CoPs on transversal themes such as migration, demography, sustainable development goals, fairness, etc., spanning across units, directorates and different thematic departments of the organisations.

In the case of participation in communities with external stakeholders, endorsement from the organisation's leadership and a clear mandate are necessary to make sure stakeholder engagement activity is an integral part of the research or policy work.

Leadership

Community leadership is both about support, investment and active participation from senior and middle management addressed earlier and about leadership from inside the CoP. A core group of CoP members taking the lead and steering the community is a key element coming up in our research. Such leaders generally and ideally emerge from within the community but they can be appointed too. The community appreciates and values their input. The community manager is part of the core group and convenes its members on a regular basis.

Community leaders need to be knowledgeable, respected and empowered. Communities may have one leader appointed by the organisation, the community or themselves. A community should allow for emerging leadership or sharing of leadership responsibilities by the core group. Community leaders give direction to the community, connect members and facilitate discussions, but they do not have authority over members or own the community. Successful communities belong to their members.

For more hands-on tips on community leadership in practice, see Community Management section.

Boundary Spanning

Evidence suggests that knowledge related to the practice of a community is regularly imported from experts outside the CoP. These experts can be from other organisations or be part of the organization to which the CoP belongs. Access to intra- or interorganisational networks not only increases members' active participation but also ensures members' diversity. Diversity of members' backgrounds and locations is desirable, but this can also mean a diversity of expectations and needs. The value proposition of CoPs needs to be defined for different personas. For instance, what is useful for a scientist may not be of same relevance to a policymaker.

Risk-free Environment: A Safe Space to Fail and Learn

Trust is the basis of a successful CoP and needs to be cultivated so that members feel safe to collaborate with each other. Within the CoP boundaries, members are no longer regarded as being under their direct supervisors' management as a CoP is a hierarchy-free, learning zone. The community leaders remind members that they will not be judged or sanctioned by their supervisors if they make mistakes, ask naive questions or admit that they have gaps in their knowledge. In a safe community environment, members can contribute openly without being judged and can always learn from others. Any negative behaviour is addressed by the community manager to keep the environment safe. The core group of members in each CoP needs to be nurtured so that they collectively own the responsibility of increasing vitality through shared community management. Core group may have a private group where any issues are discussed. Any community should have short guidelines on 'safe' participation, which may differ from community to community.

Community Management

Community management skills and sufficiently resourcing community management interms of time, budget and capacity building are crucially important for the good functioning of a community and its impact on the organisation's performance. However, our research shows that community managers have little time to fulfil their community management role, which is often squeezed within other job duties. Many organisations have made community management an integral part of job descriptions, including the European Commission and the UN's communities. McDermott

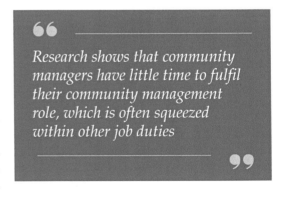

Research shows that community managers have little time to fulfil their community management role, which is often squeezed within other job duties

and Archibald research found that community leaders spend half- to one day per week on community management. The same research shows that communities provide greater value when organisations systematically train their community leaders on community management skills.

The community manager's tasks include (not exhaustively) the following:

- Promote the growth of the community and introduce and manage elements of community structure such as documents, taxonomy, knowledge mapping and events.
- Invite and stimulate different levels of participation because people will have different levels of interest in the community.
- Create and maintain a lively activity for the community (initiate discussions, meetings, video conferences, web activities, informal lunches, workshops, etc.).
- Welcome newcomers, invite them to participate, establish community relationships and promote contributions.
- Curate content by creating content types such as latest events, popular discussions, interviews and inspiring stories.
- Draw up an annual review of the CoP they manage; they can use Wenger and Trayner's assessment framework (see point 8).

Community Management: Good Practices

It is now recognised that engagement requires a systematic approach that aligns tactics with a community-centric strategy. The community manager is the voice of the organisation to the community and voice of the community into the organisation. Community managers are process facilitators, making shared knowledge visible, circulated and used. They also act as catalysts, having a good understanding of dynamic social intelligence processes such as bridging, brokering, connecting, stewarding and more.

Identify Who Belongs in the Community and 'Recruit' Them

Even though you know who the community is for, precisely identifying the right people requires analysis and oftentimes a stakeholders' mapping exercise.

Webber proposes four main questions to ask yourself when trying to determine who should join the community (Webber, 2016, p. 37):

Purpose – Does this person share a role, similar environment and overall work goals with other people in the community?

Challenges – Does this person share the same day-to-day challenges as other people in the community?

Learning – Would this person be able to learn things from other people in the community that would make them better at their job?

Teaching – Would people in the community be able to learn things relevant for their work from working closely with this person?

Working on a stakeholders' mapping is an essential step in working out the governance of a community and means identifying stakeholders with a task, file, portfolio, experience, expertise and/or keen interest in your practice field. When doing so, inquire about their needs, preferences, priorities, stakes, the "what's in it for them" to be part of the community. Extend this exercise to identify and prioritise associated stakeholders' behaviours and metrics. You can work on a stakeholders' mapping within the workshop with the core group or in the first gathering of a CoP in the early stages. Questions which help map potential members, their needs and behaviours can be used in such workshop.

- *Community Members' Associated Behaviours — Possible Questions*
- What behaviours are important drivers for this community to be successful? Can you influence them?
- What behaviours are not currently happening?
- Why are stakeholders not already doing what we want them to do in a community?

Build Strong Connections Within the CoP, A Risk-Free Environment Safe to Fail and Learn

Community management implies ensuring coordination, cooperation and collaboration in the community. The community managers coordinate the community work in order to make sure it goes towards achieving the goals and objectives agreed. It is important to have a regular rhythm and rituals for the community to ensure interaction between members and so that they know when to expect to meet up synchronously in real life or virtually and contribute asynchronously. The community manager nurtures the community by inviting and developing curiosity and nudging individuals to give their views.

Community gatherings could allow for more informal ways of connecting. Even though digital platforms nowadays link remote staff, most effective communities also hold face-to-face meetings which usually focus on specific goals often linked to concrete deliverables. Face-to-face meetings may take place physically or be facilitated by video conferencing technologies such as Zoom. Face-to-face contact fosters trust and creates the rapport that the members need to feel safe when admitting mistakes, asking for help and learning from each other. Therefore it is important to hold regular formal and informal contacts between community members and find good balance between or integration of online and offline interaction.

- *How to Convene a Community*

The more participatory community gatherings are the better they foster a sense of community and belonging. Design thinking and art of hosting methods can be used to engage and harvest knowledge from participants. Designed, run and harvested well, such meetings can create momentum and inject the energy that the community regularly needs.

When groups of people in the community are based on locations remote from each other, one needs to consider local coordinators who convene the community locally and meet regularly other local coordinators to align on community activities. Research on scientific CoPs shows that to increase international participation in a scientific community, the local coordinators should be connected among each other and that the conference location should rotate between different continents (Kienle and Wessner, 2005).

Create Community Alignment

Wenger et al. (2002) point out that a 'good community architecture invites many different levels of participation' (p. 55). Providing smooth transitions between different levels of participation allows a lively and also continuous community: new people with new ideas should be able to join the community as easily as possible; already existing members should be able to participate over a period of time and on different levels.

When a critical mass of community members feels more comfortable with each other, the community should collectively define its vision. Having a vision gives the group a shared understanding of why the community exists, which helps create common tasks.

One way to define vision is to organise a series of sessions within a longer workshop to build the vision for the community, to agree on community principles and to define the values members share. There are several ways to run such workshops, and the gamestorming.com community provides lots of ideas for games as co-creation tools used by innovators around the world. When agreeing on goals and activities, it could be useful to turn them into a shared backlog of the community to keep track of what needs to be done (Webber, 2016).

Online Tools and User Experience

Most communities need a digital place to host conversations, exchanges and repositories of knowledge. Digital tools are enablers of asynchronous community interactions for communication, connection, conversation, co-creation and coordination. They also host the community's knowledge resources. They do not replace synchronous in real life and online interactions but rather complement and reinforces them.

Digital tools hosting CoPs do not need to be complex, normally requiring functions such as forum, document libraries, expertise finder, teleconferencing and ideally video conferencing and online places where members can edit documents and discuss them. For example, the European Commission uses SharePoint, Yammer and Jive software for hosting internal CoPs and Confluence, Wikis and Drupal for CoPs involving members from outside the organisation. One can check some communities run with external partners on the JRC's Science Hub.[1]

Community managers should define a list of priority elements and functionalities that a digital community space must feature and provide. The online functionalities should correspond to the community type, its goals and objectives; they are also aligned with the members' expectations. Once the online community is set up, the community manager has to populate it with content, invite members to join, invite them to contribute to a piece of work, follow-up online on physical and virtual meetings' decisions, etc. The quality of the digital tools and the care for user experience have a profound impact on the CoP success.

Measurement: Assessing Impact and Business Value

The benefits and added value of CoPs for the organisation and stakeholders need to be assessed regularly in quantitative and qualitative ways. Guidance for measuring value of CoPs is provided in the conceptual framework developed by Wenger et al. (2011). Based on this assessment framework, communities constantly need to adapt to the evolving needs of its members and the changing thematic environment.

To measure and assess value creation, one must first frame what success looks like by identifying the purpose and strategic objectives of a community.

---

[1] https://ec.europa.eu/jrc/communities/en, accessed 05.05.2020.

Secondly, one must identify the indicators that will demonstrate fulfilment of purpose and movement towards goals and corresponding objectives.

This is only a starting point, as the day-to-day life of the community may lead you to reconsider what success truly looks like.

To appreciate the richness of the value created by communities, it is useful to think about it in terms of different cycles:

- Immediate value: activities and interactions
- Potential value: knowledge capital
- Applied value: changes in practice
- Realised value: performance improvement
- Reframing value: redefining success.

Stories are the best way to explain the linkages between community activities, knowledge resources and performance outcomes.

Questions for building value creation stories:

- What did the community do?
- What knowledge resources did they produce?
- How were those applied to get results?

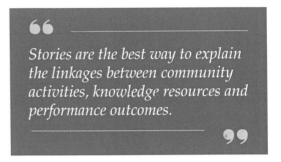

Stories are the best way to explain the linkages between community activities, knowledge resources and performance outcomes.

Communities only exist if there is an interest from members in maintaining the group. The practice of regularly checking how well the community is meeting the members' and the organisation's needs – and adapting it to ensure it does – is key for a community to survive, remain useful and relevant. The community needs to revisit its vision, goals and governance on a regular basis to see if they are still relevant, review them and adapt.

The European Commission's JRC has been managing for several years the European Technology Transfer Offices (TTO) circle,[2] a network which brings together the major public research organisations on technology transfer. Thirty-one of the largest organisations in Europe collaborate to boost innovation in Europe through a set of initiatives, including fostering the use of their knowledge portfolios; sharing best practices, knowledge and expertise; performing joint activities; establishing informal channels of communication with policymakers; organising training programmes and developing a common approach towards international standards for the professionalisation of technology transfer.

---

[2] https://ec.europa.eu/jrc/communities/en/community/tto-circle-community, accessed 05.05.2020.

> ## Community of Practice on Fairness
>
> The JRC works on an increasing number of multidisciplinary, multidimensional topics, such as fairness. One could not place such a theme in one single department to be dealt by just a handful of people. A CoP has particular potential in such cases, and the one on fairness was set up in 2017. It works through sharing knowledge and fostering an informed dialogue, across disciplines, on the multidimensional aspects of fairness to better inform policy.
>
> Researchers and policymakers from across the European Commission and relevant research agencies exchange multidisciplinary knowledge and debate issues surrounding fairness, inequality and related policy measures. As a result, the community contributed to the robustness of a report 'What makes a fair society. Insights and evidence'. Such a report, touching on various and different dimensions of fairness, from labour markets, health and education to behavioural insights, owes much to the contributions of the CoP members. Effective community management and its purposeful design, according to the principles described in this chapter, enabled this result.

Knowledge Communities and the Research Policy Bridge

Bridging the gap between knowledge production and the knowledge use remains a key challenge for the whole policy cycle, from conception to implementation and evaluation. We know from experience as we operate at the interface between evidence production and policymaking.

The hardest challenges are not about producing knowledge but rather about sharing, using and interconnecting it. Our recent audience research into the ways researchers and policymakers interact with knowledge shows clear difference between the researchers and policymakers' communities simply explained by the fact that they operate according to such different respective rhythms and priorities (Fig. 4, see also Chapter 1).

Researchers are used to engaging in communities and understand that to have more policy impact with their research, they need to reach out in new and varied ways. They are interested in finding alliances with other researchers through various platforms, as equally as they are interested in promoting their research to a policymaking audience. They are particularly concerned about the need for a 'feedback loop' – to know if, how and why their work has influenced policy. Researchers may be bound within a strict cycle in their year, particularly if waiting for new rounds of data or the update to an index.

Policymakers express concern that they cannot find the information they need, but do not tend to go outside of their current networks or traditional channels to source that information. They need to be cautious around explaining publicly how and why they have used particular pieces of evidence, or not. The political process necessitates judgements to be made about which evidence to follow or when to not follow the evidence at all. Senior policymakers see value in being connected with an expert or experts on a particular topic that is of interest to them at that moment.

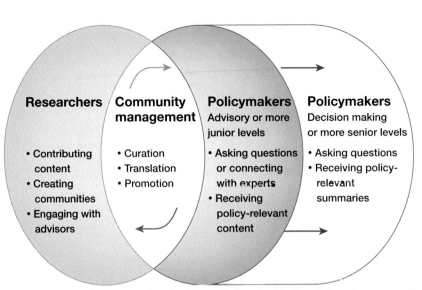

FIGURE 4 Recommended strategy for the Knowledge for Policy following an audience research – community management and interactions to bridge the gap between the two communities.

Communities have a potential to enhance the science-policy collaboration, but given the above differences, there is a strong need for knowledge brokerage and community management, defined as a form of curation and translation that makes knowledge relevant and useable for the world of policy. If you find yourself in such a role, it is useful to consult also our work on Knowledge Centres, Competence Centres and the Knowledge for Policy platform.[3]

---

[3] https://ec.europa.eu/knowledge4policy, accessed 05.05.2020.

Image: Freedomz - https://stock.adobe.com/be_en/images/young-couple-planting-the-tree-while-watering-a-tree-working-in-the-garden-as-save-world-concept-nature-environment-and-ecology/195722653?prev_url=detail
Icon in page corners: Plant icon by IconTrack, from the Noun Project (https://thenounproject.com/search/?q=planting&i=1002819)

Engaging With Citizens

Main authors: Ângela Guimarães Pereira, Thomas Völker

Contributors: Alexandre Pólvora, Paulo Rosa, Sven Schade

Key takeaways:

- Citizen engagement is a vital component of Science for Policy 2.0. It opens the science for policy relationship towards more participatory approaches, with diverse publics being meaningfully included in complex matters that concern them.

- Citizen engagement goes beyond consultations, educational efforts or tools for persuasion of the public. It is a two-way relationship of learning and reflexivity.

- Several methods exist and are sketched in the chapter, including interviews and focus groups, material deliberation and co-design, participatory modelling and scenario workshops, citizen science, collaborative ethnography, e-participation, among others.

- Citizen engagement processes should be carefully designed, taking into account context dependencies, types of publics, past and ongoing engagement activities, expectations and follow-ups.

Science for Policy Handbook
http://dx.doi.org/10.1016/D2T0-0-12-822596-7.00008-5

Copyright © 2020 European Union,
Published by Elsevier Limited.

Citizen engagement rhetoric and practices have been discussed for many decades. The literature shows that the contexts, rationales, practices, expectations, politics and cultures of citizen engagement in matters of societal concern are very varied. Sherry Arnstein wrote in a 1969 landmark paper that 'The idea of citizen participation is a little like eating spinach: no one is against it in principle because it is good for you'. Yet, citizen engagement involves much more than just organising different opportunities to mobilise citizens' knowledge into debates, co-creation or other processes (e.g., policy, research, planning, monitoring, etc.). Citizen engagement requires that policymaking institutions recognise and accept participatory governance styles and therefore create *listening* mechanisms to bring citizens' knowledge, expectations, values and imaginaries into the planning, decision or policy processes. Moreover, it means that institutions are willing to learn from citizens' engagement initiatives. For the Joint Research Centre (JRC) and similar institutions, citizen engagement can be framed with multiple lenses: (1) better framing of science for policy questions; (2) enhancement of the quality (fitness for

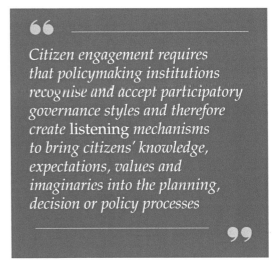

Citizen engagement requires that policymaking institutions recognise and accept participatory governance styles and therefore create listening *mechanisms to bring citizens' knowledge, expectations, values and imaginaries into the planning, decision or policy processes*

purpose) of the knowledge basis to address societal issues; (3) co-creation or co-design strategies to address societal issues and (4) empowering communities to address collective matters of concern. In this chapter, we first provide guidance about where this idea comes from and how it is framed, followed by a brief review of possible models of engagement. The chapter then gives some guidance on widespread methods, with an example of a JRC project.

Participatory Governance: A Quick Historical Review

There has been a worldwide endeavour for the past 50 years to involve different publics in knowledge production that interest research and governance processes.

The 'ladder of citizen participation' (see Fig. 1) developed by Sherry Arnstein in the late 1960s (Arnstein, 1969) is a very useful heuristic to situate citizen engagement practices. There is a broad range of methodologies and approaches that can be distinguished roughly by the degree to which they aim for a redistribution of power in the decision-making process. Clearly, the upper levels of the ladder describe initiatives where citizens' agency is higher.

The expression 'Public Understanding of Science' (PUS) is commonly used to summarise a debate that started in the late 1980s in the United Kingdom, when UK science policymakers faced a crisis in which the so-called 'public' **seemed to lose trust** in science, which in turn risked losing legitimacy (and funding). Scientists and policymakers argued that the reason for this lack of trust was that the public did not understand scientific facts, i.e., that members of the public suffered from a **cognitive deficit**. This was backed by surveys that demonstrated citizens' lack of knowledge of 'basic scientific facts'. In fact, given this framing, the only possible solution was to **'educate'** the public and **science communication** was given a new function,

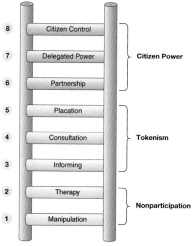

FIGURE 1 Arnstein's ladder of citizen participation.

with purposefully allocated funding *scientists* embarking on a pedagogical mission.

The expression PUS implies a condescending assumption that any difficulties in the relationship between science and society are due entirely to ignorance and misunderstanding on the part of the public. Many people have tried to demonstrate that this framework is simplistic given that it rests on the assumption of a somehow 'deficient' public (and science as universally comprehensible). In that perspective, such public needs to be either informed (cognitive deficit) or given a voice in decision-making processes (democratic deficit), which are often described as 'deficit models' about science–public relations (Wynne, 1993; Gilbert, Stocklmeyer and Garnett, 1999; Irwin and Michael, 2003).

The *urgent* call for citizen engagement in science for policy came prominently from scientific controversies that had serious implications for public life, such as for example the infamous BSE case – see Box 1 – and so, as a reaction to this criticism, new forms of relations have emerged that can be described by the label of '**Public Engagement in Science and Technology**' (**PEST**).

The PEST framing aims at channelling public voices and enabling democratic participation in decision-making processes. This can be regarded as a necessary step towards acknowledging the complexities involved in attempts to integrate science, society and policy. However, such 'formalised mechanisms of voicing' (Felt et al., 2009; Michael, 2012) also have particular shortcomings: it is often not clear how engagement exercises actually **link to governance** or in what ways they become **consequential** for scientists or policymakers. In this sense, such 'mechanisms of voicing' need to be understood as a particular '**mode of governmentality**', which even runs the risk of **foreclosing more active forms of citizenship**, such as activism or grassroots movements.

← A key moment was the publication of the 2000 House of Lords Report *Science and Society*, followed a year later by the European Commission's *Science and Society Action Plan (2002)*.

Box 1: BSE: bovine spongiform encephalopathy

At the end of the 90s, the spread of the so-called 'mad cow disease', i.e., the bovine spongiform encephalopathy (BSE), a chronic neurological degenerative disease that has affected thousands of animals in various European countries, broke out. It was discovered that BSE was transmissible to humans and, in fact, several people died shortly thereafter. This event is considered by many social scientists as pivotal of the transition to a different way of conceiving the relationship between science and society. The incident led the House of Lords, one of the two chambers of the British Parliament, to publish in 2000 a report entitled Science and Society, which states that faced with a clear crisis of confidence in science advice, the relationship with the public must change. We can no longer think of giving the public only information on what to eat, but we need to build a dialogue based on mutual trust (House of Lords, 2000).

Citizen Engagement Institutionalisation

Challenges and Possible Responses

The institutionalisation of citizen engagement not only comes with different narratives – see Fig. 2 – but also may bring with it the increase of one-size-fits-all recipes engagement practices that try to circumvent the *situatedness* of those events and mainly frames them as 'technologies of elicitation' (Lezaun and Soneryd, 2007) and 'technologies of participation' (Soneryd, 2015). In such exercises, which function mainly as 'formalized mechanisms of voicing' (Michael, 2012), the problems are mostly predefined either in the form of a technological fix or as a social innovation. Citizens are brought into the process mostly for assessing potential impacts and ethical issues. This is a serious temptation, which could only discredit the exercise. Alternatives to this approach are available:

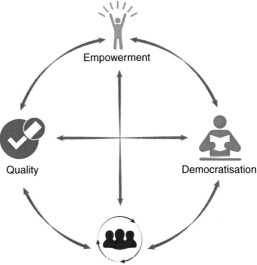

FIGURE 2 Narratives commonly found to justify citizen engagement: democratisation of expertise, governance, quality of evidence, empowerment and social change, social learning and social justice.

- *Publics as Collectives*

If engagement is an 'event' co-constituted with issues, publics and subject positions, where opinions and values can be negotiated and potentially changed within discussions, then understanding publics as *collectives* that interactively develop and contest various perspectives on certain issues is rather useful. If publics are understood as not stable but rather dynamic, then there is also not one *general* public with coherent and stable views that can be 'surveyed'. Engagement in this understanding is not just about exploring opinions and interests, but about openly discussing 'matters of concern' (Chilvers and Kearnes, 2015).

- *A Participatory Model of Science for Policy*

A participatory model of knowledge co-creation is particularly relevant for the remit of the JRC and similar institutions. In his review of models of science and policy, Funtowicz (2006) suggests that one of the models to *cure* tensions on the current relationship between science and policy requires that 'the ideal of rigorous scientific demonstration is succeeded by that of open public dialogue, in which citizens become both critics and creators in the knowledge production process as part of an extended peer community' (*Op. cit.*, 139). This 'extended participation' model acknowledges that in the current state of affairs, different types of knowledge are produced and need to be circulated to underpin policymaking.

In Post-Normal Science (Funtowicz and Ravetz, 1990; see also Chapter 2), this extension will be carried out by an 'extended peer community', 'consisting not merely of persons with some form or other of institutional accreditation, but rather of all those with a desire to participate in the resolution of the issue' (*Op. cit., 651*).

- *The Co-creation Turn*

Co-creation ideas are visible everywhere, from research agendas, policy design, regional planning and assessment framings; a lot of experiments are being done. The co-creation turn sets a much respectful relationship, which sees fellow citizens as partners (see Fig. 1).

Upfront Recommendations

- *Humility and Reflexivity*

The objective of engagement exercises is neither to simply educate or convince the public about certain policy or technology options nor to produce better engagement methods to learn more about opinions or even just concerns and expectations. Rather the strength of engagement is that it can function as a technology of humility (Jasanoff, 2003) about the use of scientific knowledge in decision-making and also increase the reflexivity of institutions in regards to their problem-framings and governance models (Stirling, 2008).

- *Reinvent the Wheel We Shall Not*

There is a great deal of citizen engagement already out there, organised by other institutions and organisations, such as academia and NGOs but also grassroots initiatives in the form of activism, 'community' action, making and hacking. Hence, space needs to be made to engage with ongoing engagements and organise citizen engagement on matters that have not been previously addressed.

- *Respectful and Honourable Relationships*

Engagement of citizens needs to be from the outset accompanied with respectful mechanisms, to listen, make sense and voice the engagements' outputs. Any failure to channel those outcomes may compromise subsequent attempts to engage citizens in policymaking in any of its phases.

Exploring the Policy Cycle Opportunities

There are many ways in which citizen engagement can meaningfully contribute to the quality of policies. Institutions like the JRC can from the start ensure that the evidence provided in different steps of the policy cycle is inclusive of and open to citizens' voices. In general, bringing different voices, especially those that usually do not find space to be heard, into a policy process enriches the quality of the knowledge base. Such quality is necessary to ensure the social robustness of a policy, as well as avoiding a Type III error, i.e., addressing the wrong societal problem. The types and formats of citizen engagement inputs are not a closed matter; they can range from collected data, experiential knowledge to structured recommendations.

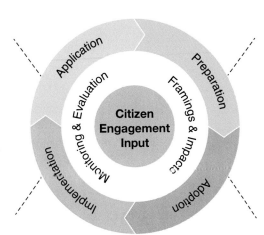

- Involve grassroots movements for dialogue and deliberation
- Co-produce counter-knowledge
- Collect monitoring data
- Employ dialogue and deliberation to evaluate implementation strategies and outcomes
- Contextualise the policies with situated and experiential knowledge

- Open up framings (research and policy) though upstream engagement
- Explicate expectations in deliberative settings
- Identify matters of concern and care
- Futuring
- Co-design policy
- Co-produce knowledge
- Involve grassroots movements for dialogue and deliberation
- Add situated & experiential knowledge
- Collect and crowdsource data
- Identify potential impacts and ethical issues through dialogue and deliberation
- Bring in situated knowledge
- Bring in experiential knowledge

FIGURE 3 Function and types of input at all phases of the policy cycle. Policy cycle scheme adapted from the 'Better Regulation Package'.

Fig. 3 shows the function of citizen engagements inputs in the different phases of the policy cycle as described in the 'Better Regulation Package'.[1] It maps the types of inputs that citizen engagement can provide to the policy cycle. It is important to include upstream engagements, i.e., deliberations in the early stages of the policy cycle but equally important are engagements that help with monitoring and evaluation of outcomes, which occur later in the policy cycle. In the former, the function of engagements are mainly co-creating the framing of policy, exploring expectations and concerns and discussing outcomes of policies, relevant institutions and actors as well as challenges and possible solutions. In other words, citizen engagement can help not only with the design of policies but also in their monitoring and evaluation.

Methodologies Rough Guidance

In our institutional context, we understand citizen engagement practices as a reflexive action that provides the means to share and structure participants' knowledge, values and matters of concern into input to the research/planning/evaluation/policy process.

Planning

- *Before You Even Start*
  A number of activities need to be carried out to avoid some pitfalls of engaging citizens, for example, avoid type III error, fatigue and reinvention of the wheel:

- identify existing citizen engagements on the same subject, taking stock of existing insights; these could include problem framings, matters of care, methodological aspects, recommendations, imaginaries, action, etc.

---

[1] https://ec.europa.eu/info/law/law-making-process/planning-and-proposing-law/better-regulation-why-and-how/better-regulation-guidelines-and-toolbox_en, accessed 05.05.2020.

- proper preparation for citizen engagement should build on a wide array of social sciences practices that include analysis of policy and (new and traditional) media narratives, institutional analysis, mapping and identification of the extended peer community.
- identify useful partnerships with people and organisations that could facilitate citizen engagement practices, such as citizen science networks, makerspaces, museums of science and technology, NGOs and communities.
- ensure that there is a mechanism through which citizen engagement activities will inform the process they were designed for.
- establish the mechanism through which citizens are informed about it.

- *Understanding Context Dependencies*

FIGURE 4 Interdependencies of context, methodologies, participants and expectable outcomes.

Fig. 4 illustrates the interdependencies of context, citizen engagement methodologies, participants and planned outcomes.

The context in which citizen engagement develops determines everything else. For example, the legal mandate, the stage at which citizen engagement is required in the policy cycle, geographic and temporal specificities, situation, etc.

Hence, context sets who the participants are, their level of involvement in the 'process' (early stages may mean co-design and sharing responsibility; final stages may mean seeking for legitimacy from the side of the organisers), the participatory methodology and the *contract* with participants. The latter is key to settle a priori expectations from both sides, organisers and participants. It is basically mutual understanding of what organisers expect from participants and how organisers expect to use the outcomes of the process (Box 2).

Box 2: Moderation of events

- Style of moderation: role should be explicit and open to discussion – negotiator, mediator, facilitator, arbitrator, etc.
- Number of moderators and composition of the moderators team – depends on case. More than 2 moderators in a group of 10 is a crowd.
- Rules of moderation agreed within the organising team before the engagement activity takes place
- Moderators should use the language of the country
- The importance of being 'local' needs to be considered
- Methodological choices

- *Identifying Who Should Be Involved*

Who are the citizens? Those concerned, the 'getroffen' (sufferers), stakeholders, voiceless and disempowered, community members?

The following tasks need to be carried out:

- Design the invitation
- Define recruitment criteria
- The number of participants (which varies, e.g., according to issue of concern and methodology employed)
- Tokens and 'contract'

- *Methodological Choices*

The methods and tools to carry out citizen engagement activities are heavily dependent on the situation, context, issues, the participants involved, requested inputs, imagined outcomes and on the process (whether policy, research or grassroots activism), where inputs from citizens shall be used. There is a myriad of methodologies, and whilst the choice is strongly linked to the factors above, one can say that they are also strongly linked to the model of participation; a citizen science project where participants help with collecting data does not require in principle deliberative formats; a co-creation model requires different approaches compared to a public hearing model. There is no definitive toolkit, but there are many tools and practices that can be deployed in a policy context. Ideally, citizens should be asked how they would like to be involved and in what terms. For a successful process, some aspects need to be thought through, namely

- Format of the participatory process and level of "orchestration" (e.g., participatory scenario development, participatory modelling and prototyping are strongly orchestrated approaches)
  - Who does the particular method exclude?
  - Should we be employing an array of formats rather than just one to address different situations?

- Organisation of the event(s) (duration, venue (offline, online and hybrid), draft agenda)
  - Does the process require continuous engagement activities or different phases?
  - The importance of the space where the engagement takes place, preferably
    - where citizens already meet (e.g., the pub or particular social media);
    - avoiding places that are alien or intimidating (e.g., a court building perhaps can be intimidating; online dialogue spaces—not necessarily 'comfortable' for everybody);
    - places related to the issues of concern (e.g., school and particular locations in the city, farm);
    - places which function citizens can recognise and connect to (e.g., museum of science and technology, garden, makerspace and library).

Definition of citizen, according to Collins Dictionary online:
1. a native registered or naturalised member of a state, nation or other political community
2. an inhabitant of a city or town
3. a native or inhabitant of any place
4. a civilian, as opposed to a soldier, public official, etc.

- Organisation of prior knowledge that informs the participatory process (discursive vs. experiential or both)
  - Tools and props with which participants will reflect, deliberate and co-design the outputs of the engagement exercise;
  - Bringing in the expert;
  - 'Progressive disclosure of information' principle should be applied to deal with the complexity of the issue of concern: layers of growing complexity are progressively made available to participants possibly in different formats.

- Organisation of participants' knowledge around the issues of concern
  - Desired outputs need to be envisaged, on the understanding that these frame the organisation of the activity;
  - The types and formats of citizen engagement inputs can range from *crowdsourced* data, experiential knowledge to rather structured recommendations or proposals for action, policymaking;
  - Expectations about formats should be aligned to participants' resources and also to the operability of such formats within the institution – e.g., reports, manifestos, recommendations, multimedia materials, scenarios, model outputs, prototypes, data or simply moderator notes.

- Language: in the EU or any multilanguage context, language is an issue. Citizen engagements should be done in the language of the country, where it takes place – whether the engagement takes place *offline* or online.

- *Outcomes and Feedback Loops*

The expected or desired outcomes depend upon context and participants. The key question to ask is how those outcomes will influence the process for which they were planned. In any process, a key question is about the degree of influence that is promised in the 'contract' with the participants. For example, in the context of the European Commission, this could be articulated as policy binding or nonbinding outcomes. In a context of a research process, this could be articulated as framing of research questions.

The other key understanding with regards to the accomplishment of citizen engagement activities is feedback to those engaged. The outcomes and their use in the processes for which they were produced need to be known to the participants. This is one of the basic guarantors of both trust and continuity. Citizen engagement involves using other people's time and people' expectations of influencing the process they are engaged in. In practice, this realisation includes both a reflection and concrete steps on the following:

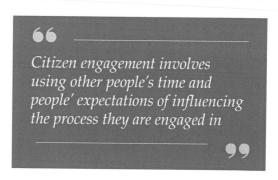

> Citizen engagement involves using other people's time and people' expectations of influencing the process they are engaged in

1. Institutional arrangements that voice outcomes to the process.
2. Feedback activities to get back to the citizens and explain how their input was used.
3. Accountable institutional mechanisms that ensure continuity.

Frequently Used Methodologies

- *Qualitative Social Research Methodologies*

There is a great variety of methodological approaches with an equal number of variations, and so this listing is incomplete. Below we focus on qualitative research methodologies that have inspired citizen engagement activities at the JRC, but that are widely used in contexts that intersect science, policy and society. The methodologies are also often used together; hence, they are presented here as rough guidance for the future practitioner.

*Resource: https://participedia. net/

In-depth Interviews	Focus Groups
In-depth interviews are one of the most widely used qualitative methods to explore individuals' opinions and insights about a specific issue or idea (Kvale, 2008). They are useful to investigate a certain topic with more in-depth information (Boyce and Neale, 2006). In our context, this methodology has been particularly interesting in cases where there was genuine difficulty in having an a priori understanding about who is behind knowledge claims that inform policy, allowing for a deeper scrutiny of knowledge production and circulation. It has also been very useful, in cases, where different actors would not seat at the same table for mere logistic reasons or because of genuine tensions.	Focus groups are 'a research technique that collects data through group interaction on a topic determined by the researcher' (Morgan, 1996, p. 130), also described as a form of group interviewing (Gibbs, 1997), used as a social research method (Morgan and Krueger, 1993; Bloor et al., 2001) but also as a social event. FG help with collecting knowledge, experiences, expectations, feelings, tensions, beliefs, and hints on opinion formation that cannot be collected by other social research methods, such as observation, one-to-one interviews or questionnaire surveys (Morgan and Krueger, 1993; Kitzinger, 1994; Gibbs, 1997). FG can take on very different formats and can develop with variable duration; the most typical is 2 and ½ hours but e.g., in-depth groups, a term coined by Burgess (1996), refers to a lengthy process, where the relationship of researchers and participants develops over time through their participation in several events (e.g., Darier et al., 1999).

Material Deliberation	Co-design
Material deliberation emerged to counteract the idea that a great deal of citizen engagement practices was based on notions of 'reasoned discourse' (Elam and Bertilsson, 2002), in other words that valued the spoken word and rational argument (Davies et al., 2006).	Co-design or participatory design for policy-making or within policy advice contexts is a participatory approach that uses design methods and tools to actively engage multiple stakeholders in the collaborative production of shared visions, solutions, projects, programs and other policy-related outputs.

MD acknowledges dimensions which go beyond the discursive, such as: embodiment and materiality, emotion and affect, (undervalued) genres of talk, openness to diversity, as well as the situated and relational nature of the deliberative process. Hence, "material deliberation' is used as a shorthand for processes of deliberation and citizen engagement, which incorporate an awareness, openness or sensitivity to nontraditional modes of deliberative interaction, including, but not confined to, the sonorous (music, singing, laughter, shrieks and noise), the discursive (gossip, storytelling, anecdote, polemic and drama), the material (objects, bodies, sites and places) and the affective (hate, love, fear, attachment, nostalgia, intuition and pleasure). Such engagements show a sensitivity to the situated nature of all encounters, deliberative or not, as embedded in particular spaces, material configurations, and temporalities' (In Davies et al., 2012). The techniques that support the access to these dimensions recur to art, games, immersive environments, walking tours and other experiential methodologies that value the contextual dimensions in which the engagement takes place. Emblematic examples of these methodologies are the Futurescape City Tours project around technology in the city (Selin and Pillen Banks, 2014) and also more recently the Food Futuring Tours project around food futures (Guimarães Pereira et al., 2018).

The main goal is to get results that are closer to the needs and requirements of those who might be impacted by the policy decisions in discussion, and ultimately reach conclusions which represent as many perspectives as possible, while also ensuring any outcomes generated become more than the sum of its original inputs (Stappers and Sanders, 2012; Bson, 2016; Nascimento and Pólvora, 2016; Nascimento et al., 2016). One of the multiple frameworks co-design approaches can make use of to inform or support policy is prototyping. For policy purposes, piloting and testing of services before implementation or scaling up stages needs to happen at multiple phases of a research project or experimental intervention. Participants may be called into trial prototypes through role playing, user journeys, contextual mappings towards fine tuning and possible iterations and a search for the best possible evidence on how to move plausible proofs-of-concept into working solutions (Selin et al., 2017; Blomkamp, 2018). Other approaches include the creation of fictional artefacts meant to trigger forward looking discussions into the possibilities of yet to be fully fledged realities. The outputs are learning devices attached to imaginative leaps, which question potential policy realities to come (Kimbell, 2015). More on design for policy can be found in Chapter 13.

Participatory Modelling

Applying tools typically used in expert realms in participatory settings has been proliferating since the early 1980s. Typically, issues where there is a strong component of scientific knowledge involved in the evidence and reasoning to use. Many experiments have been carried out, with for example participatory modelling (Videira et al., 2003), participatory multicriteria analysis (Salgado et al., 2009; Guimarães Pereira et al., 2005), participatory foresight and so on. In practice, this amounts to tailor technical analytical tools to be used in participatory settings as the properties that guide, structure and, therefore, also frame the discussions. Examples of this usage have been in environmental governance, where models have been co-developed with participants.

Scenario Workshops

Scenario workshops practices raised during the middle 1990s as a means to foster democratisation of urban planning (see e.g., Andersen and Jæger, 1999; Mega, 2000) or land-use change (Van Asselt et al., 2005; Herivaux et al., 2018), but is now a widely used practice in policy settings, under different names or a part of compound engagement methodologies. It is in itself a compound methodology, given that it combines ideas of scenario development and workshop. It is also strongly linked to quite structured ways to think about the future, such as foresight. Typical outputs are future narratives which include a temporal vision, a reflection on drivers and uncertainties to achieve that future vision, and key actions to attain or to avoid the developed vision. More on scenario analysis can be found in Chapter 12.

Participatory Games

The use of games and the more relatively recent hype around serious games (Sawyer, 2003) as properties in participatory events is quite a debated practice, even before the widespread use of digitally implemented games. Games are an appealing way to structure participatory events, also allowing to explore trade-offs in 'role play' fashion. The use of games in urban planning e.g., has been widely published. See, e.g., this database for games for city planning: http://games-forcities.com/database/.

- *Crowdsourcing Methodologies*

Citizen Science

The practice of citizen involvement in scientific projects as citizen scientists is not really new (Cohn, 2008); in some fields, e.g., in environmental monitoring projects, including biodiversity the practice has more than one century and it has been on the rise (see e.g., Gouveia and Fonseca, 2008; Catlin–Groves, 2012; Morzy, 2014) because of information technologies, engaging citizens in larger numbers.[2] In the middle of the 1990s, two quite different perspectives on citizen science developed independently. Whilst for Irwin (1995) citizen science implied a form of science developed and enacted by citizens, for Bonney (1996, 2004) citizen science was a method to involve individuals in scientific studies, 'either by providing opportunities for people to serve as research assistants or by enabling them to conduct their own original investigations' (Bonney, 2004, p. 201). The two models, which we can roughly describe as bottom up and top down citizen science co-exist today. More recently, the ambition that citizen science becomes part of the scientific evidence base to inform policy has gained prominence. Many projects emphasise one or more of these opportunities (1) data gathering, e.g., to retrieve early warnings about the occurrence of invasive species (see: https://easin.jrc.ec.europa.eu/easin/Citizen-Science/About and Roy et al., 2018) or localised information about air pollution (see box – making sense project and Schade et al., 2019); (2) models quality assurance by e.g., including citizens in the identification of species or in ground trothing (fact checking) the results of environmental models in their local neighbourhood; (3) data analysis and interpretation, e.g., to identify damaged images from buildings, or the blooming season of a certain crop. In addition, citizen science activities might result in new research framings, including research questions and methodologies to deal with them. See also the JRC citizen science projects inventory: http://data.jrc.ec.europa.eu/dataset/jrc-citsci-10004 and the related study on citizen science for environmental policy by Bio Innovation Service (2018).

Collaborative Ethnography

A particular example of other forms of collaborative work is collaborative ethnography (see e.g., Lassiter, 2005). This framing of collaboratively enquiring one's environment has inspired some citizen engagement activities, such as those promoted by the OpenStreetMap project (see: https://www.openstreetmap.org/)

[2]Terminology around citizen science is also varied–see e.g., Nascimento et al. (2014).

- *Digital Participation*

e-participation

By e-participation, we mean here digital tools and platforms, connected to the Internet through which citizens can engage with different issues, through direct invitation by the institutions or by any organisations that invite them to do so. e-participation carries the promise of both e-democracy and also great citizen outreach. This includes both platforms and applications that facilitate citizen engagement. Many e-participation platforms attempt to mimic physical meetings, others work as working places, discussion forums, voting places, etc. The technologies have been constantly evolving and can include chatting, video conferencing, online gaming and scenario development. See, e.g., https://decidim.org/. https://ec.europa.eu/futurium/en.

- *Deliberative Methods*

In deliberative democracy, the concept of mini-publics (Goodin, Dryzek, 2006) is key to describe methods where randomly selected citizens, chosen through sortition by lot from the electoral roll which function as a representative sample of the relevant population[3] affected by the topic of concern. There are different formats that include Citizens' Juries, Consensus Conferences, Citizens' assemblies, Deliberative polls, and Planning cells.

Citizens' Juries	Consensus Conferences
'Alhough they may produce rich qualitative insights, focus group and participatory appraisal techniques do not in themselves change the passive status of the people being studied. Drawing on the symbolism of the system of trial by jury, citizens juries have been seen as potentially challenging this separation between analyst and subject'. (In Wakeford, 2002, p. 1) CJ were described as potentially helpful to deal with matters of social justice and the legitimisation of nonspecialist knowledge. In this method of participatory research, panels of 12–20 nonspecialists meets for a large number of hours to examine carefully an issue of public significance. The method by which members of the jury are recruited is key to maintain their potential representativeness – e.g., randomly from the electoral register (Wakeford, 2002). An important application of CJ was about nanotechnology in the UK (Singh, 2008). Citizen juries are a form of the so-called mini-publics.	Consensus conferences also known as 'citizens panel' was a methodology widely used by the now extinct Danish Board of Technology (then an independent institution established by the Danish Parliament), but it was also in use in the Netherlands and the UK. Citizens were involved in the assessment of socially sensitive topics, namely new and emerging technology, through a recruitment procedure that included random invitation based on the telephone directory. 14 members that included experts as well typically composed the panels. The first consensus conference was organised in 1987 in Denmark focussing on 'Gene technology in industry and agriculture'. (See, e.g., Joss and Durant, 1995 and Kliiver, 1995).

[3]See https://www.newdemocracy.com.au/2017/05/08/forms-of-mini-publics/, accessed 05.05.2020.

We need to mention here other formats of addressing citizens, which are used with expectations of representativeness. Our view is that they could be helpful if they were combined with qualitative work to solve their major pitfalls such as: framing (who decides what issues need to be consulted with the publics?), exclusions (who gets excluded from these types of methodologies?), uninformed and misinformed engagement processes (what knowledge needs to be shared before one can even start thinking about the issue?). These methods also assume that there is a public out there to be surveyed, which is in contrast with the view that participatory activities create both 'publics' and their relationships to institutions. Hence, beware of standalone usage of these methods as citizen engagement methods.

Surveys and Opinion polls	Consultations
Randomly sampled citizens are interviewed by means of questionnaires, usually in person. Sampling criteria need to be defined. In the EU, the Eurobarometer surveys are quite well-known. See: http://ec.europa.eu/commfrontoffice/publicopinion/	These can occur in a myriad of formats. In the European Commission, consultations made online are done through questionnaires in specific policy topics, during the policy development stage. The important thing to note is that the outcomes are not binding, even if as in the case of the Commission, consultation is done under legal mandate. See e.g., the Commission portal: https://ec.europa.eu/info/consultations_en.

Spaces

Here, we briefly refer to three prominent types of spaces that we have been experimenting with at the JRC and could be a source of inspiration for those interested in engaging with citizens. These (physical and online) spaces are the JRC starting infrastructure to carry out citizen engagement. Evidently, they do not exist in a vacuum as they purposefully resonate with kindred projects outside the commission (Box 3). Besides these, we use different public spaces to carry out citizen engagement, schools in school matters, the city if we engage citizens on city affairs, etc.

The EU Policy Lab	The JRC makerspace	The JRC Citizen Science Platform
The EU Policy Lab is a physical space designed to foster creativity and engagement, develop interactions, processes and tools contributing to bring innovation in the European policymaking. Like other policy labs, the emphasis is on testing, experimenting and co-designing with stakeholders by using tailored made approaches and relying a lot on visualisation. The Policy Lab explores, connects and designs for better policies. More on this can be found in Chapter 13. See also: https://blogs.ec.europa.eu/eupolicylab/	The JRC makerspace was imagined as a networked thinking and tinkering space, resonating with similar grassroots initiatives. Like other makerspaces, it is designed as a collaborative open space, designed to promote active participation, knowledge sharing, and citizenship through experimentation and prototyping. It is a place of material deliberation, allowing complex techno-science developments to be deliberated through an experiential (as opposed to discursive) approach. Also, being networked by default, it facilitates multisite projects with different communities. The JRC makerspace is also available as a van, allowing it to travel different locations. See: https://ec.europa.eu/jrc/en/publication/jrc-thinkers-n-tinkers-makerspace-concept-note	The Citizen Science Platform is a customisable tool to facilitate data collection, particularly supporting citizens' contributions. The received inputs are used to extend the evidence base for European policies. The idea is to improve the chances of providing timely and impactful citizen science inputs to European policymaking. In this way, policy debates are not supported only by scientific advice of a few selected experts, but can also benefit from targeted contributions from citizens. The citizen science platform especially welcomes data collected via mobile applications. See: https://ec.europa.eu/jrc/communities/en/community/citizensdata.

Box 3: Makingsense project

Making Sense was an H2020 project funded under the CAPS 'Collective Awareness Platforms for Sustainability and Social Innovation' programme. It ran between 2015 and 2018, and combined the efforts of Waag Society (NL), Institute for Advanced Architecture of Catalonia (ES), Peer Educators Network (KS), University of Dundee (UK) and the Joint Research Centre (BE).

The project was focused on how open source hardware and software, digital maker practices and participatory design could be used by local communities to make sense of their environment and effectively address problems such as air or noise pollution in urban settings. This was achieved through nine community-driven pilots in the cities of Amsterdam, Barcelona and Prishtina.

The project's main results, best practices and lessons learnt can be found in Making Sense: Citizen Sensing Toolkit, a Creative Commons licensed on-line and printed book.

The Making Sense team developed the toolkit as an entry point for the project's approach to citizen sensing, aimed at both deepening and disseminating its understanding of sustainable processes, which can enable collective movements from sensing to awareness to action. The toolkit contains multiple portraits and stories from citizens involved in the project, together with a presentation of an 8 steps framework, 6 cases and 25 tools and methods drawn from the pilots, and 7 key overall insights. It is a guide for citizens, communities and middle ground organisations who would like to build or be engaged in similar projects, and ultimately transform their surrounding through a collective, participatory, and bottom-up hands-on approach.

Links:

Toolkit for download: http://making-sense.eu/wp-content/uploads/2018/01/Citizen-Sensing-A-Toolkit.pdf.

Project Website: http://making-sense.eu/

Twitter: https://twitter.com/MakingSenseEU#MakingSenseEU.

Facebook: https://www.facebook.com/MakingSenseEU/

A Case Study

- *Final Reflections*

This chapter aimed to give context of citizen engagement activities in science for policy milieus and food for thought to practitioners, when they attempt to implement citizen engagement. We would like to finalise this chapter with some recommendations and a reflection on expectations about citizen engagement.

Unreasonable Expectations: What You Cannot Expect From These Types of Citizen Engagement

A recent reflection within our Community of Practice on Citizen Engagement has brought light to the challenges that political ambitions for and expectations from citizen engagement practices in institutions like ours could put in jeopardy the whole endeavour. These are, for example:

- **Representativeness:** Whilst this is a perfectly legitimate ambition, it is unlikely that many citizen engagement practices can aspire to deliver outcomes representative of entire populations. First, the practitioner needs to decide whether representativeness is a relevant issue. In many citizen engagement projects, the objective is to collect other *knowledges* into the evidence base, or insights to establish possible framings to address the issues, and so on (see Chapter 10 to read more about how interests influence the knowledge pool) .
  If the issue requires representativeness, then some practices are more suitable than others to attain this ambition; electronic formats of participation promise wider scopes. By combining qualitative and quantitative methods, for example, one can test with a survey the outcomes of a qualitative research study. It must be noted that by reaching out wider numbers of citizens does not guarantee representativeness. *Recommendation: the practitioner needs to reflect on whether this is needed.*
- **Scalability**: There are no methodological panaceas and scalability might not be possible or even desirable. In the EU itself, we have 28 Member States with different histories and diverse cultures of civic engagement. For this aspiration to materialise, the practitioners

need to embrace large scale experiments before scalability becomes a goal in itself. In other words, scalability could turn out to be a great end-result but should not be a guiding criterion for development.

- **Publics**: Publics are not out there to be discovered or engaged; publics are constructed by the participatory events.
- **Replicability:** Methodologies and outcomes are greatly dependent on context. As for scalability, replicability could turn out to be a great end result, but should not be a guiding criterion for development. However, one should still investigate the contextual conditions for a particular citizen engagement initiative.
- **Consent fabrication and politics of acceptance**: Citizen engagements should rather be opportunities to understand why and how particular configurations of contestation emerge. They should also explore ways in which policymaking is creating unexpected and implausible normativities, or can help with those, namely by supporting the inclusion of different types of knowledge and evidence, relevant for the issue of concern.

Some Guiding Principles

- There is no definition of the 'citizen'; he or she can be anyone or be very specific people.
- Realise who is included and who is excluded.
- Community is not 'tabula rasa': all citizens have resources that need to be respectfully recognised.
- Take stock of engagements organised by civil society; do not start from scratch and work in partnership if possible.
- Citizen engagement is about respectful knowledge sharing; participants are epistemic actors.
- Social contract: the requirements from those we engage with and the outcomes usage of those engagements is negotiated a priori.
- Trust: condition *sine qua no* for effective and creative collaboration.
- Diversity: aims at co-existence of methodological approaches.
- Mind the Arnstein ladder (1969): know what you are busy doing when you organise citizen engagement activities

Finally, Chilvers and Kearnes (2015) offer a framework for 'remaking participation', which we find particularly useful. Participation should be reconsidered as the following:

- 'Experimental and reflexive': this means paying attention to framing, but this also means preparedness to change.
- 'Open up to wider systems and ecologies of participation': recognise diversity.
- 'Responsiveness': Cultivation of institutional responsiveness to diverse forms of *public relevance*.

Image: NaturePicsFilms - https://stock.adobe.com/be_en/images/bait-ball-in-coral-reef-of-caribbean-sea-around-curacao-at-dive-site-playa-piskado/272884060?prev_url=detail
Icon in page corners: Shoal icon by Juan Pablo Bravo, from the Noun Project (https://thenounproject.com/search/?q=shoal%20fish&i=75587)

The Big Data and Artificial Intelligence: Opportunities and Challenges to Modernise the Policy Cycle

Authors: Massimo Craglia, Jiri Hradec, Xavier Troussard

Key takeaways

- Big data is not just another type of evidence: with AI developments, it offers potential for radical transformation of policy environments, making them more in tune with a fast-changing world.

- If designed with accountability and transparency at their core, big data and AI can modernise the policy cycle, e.g., by customising policy interventions and offering their faster evaluation and adaptation.

- By putting individuals' needs in the centre, these innovations can help design policies more attuned with diverse needs or location specificities, also helping solve the problem of silent and overlooked groups.

- Such methods can only succeed if a trustworthy social contract for sharing and using data by governments is established. In turn, a more responsive policy environment can strengthen active citizenship and communication between the authorities and the public.

Science for Policy Handbook
http://dx.doi.org/10.1016/B978-0-12-822596-7.00000-7

Copyright © 2020 European Union,
Published by Elsevier Limited.

We are living through a period of intense digital transformation of our society, in which the integration of different technologies, such as artificial intelligence (AI), sensor networks, blockchain, 3D printing and others, with digital data is changing every aspect of our daily lives. The power of integrating different data streams to profile customers and users, predict their behaviour and customise services is becoming increasingly evident to business and some government agencies with both positive outcomes in terms of personalised services and also negative ones in terms of manipulation and control for both commercial and political gain (see for example, Krumm, 2011; Zuboff, 2015).

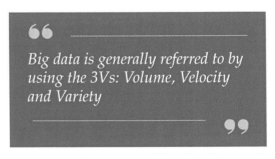

> " We are living through a period of intense digital transformation of our society, in which the integration of different technologies, such as artificial intelligence (AI), sensor networks, blockchain, 3D printing and others, with digital data is changing every aspect of our daily lives. "

In this chapter, we discuss the opportunities and challenges of using big data and AI to modernise the entire policy cycle, from anticipation to design, implementation, monitoring and assessment. It could be a peculiar example of cocreation of knowledge and making policymaking, as well as evidence, more dynamic. We show in particular how the concept of profiling can be applied to official statistics and other data sources to develop policy interventions targeted to the groups and areas needing them the most. This form of 'personalised' policy recognises the need to put individuals at the centre of the policy debate, addressing their needs, expectations and perceptions. The approach described shifts the traditional knowledge used to inform policy by combining both objective and subjective measures of need and by increasing the granularity of evidence to the level of the individual. This may have consequences to how we define knowledge gaps, commission new research or request scientific/research support. Before exploring the topic, it may be useful to briefly introduce the two key concepts, big data and AI, because they do not always have agreed definitions.

Big data is generally referred to by using the 3Vs: Volume, Velocity and Variety (Laney, 2001). This definition points out that big data does not simply mean big datasets or many datasets (big Volume) but also rapidly changing, next to real-time data (big Velocity) and great heterogeneity (big Variety). In general, it refers to the enormous increase in range of data sources, from space, social media, the public and private sectors and the ability to integrate

> " Big data is generally referred to by using the 3Vs: Volume, Velocity and Variety "

the data and generate new insights typically for commercial purposes. This definition and others that have added other Vs, such as Veracity, Value and Visualisation (Nativi et al., 2015), are based on a technical perspective. Other authors take a more social and political perspective focussing on Big data and 'datification' as the transformation of our everyday life into quantifiable, measurable and therefore controllable data (Mayer-Schoenberger and Cukier, 2013; van Dijck, 2014), which may lead to forms of surveillance capitalism (Zuboff, 2015).

The definition of AI also lacks clear boundaries. Traditionally, AI refers to machines or agents that are capable of observing their environment, learn, and based on the knowledge and experience gained, take intelligent action, or propose decisions. This is a rather old-fashioned definition, and with the emergence of new algorithms, the definition has become rather blurred to include areas of AI, such as machine learning (ML), deep learning, reinforcement learning, neural networks and robotics, and key fields of application such as natural language processing, image and speech recognition, computer vision and so on.

The interest in AI is rather recent even if the underlying methods date back to the 1950s. This new found interest in AI, and ML in particular, results from the convergence of three developments: (i) increased access to cheap computing storage and processing capabilities, (ii) increased availability of big data on which to train algorithms and address previously hard problems such as object recognition from digital images and machine translation and (iii) improved algorithms and increased access to specialised open source ML software libraries that make the creation and testing of ML algorithms easier. These trends started to come together around 2012, and since then, we have seen a rapid development of AI.[1] As in the case of Big data discussed above, we can contrast this technical perspective of AI with more political ones, which see Big data and AI as part of the same narrative of 'dataism', as the new authority of data and algorithm on human society (Harari, 2015; van Dijck, 2014).

In this chapter, we want to consider the potential use of Big data and AI to modernise the policy cycle. Why would we want to do that? Because there is an increasing gap between the speed of the policy cycle and that of technological, and social, change. Using the example of the INSPIRE Directive (EC, 2007), which addresses data, standards and technology to share environmental information, it started being discussed in the year 2000, was formulated in 2002–03, was adopted in 2007 and has an implementation roadmap that will end in 2019–20. During these 20 years, computing power has increased about 10,000 times and data availability more than 100,000 times (based on Kambala et al., 2014). Many jobs of today did not exist 20 years ago, and over the next 20 years, we will see even further changes in the job market and social practices. How can we formulate meaningful policy in this context? We are always playing catch up rather than being able to guide the processes. Therefore, the question is can we leverage AI and Big data to govern *with* the digital transformation, in addition to shaping the governance *of* digital transformation? What would governing with AI and Big data look like?

We sketch a scenario below starting from the assumption that computing is not an issue as it is now ubiquitously available through different forms of cloud computing. In the near future, more decentralised forms of computing at the edge of the network will also emerge by preprocessing data at the level of sensors, vehicles and mobile devices. We also start from the assumption that data, whether collected by or contributed to public authorities, will be linked and exploitable for public good without jeopardising the rights of companies and individuals, including the protection of private data. Finally, we recognise that AI is at the present time largely focussing on ML and related algorithms that are trained on the data to find patterns and rules, predict future behaviours and responses and adapt or 'learn' based on feedback loops.

---

[1] For further reading on the subject, see http://publications.jrc.ec.europa.eu/repository/bitstream/ JRC113826/ai-flagship-report_online.pdf.

A first step for transforming public policies would be to exploit the full potential of administrative data to orchestrate policy evaluation into regular and short feedback loops. Through fine-grained administrative data, it is possible to individualise key characteristics like age, gender, residence location and socioeconomic profile and start measuring the impact of public policies on different groups, going beyond correlation towards causality. A new short cycle of adaptation could be foreseen in new types of regulatory instruments sensitive to impact results. There is already available experience in implementing counterfactual impact evaluation and exploiting the potential of administrative data linkages. Future developments will depend on data availability as well as changes in legislative approaches, aligning with the requirements associated to the regulation of complex systems: probe, test and adapt.

When bringing AI into the picture, we can progress the transformation of public policy-making even further. We are concerned at the present time with the notion of 'algorithmic' governance, i.e., being ruled by decisions taken or informed by machines on the basis of algorithms (i.e., rules) that we do not understand and are not accountable. There is a clear need for accountability, transparency, oversight, testing for biases and explainability of algorithms but that does not mean that we should reject the use of algorithms outright to support decision-making processes. In fact, we can posit that a set of legal implementing rules expressed in computer code (i.e., as algorithms) could be clearer and more verifiable than expressed in legal language, with the advantage of being more programmable and adaptable, for example, to maximise effectiveness and fairness of implementation whilst maintaining the objective of the legal act constant.

We can think of this with analogy of European Directives, where we agree on the objective to be reached (the *What*) and then leave the Member States to transpose the Directive in their national laws so that they can adapt the implementation (the *How*) to their institutional system and national characteristics. So why not think of redesigning the policy so that we agree on the objective in such a way that the implementation shall vary according to different circumstances, for example, different areas and different groups of people or firms, to maximise efficiency of resources, effectiveness of outcomes and fairness in implementation? If the implementing measures (rules) were expressed as ML algorithms, we could also from the outset design the policy so that it does not need revision unless the objective has changed, but is constantly adapting to changing reality and 'learning' based on the feedback loop from implementation.

Aside from more flexible, adaptive and responsive policies, we can also think of more targeted policies based on needs and location. We may be comfortable with personalised services (e.g., loans, insurance, recommendations about books, films or music and in the near future personalised medicine) and less so with personalised/targeted marketing, but how would we feel about 'personalised' government policies? The answer may well be more about our trust in government and whether we feel it has our best interest at heart, than about concepts, methods, or technology. Therefore, it probably varies from country to country, level of government and historical period.

The issues about designing 'personalised', 'need-based' policies are being addressed in the Digitranscope[2] project and in leading centres like the Alan Turing Institute in the United

---

[2] https://ec.europa.eu/jrc/communities/community/digitranscope.

Kingdom, which has a dedicated programme about data science for public policy.[3] The key point is to identify individual needs and then target policy intervention around such needs whilst being in full respect of privacy protection. This can be done through anonymised processes and under governance protocols protecting from various types of potential abuses or violations. Administrative data management and new forms of social contracts around data sharing between citizens, public authorities and private companies are key aspects of this area of development, and many countries are exploring innovative approaches as a result of the AI revolution.

To identify the needs of individuals and groups in specific geographical areas for different public policy areas of intervention such as housing, social care, education or energy, we can use several data sources and strategies:

- Infer need by integrating and analysing all the data relevant to a policy issue that are already held by government at different levels: This is technically possible as we (almost) all have unique identifiers like tax codes or digital IDs that allow to link the files held by different government departments (the so-called administrative data linkage). In most countries, it is not done because of legal, cultural and organisational barriers/sensitivities although there is a policy push by European Commission to introduce the 'Once Only' principle, already applied in Estonia, whereby a government should not ask citizens or firms for information it already has. This implies a much greater degree of good data management and data sharing across government than is the case in most countries at the present time, but it seems to be a direction for future development.
- Infer need by disaggregating anonymised group data that are published by statistical offices: National and local statistics are typically published at small area units of approximately 200–500 people. For each area, many variables are available about the population, households, families and buildings. These variables can be disaggregated to the level of (artificial) individuals based on a set of rules, so that when reaggregated at the small area unit, they give the same set of statistics as those published. The (imputed) characteristics of these (artificial) individuals can then be aggregated into families and households and assigned to buildings and dwellings, so that again when reaggregated, they return the official published data. This technique is already well used for policy modelling and assessment, for example, to compare the outcome of a policy intervention on a certain group with nonintervention on a group having similar characteristics or for modelling emissions from individual transportation (see, for example, Chapter 18).
- Ask people to express their needs: Traditionally, this is done through postal, telephone or online surveys, which can be done more frequently and on questions already targeted on different groups based on some degree of profiling from one or two above. This would have the advantage of making the questions more pertinent and eliciting not just 'need' but also the equally important 'perception of need'. As an example, there could be a set of questions about level of satisfaction with the local school, and journey to it only addressed to families with young children, and access to healthcare targeted to the elderly, etc., and avoid questions that do not apply to the groups imputed from one to two above.

---

[3] https://www.turing.ac.uk/research/research-programmes/public-policy.

- Establish a social platform, encourage people to create their profiles and then gather data from the interaction among people and between people (or firms) and the platform: This is equivalent in a public space to what is done by all social media platforms that are based on content created by the users and then enriched with labels and context by the user interactions. This is crucial for training ML algorithms: not just raw data but semantically enriched, contextualised data. Public administrations cannot do that on their own, they need users to do it, but of course, they need to provide the right incentives to get people (or firms) to create and maintain their profiles and use the platforms, maintain accountability and trust and so on. This is a rich matter of ongoing research also in many experiences with citizen-generated content and citizen science where motivation, incentives and sustainability are key concerns.

Unlike traditional surveys, the combination of the methods highlighted above would also allow to identify the groups that do not respond or participate and try to understand better the reasons behind this, reducing the problem of the 'silent and overlooked' groups. If carefully developed and adequately communicated and explained, these methods could be used to customise policy intervention according to the need (and perception thereof), develop powerful feedback mechanisms to policy planning and implementation and reinforce bidirectional communications between citizens and the government leading to greater accountability, increased trust and more active citizenship. Algorithms finding commonalities among the citizens will help us identify 'communities' of shared needs and interests, to which we can tailor policies so that they do to impose obligations on those that do not need to be affected.

Last but not least, it is now possible in a digitally transformed society to do any of the points above considering real people in the real physical world, artificial individuals in the real world, artificial individuals in a virtual world (e.g., avatars) or real individual interacting with a virtual replica of the real world. An example of the latter is the Digital Twin of the Netherlands created in Minecraft by a public–private partnership between the Dutch Cadastre, Dutch Waterboards, the Free University of Amsterdam and Geodan, a private company. Geocraft.nl[4] is a 1:1 model of the Netherlands where every building is represented based on the official cadastre and recreated by more than 20,000 children over a period of 4 years. The opportunities for a new form of participation and policy design are illustrated from an experiment done in June 2018 in the south of Amsterdam, where 500 children came together with the local administration, industry and academics to use this virtual model in Minecraft to help design their vision of the future for their neighbourhood.[5] This experiment is now being replicated in Warsaw with the engagement of local schools.

Combining the approaches described above, it is possible to gather knowledge about objective/relative and perceived needs and design policy interventions that address those who need them most in the geographical areas that need them most.

These policy interventions can be modelled and tested in advance using randomised control trials techniques in both physical and virtual environments and then deployed and monitored so that the feedback from implementation adapts the policy intervention in next to real time, a form of 'policy that learns' similar to the approach in ML, where algorithms learn from the

[4] https://www.youtube.com/watch?v=R-xVyyliS4ghttps://geocraft.nl/.
[5] https://www.youtube.com/watch?v=WkKHReQ8wyE&feature=youtu.be.

data. Moreover, because we are designing from the outset policies that target specific groups in specific areas, we can assess with much greater transparency their impacts and include also the feedback of the policy recipients themselves. This creates new opportunities for public participation also in the ex-post policy assessment described in Chapter 18. Last but not least, as the case of South Amsterdam mentioned above, we can involve the recipients of intervention in the policy design process, and who better than children are the most impacted by the future.

Of course, using AI and Big data for new forms of policy design and evaluation as described here may have negative and unintended consequences from the point of view of security, privacy and social equity. It is for this reason that we are running policy experiments to ask the questions that may help us identify positive directions of travel, blind alleys or no-go areas. On the other hand, more targeted and transparent policy design and impact assessment could force politicians and decision-makers in the industry to be more accountable about their promises and citizens and firms to become more conscious about their responsibilities. This in turn could contribute to improving that dialogue between citizens and institutions that Vesnic-Alujevic et al. (2019) advocate as crucial in meeting the future challenges in society.

Image: https://stock.adobe.com/be_en/images/cape-buffalo-with-lesser-white-egret-looking-for-insects/136472725?prev_
url=detail
Icon in page corners: Mutualism icon by Nithinan Tatah, from the Noun Project (https://thenounproject.com/search/?q=
mutualism&i=2369116)

Navigating Interests in a Science for Policy Environment

Main authors: Marta Sienkiewicz, Marton Hajdu, Pieter van Nes, Marie-Agnes Deleglise

Contributors: Sharon Munn, Serge Roudier

Key takeaways:

- Science for Policy 2.0 implies close relationships between different actors involved in policymaking. This inevitably creates a space where multiple interests intersect, to a much higher degree than in a basic scientific environment. As such, scientists need to be prepared that their science can be contested and attempts can be made to influence and instrumentalise it for achieving particular goals.

- These interests are of various nature: some are personal interests, values and convictions of the scientists; some come from policymakers, while others from lobbyists, stakeholders or institutions.

- Maintaining a culture of openness, honesty about expectations and entanglements and committed to efforts to increase both legitimacy of expertise and vigilance to undue use or influence is our suggested way forward.

Science for Policy Handbook
http://dx.doi.org/10.1016/B978-0-12-822596-7.00010-7

Copyright © 2020 European Union,
Published by Elsevier Limited.

Participating in policymaking requires actively engaging with policymakers and other non-scientific stakeholders. Sometimes this can create a sense of unease in some scientists, for fear of trespassing the norms of scientific integrity. Science for policy is different than the science communicated to academia, in that it becomes part of a system in which different actors, with different interests, participate. Policymakers, stakeholders, institutions and lobbyists all have their interests, and scientists themselves are not free from them.

In a policy context, science is also contested in different ways than in academia. It is scrutinised by lobbies and citizens, often coming under attack. Lobbyists, be it corporate or non-governmental organisations, seek to influence and instrumentalise science for achieving their own goals. The presence of interests in policymaking is inevitable. Therefore, those aspiring to work in Science for Policy 2.0 need to acknowledge and carefully manage them to maintain integrity.

Before considering specific interests in detail, it is vital to stress that the basic principles of scientific integrity must still be applied. Robust science is the precondition for any policy engagement discussed in this book. Therefore, nothing justifies playing with data to fit any particular interest in the policymaking ecosystem. It can happen that scientists may feel the need to artificially fit the scientific facts to policy agendas, to preserve a long-established relationship, gain new influence areas, and secure more impact or funding. The pressure can even directly come from policymakers. This is both ethically inadmissible and diminishes scientists' credibility given that policies and their background science are scrutinised by other actors and observers in the process. Institutional arrangements are important ways to help properly manage such pressures.

Personal Interests, Values and Emotions of Scientists

Traditionally, scientists' role is seen as one of impartial and objective producers of knowledge, removing themselves from any outside influence. However, this understanding of their role has been changing. The value-free ideal of science understood as a fully objective and rational process devoid of emotional and normative entanglements is questioned by science and technology studies (Douglas, 2009; Elliott, 2017). There is a growing understanding that facts are established through a social, culturally-dependent process: which types of claims become facts, with how much evidence behind them, is not universally agreed (Latour and Woolgar, 1979). The complexities and social character of scientific debates, the dynamics between conformism and dissent (de Melo-Martín and Intemann, 2014), make it difficult to make observations outside of a paradigm, which is, however, not infallible (Kuhn, 1962). Scientists have to decide how much evidence is needed for a claim to be accepted and trusted, and the criteria for it are not universal (de Rijcke et al., 2016).

This was visible during JRC's work on defining the scientific criteria for the identification of endocrine disrupting chemicals. Endocrine active substances (EASs) are substances that can interact or interfere with normal hormonal action. When this leads to adverse effects, they are called endocrine disruptors (EDs). The endocrine system is important because it regulates and controls the release of hormones. Scientific knowledge in this area is still growing and, therefore, understanding of what is an EAS/ED continues to be the subject of scientific debate.

The diversity of experts from the Member States tasked with implementing this particular legislation and involved in the process meant a diversity of social and moral values and cultural backgrounds. It is clear that these values influence the judgement on accepting a body of evidence as conclusive and robust enough to make a decision. The other side of the evidence base (what is known) is what is not known, as well as the extent of conflicting evidence or uncertainties. How to conclude in the face of the uncertainties again comes down to value and expert judgements and lies firmly in the centre of the science–policy interface.

Values enter the scientific process in the framing of research questions and objects of study, in decisions about what gets funded, in the selection of data to be collected, the selection of analytical methods and scope of the analysis. They also play a role in deciding what is deemed pertinent to be communicated as important scientific findings, and how they are framed. Therefore, there is also no objective 'view from nowhere', because science cannot insulate itself from value judgements and decisions.

Values and emotions can also influence the understanding of one's role as a scientist, and expectations the public or (some) policymakers place on them. With a common framing of science and technology as the ultimate answer to today's global problems, scientists can end up feeling the illusion of the 'white knight'. The interaction between science and policy can appear as an arena to fight against the rise of anti-intellectual, antiscientific and antimed-

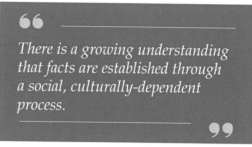

> *There is a growing understanding that facts are established through a social, culturally-dependent process.*

ical positions, where scientists are encouraged to speak truth to power (even though this notion has been criticised, see Chapter 8). This can involve strong emotions, create conflicts of interest (or their perception) in a more ideological and political sense or create pressure and undue influence of values on the scientific process.

None of the above presents a reason to reject science. Deliberate misconduct and willingness to deceive are rare (Fanelli, 2009; Martinson et al., 2005) and overt scientific fraud remains an antivalue for the scientific community. However, scientists must consider that attaining the value-free ideal of scientific pursuits is not realistic and be more transparent about the role of values in scientific production. Embracing this helps to design mechanisms to keep these interests and values in check and maintain trustworthiness and credibility of researchers involved in policymaking. Below are some suggestions on how to navigate this difficult space, based on JRC's experience.

- Scientists should work on gaining legitimacy in the policy process

In a policy context of power relations, values and interests, the legitimacy of scientific expertise does not come only from the authority of the scientific process. Scientists need to work to win legitimacy, and especially the democratic legitimacy needed in a policy process.

One way to do it is to become more open to debating one's results in contexts other than the scientific community, including scrutiny by contesting audiences. Another is to include the diversity of different value positions already at the stage of defining the objects of study. This means opening a space of debate not just about the facts but how they are produced, thus helping to mitigate the risk that the scientific process and uncertainties become weaponised in policy debates. Trust in science increases if scientists are engaged and open with the people they want to reach (Oliver and Cairney, 2019). Much of this can be achieved through stages described earlier in this book: working with knowledge communities (Chapter 7), engaging with citizens (Chapter 8) and better communication (Chapter 15).

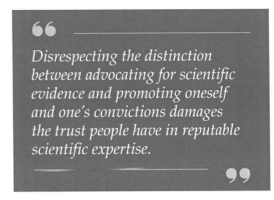

Disrespecting the distinction between advocating for scientific evidence and promoting oneself and one's convictions damages the trust people have in reputable scientific expertise.

- Scientists should clearly distinguish when they speak as scientists, and when as citizens or policy advisers

Scientists are just humans embedded in social processes. They have convictions and values which may push them to act more decisively on the basis of their research, whether consciously or not. However, there is a difference between *presenting* scientific results and *concluding advice* on what should be done on their basis. Scientists should not hide from the fact that they have opinions, but their ethos requires that they cultivate self-awareness about where their science ends and their normative opinion on its basis begins. They also must be advocates for the scientific evidence, not for themselves and their convictions. Not all opinions of scientists are 'the voice of science' just because they are expressed by representatives of the scientific community. Disrespecting this distinction damages the trust people have in reputable scientific expertise. It has to be clearly communicated, even in informal settings.

- Scientists should not shy away from emotions, especially while presenting their results to nonspecialist public

Emotions and emotional narratives offer potential benefits in communications and engagement with policy actors. The conclusions can be attuned to each audience, their framing, interests and concerns regarding the issue, provided that different messages are not contradictory and misleading. Emotions may help an audience better relate to the facts and grasp their relevance. They also give scientists a good indication of values that lie behind the emotional reactions of policy actors or citizens.

Scientists, just as all humans, cannot switch emotions off, even if disinterestedness is one of the foundational norms of scientific community (Merton, 1942). Trying too hard to suppress emotions in the name of impartiality may counterproductively contribute to biased thinking (Siegel et al., 2018; van 't Wout et al., 2010). It is better to train in self-awareness of our emotions and be open about them when they play an important part in our behaviour or narratives.

Policymakers' Interests

First and foremost, contrary to science, policymaking is highly value-based. Expertise plays a role, but any knowledge for policy deriving from science is clearly embedded in society and policy considerations, and thus inevitably gets entangled into debates about values, norms and political priorities. Policy problems are rarely neat enough to bend themselves to isolated hypothesis testing away from social and political implications (more on this tension in Chapter 6).

Moreover, policymakers often expect definitive answers and advice on what to do, what course of action to take based on the science. However, science can by definition answer only analytical questions, not the normative ones. A push for decisive policy answers from scientists not only overlooks uncertainty but lies beyond the competence of scientists.

Furthermore, scientists working for policy can discover an 'inconvenient truth', i.e., the results which present undesirable knowledge complicating a policy response, or a politically sensitive conclusion. Such a problem has two facets.

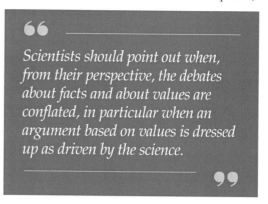

> Scientists should point out when, from their perspective, the debates about facts and about values are conflated, in particular when an argument based on values is dressed up as driven by the science.

One is the difficulty of communicating an unexpected, disturbing result to the policymakers, which creates a problem for them and potentially disrupts the relationship scientists have with them. The other is the dilemma of whether to publish such results, which can understandably be motivated by a sense of responsibility towards the public and the scientific community, as well as by the career incentives in science.

Ultimately, each organisation defines the conditions of their relationship with policymakers according to the objectives and expectations. The JRC is independent from EU Member States and any industry or special interests, but is an integral part of the European Commission. Below are the reflections based on our practice.

- Scientists and scientific organisations should choose which type of scientific advisory role they want to occupy

Even when they clearly distinguish facts from opinions, scientists in the policy context operate in a grey zone between informing and aiming to persuade. Roger Pielke Jr. (2007) introduced a useful typology of four roles which scientists working in policy can occupy, depending on their relation to influencing. Those who do not want to attempt any influence are 'pure scientists' and 'science arbiters', who deliver only the facts, with different levels of attention to the needs of policymakers (the former less, the latter more). 'Issue advocates' act without presenting all evidence, instead they tailor the response to sway a decision to one preferred policy solution. 'The honest broker' is a scientist who presents a range of relevant facts to different policy alternatives, adapting to what the policymakers want to know, but leaving the choice of solutions to them. In our experience, the honest broker is the most appropriate approach that allows to be useful to policymakers and not overstep scientific impartiality or damage credibility. One can respond with our opinions about the options if requested, but never start from being an issue advocate, especially not a stealth one.

- Scientists can add value as arbiters against the misuse of facts and engaging them as proxies in value-debates

The inferential gap between scientific results and their 'real-world' conclusions (i.e., what science says and what it means for policy or society) can cause misuse of scientific evidence, whether deliberate or accidental. One of the strongest arguments for scientists having a role in policymaking discussions is their ability to help policymakers spot misperceptions and distinguish between debates about facts and debates about values. Scientists should point out when, from their perspective, these debates are conflated and in particular when an argument based on values is dressed up as driven by the science. This happens, for instance, when a political disagreement over the objectives of a policy is hidden behind facts brought by different sides to support their preferred, value-motivated option.

Of course, scientists are not always present for those discussions. Policymakers can attempt to mould scientific results to fit their political argument even without the involvement of the scientists. However, researchers working for policy should scrutinise the conclusions drawn from their research and used in public discourse, speaking up in case of inaccuracies or manipulations.

- Scientists should explain the weight of evidence for different policy goals and objectives, instead of giving general advice for action

Due to the inferential gap between what science describes and what these descriptions imply, scientists should not try to make universal policy conclusions from their data. Uncertainty should also be properly communicated in order neither to stall nor to push a policy process too decisively. After all, politicians are used to taking decisions under conditions of uncertainty, indeed almost all political decisions involve some uncertainties. Different policy options for action depend on the end goals and evidence should be discussed in their context, though of course not deliberately prepared to fit them. It should be clear to which goals and values given recommendations apply, with what level of uncertainty.

- Scientists and policymakers should anticipate sensitivity and together agree on ways to manage it

Scientists and policymakers should anticipate if an issue and related research can become sensitive. Gathering policy intelligence (see Chapter 5) can help scientists to assess it, but communication risks should be carefully discussed together. Safeguarding independence does not mean waging public wars with policymakers who disagree. They should not be surprised by a publication, especially one that challenges their lines. Instead, communicators from both sides should prepare for any public response that may come to it, including defensives, and together decide a position in light of the evidence.

It is best to clarify with policymakers in advance whether researchers will be able to publish these results in scientific papers: the expectations must be made clear. If certain analysis is requested as highly sensitive with restricted access, this should be agreed upfront, not required only after the results.

- Scientific publications must be crafted carefully, focused on evidence and not political assessments

If scientists decide to publish, especially in more risky and politically sensitive areas, it is vital that their papers withstand the harshest scientific scrutiny. This includes both the logic and quality of the methods and data, but also the language. Unnecessary hyperbole falling outside normal scientific language would not pass the test. The JRC is working on an authorisation process for all publications, which is geared towards verifying the scientific quality of our outputs, as this is the primary source of risk to our reputation. In any sensitive cases, it is advisable to extend the usual internal peer review even beyond a normal procedure, to include a wider variety of perspectives, also nonscientific ones, such as that of communicators.

Unfortunately, the quality of a scientific argument is not something easily translatable to legal criteria. Scientific organisations need to rely on the collective expertise of their teams and their continued commitment to scientific integrity. It is crucial to build a culture of collaboration, debate and internal peer review, even if partly informal. It is therefore best to complement the external, formal peer review with internal mechanisms of help and scrutiny. For optimal results, such review should go beyond scientific scrutiny, to include also advice from communications and policy liaisons, to ensure that the message intended by the scientists will be understood by other audiences.

The advice on the two points above applies to scientific publications of our results, not opinion pieces, especially those commenting on specific proposals for EU policy lines. The exceptions to these rules are much more black-and-white situations: revealing information that has not been made public, causing prejudice to the interest of the organisation, or violating the principles of loyalty and impartiality. The last two points most likely would require a case-by-case judgement which is determined by the cultural context of a specific organisation.

- Scientists should weigh pros and cons of policy engagement in particular situations

Organisations can also consider not engaging in policy support, if the pressure is too big or the risk of distortion of science for 'policy-based evidence' too high. There are multiple sources of evidence and if scientists suspect misuse of the results, or are adamant about publishing regardless of the sensitivities, there is no obligation to accept a request for policy collaboration. Developing in-house integrity codes conforming with international standards gives a transparent reference point to the acceptable conditions in which an organisation engages in policy support.

External Interests: Lobbyists and Other Interest Representatives

When a scientific organisation gets more involved in policymaking and moves towards Science for Policy 2.0, it gradually becomes more influential in the policymaking process. As such, it will increasingly become the target of influencing attempts itself. Corporate lobbyists, NGOs and other interest representatives will inevitably seek to engage it to further their own goals. It is therefore vital that scientists become aware of the issues that can arise with regards to external lobbying (lobbyists and lobbying should be understood here as catch-all terms for anyone involved in advocacy on behalf of any organisation or particular interest and for the activity they carry out, be it classical lobbying, interest representation or advocacy).

The Place of Lobbying in the Policymaking Process

Lobbying to influence the policymaking process is not inherently wrong or illegitimate. Quite the contrary, in a democracy, people and organisations should have a right to know and influence how policies that will affect their life and their bottom line are made. Article 11 of the Treaty on the European Union prescribes that 'citizens and representative associations [shall have] the opportunity to make known and publicly exchange their views in all areas of Union action' and the EU 'institutions shall maintain an open, transparent and regular dialogue with representative associations and civil society' while the European Commission (of which the JRC forms a part) 'shall carry out broad consultations with parties concerned in order to ensure that the Union's actions are coherent and transparent'.

Lobbyists can bring to the table legitimate viewpoints, including aspects of the science that may otherwise be overlooked or simply not available – this is especially true for corporate scientists who often benefit from generous funding and access to proprietary data. However, unlike scientists providing policymakers with impartial evidence, lobbyists will always serve a particular interest. Sometimes this means engaging in illegitimate activities and exploiting scientific uncertainty to frustrate legislative efforts aimed at regulating their industries (Bramoullé and Orset, 2018). It is true that regulation is often a zero sum game with serious amounts of money on the line, and lobbyists have been known to exploit scientific uncertainty and produce narratives based on 'bad science' to convince the public, politicians and policymakers to alter, delay or completely halt regulation. This has been the case, for example, with tobacco and lung cancer (Proctor, 2012) or more recently with climate change and fossil fuels (Hoggan and Littlemore, 2009).

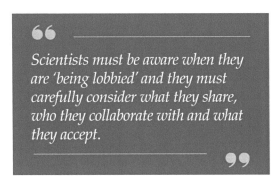

> 66
>
> *Scientists must be aware when they are 'being lobbied' and they must carefully consider what they share, who they collaborate with and what they accept.*
>
> 99

Why Are Scientists Lobbyists' Potential Target?

In representing their organisations or clients, lobbyists aim to achieve two main objectives: gather intelligence about the policymaking process and sway policymakers and politicians and the public by providing relevant information and arguments. As argued in Chapter 5, intelligence gathering is important because it helps to prepare and fine-tune further lobbying activities and it also helps the organisation, for example, a manufacturing firm, to adapt to upcoming legislative or regulatory changes, such as the ban of certain ingredients used by the firm.

Given these two objectives, engaging scientists as evidence providers can be beneficial for lobbyists on both counts. Scientists closely involved in the policymaking process will typically possess privileged information that they provided to or received from policymakers or that they become aware of through their cooperation with them. This can include information on the policy options being considered or already discarded; the assessment of their expected impacts; the stakeholders being consulted and even the arguments other stakeholders presented in the process, possibly including trade secrets.

Furthermore, the evidence scientists provide to policymakers can also be influenced, for example, by calling attention to and explaining research results previously unknown to the scientist; sharing proprietary data and research results otherwise inaccessible to the scientist or merely providing compelling arguments and narratives in support of a particular course of action.

None of the above is inherently problematic or illegitimate. Scientists, however, must be aware when they are 'being lobbied' and they must carefully consider what they share and what they accept.

Who Are Lobbyists?

There is no universal job description for a lobbyist: anybody could be considered a lobbyist if he or she advocates for a particular interest and seeks to influence policymaking or gather intelligence for their organisation's benefit. They are often highly skilled experts in their field. They may wear a suit and present a business card with the logo of a company or an industry association, but they may equally wear jeans and work as a journalist for a trade publication, or as a blogger, an NGO activist or a think tank analyst. And they may just as well wear a white coat and do research in a laboratory – possibly funded and steered by private interest (Steele et al., 2019).

While scientists aim to spend most of their time doing research, lobbyists spend most of their time building and managing their network to establish and nurture long-term relationships. Classical lobbyists are easier to spot, but interest representatives wearing multiple hats are more difficult to identify. This is also the reason why the EU transparency register puts an emphasis on what one does rather than who they are, but it is by no means certain that all the people who do lobbying register. Developing policy intelligence, or a 'helicopter view' can help identifying lobbyists, because certain positions will be more typically held by representatives of certain interest groups. For example, for profit health care providers or paying organisations would care more about the economic impact of legislation while patient groups would focus on health outcomes.

With many different stakeholders in the field, scientists and their organisations should learn a little bit about the main issues, opinions and constraints of each group in order to be able to identify them but also to better understand their positions and possibly benefit from their insights.

Dealing With Lobbyists

In general, a public policy organisation should be open to overtures by lobbyists for the reasons detailed earlier but risks as well as costs should be carefully considered in defining an organisation's own rules of engagement with lobbyists. In the case of the JRC, our staff must comply with financial, ethical and other rules and guidelines of the European Commission which, as a political and policymaking body, is a major target for lobbying activities. For any organisation it is true that staff must be made aware of the relevant rules through continuous training, and regular discussion of specific cases is advisable with management if doubt arises.

Within those constraints, the prevailing practice in the JRC is to be open and willing to engage with lobbyists. In order to manage the risks inherent in such engagement, conducting due diligence on partners and professional acquaintances is a must: it is a good idea to enquire about who they work for and who they receive funding from and verify if they are listed in the relevant national or EU level registers for lobbyists. Different levels of engagement will require different levels of scrutiny, and overly bureaucratic approaches should be avoided, but a critical approach to industry-funded research is important (Steele et al., 2019).

At the lowest level of sensitivity, it is advisable to maintain summary records of meetings and exchanges with lobbyists. As the level of sensitivity increases, more stringent record keeping, including the registration of written exchanges, is advisable as well as advance consultations with policymakers. Finally, in cases where stakeholders are involved in decision-making processes, clear, transparent conflict of interest rules must be put in place to safeguard scientific integrity and ensure the citizen centricity of the scientific process.

Going beyond procedural safeguards, and keeping in mind that 'lobbyists' also include top scientists and experts employed by organisations trying to promote their own narratives, the importance of ensuring scientific integrity and scientific excellence cannot be emphasised enough. In order to be perceived as credible by all stakeholders, a science for policy organisation cannot afford to be seen as offering anything less than sound evidence based on the best available science. Those with opposing interests will scrutinise our advice for possible flaws or shortcomings and use them to attack the policy itself. This includes issues in the grey zone of scientific uncertainty or issues that arise because of differences between the EU and other regulatory systems. In such cases, scientists must be prepared to supply policymakers with sound counterarguments as to why alternative approaches may be feasible in other jurisdictions but not in the EU. This approach requires that science for policy organisations develop the already mentioned policy intelligence which allows them to see beyond the science and anticipate policy issues.

Finally, trust is important throughout the science–policy interactions, and not less crucial in this respect. Strong, trust-based relationships with policymakers can help to anticipate lobbying efforts and provide guidance in responding to them as well as identify narratives used by lobbyists which are based on 'bad science'. It is particularly useful when scientists are able to explain to policymakers the uncertainties and half-truths behind them and purposes they serve.

Managing Conflicts of Interest

Personal Conflicts of Interest

Strong collaboration between science, policy, citizens and relevant stakeholders heightens the risk of conflicts of interest. The OECD (2005, p. 13) states that a conflict of interest involves 'a conflict between the public duty and the private interest of a public official, in which the official's private-capacity interest could improperly influence the performance of their official duties and responsibilities'. It can be extrapolated to scientists working for policy, whether they are officially public servants (like scientists in the JRC) or external collaborators.

A conflict of interest often creates uneasiness, it is considered as something irregular to stay away from. In fact, the term only describes a situation without giving any value judgement. The real issue with conflicts of interest is not to avoid it, but to recognise and manage it (see OECD, 2005 for a detailed toolkit, and Thagard, 2007 for some strategies). Any conflict of interest can be discovered and voluntarily defused before any corruption occurs. As Ravetz (1999, p. 648) puts it, the integrity of scientists 'lies not in their "disinterestedness", but in their honourable behaviour as stakeholders'.

Conflicts of interest can be considered in terms of economic drivers, but the ideological and political aspects are particularly worth considering in science for policy collaborations. Ensuring diversity of advice is important, albeit without falling into the trap of false representation of the 'two sides of the argument' (Oreskes and Conway, 2010). Members of the experts groups working with the European Commission need to declare more than just their financial incentives, namely also their intellectual property rights, membership of managing bodies, public statements and positions and interests of their immediate family (Group of Chief Scientific Advisors, 2019).

Culture, risk appetite and 'the tone at the top' are vital aspects in how an organisation tries to manage conflicts of interest. Once the interests are declared, people in question may need to refrain from trying to influence the decision process, act on the side line or even give up the role for a particular file. Even the perceptions or suspicions of conflict of interest can be damaging, putting in question the credibility of the scientific input. Sometimes, not all parties can agree on what constitutes it, and can contest the declarations.

Institutional Conflicts of Interest

Conflicts of interest arise not only on the personal level but also need to be managed as part of the co-creation with institutional stakeholders involved in a policy or scientific advice process. In response to these, we have developed a successful 'Sevilla process', to manage various interests by involving all stakeholders.

The process concerns establishing secondary legislation on complex technoeconomic issues including on product policy, industrial emissions or waste. The 'Sevilla process' is particularly applied for establishing the Best Available Techniques (BAT) under the Industrial Emissions Directive (2010/75/EU). BAT are the most effective technique of achieving a high level of protection of the environment when it comes to industrial emissions. We create spaces where all stakeholders involved are treated equally and their input, which is based on robust technoeconomic evidence, is impartially taken into account. The key principles are

- All stakeholders are actively involved from the very start of the work up to and including the final decisions on BAT.
- Co-creation with stakeholders (of the BAT reference documents – the so-called BREFs) and consensus decision-making (on the BAT conclusions) are at the heart of the process.
- The roles and responsibilities of stakeholders (including of the JRC) in the process are clearly assigned and laid out.
- A rigorous, open and participatory process is in place to collect and verify the necessary information and data from which the BAT conclusions are derived.
- The complex technoeconomic discussions are led by a highly competent, neutral and credible entity, in this case the JRC's European Integrated Pollution Prevention and Control (EIPPCB) Bureau, and sufficient time is provided for the discussions to decide on BAT.

Making Things Public: Open and Transparent

In an environment in which science is often contested and forcefully entangled in policy battles, being open gives a chance to win legitimacy and build trust in the evidence-informed nature of the process. It is vital not only for presenting final results of research or policy design; the process used for arriving at these results should also be open for scrutiny, and inclusive of citizens and stakeholders voices, given that the impact of policy is public and concerns many.

> Being transparent is not synonymous with being open and willing to engage.

While 'transparency' is a well-known and codified principle, we prefer to talk about fostering an open attitude and making things public, rather than making them transparent. Being transparent is not synonymous with being open and willing to engage, and brings a connotation of making things close to invisible.

Openness is crucial, especially for science for policy: because of the impacts of policy on the public, both the policy solution and the science behind it must be discussed in the public space. It helps to guarantee legitimacy of the scientific input by minimising the unfounded perceptions of conflicts of interest. It also presents a fuller picture of a policy co-creation process and prevents blaming scientific inputs for policy failure. It is an underlying principle of Science for Policy 2.0, one that is realised through citizen engagement, inclusion of diverse actors in defining research questions, collaboration with knowledge communities, among others. It helps increase the quality of evidence-informed policymaking, in an era where facts are often disputed.

Backbone tools of Science for Policy 2.0

Image: Ead72, https://stock.adobe.com/be_en/images/giant-redwood-forest-canopy/66538109?prev_url=detail
Icon in page corners: Leaves icon by Made x Made from the Noun Project (https://thenounproject.com/search/?q=ecosystem&i=1759605)

Complexity Science in the Context of Policymaking

Author: Vera Calenbuhr

Key takeaways

- In order to understand the complexity of many real-world phenomena such as resilience, emergent properties, collective decision-making, evolutionary change and many others, it is necessary to change the perspective from the parts of the system to the connections between the parts and to the system as a whole, i.e., from reductionism to holism.

- Reductionism and holism are complementary.

- Effective policymaking benefits from appreciating this complementarity.

Science for Policy Handbook
http://dx.doi.org/10.1016/B978-0-12-822596-7.00011-5

Copyright © 2020 European Union,
Published by Elsevier Limited.

Introduction: Why Is Complexity Science Relevant?

In economics and policymaking, many concepts and models talk about equilibrium, masses and centres of gravity (EU, 2019a; EU, 2013). They talk about linear cause and effect chains, prediction and precision. One consequence of this worldview is that many policymakers assume that having more details and more precise figures help them to make better policies.

Many organisations amongst them the OECD, the European Commission's Joint Research Centre, think tanks and academic institutions have recognised that this reductionist worldview concentrating on the parts of a system is no longer sufficient in accounting for the complexity encountered in the economy, society and the environment.

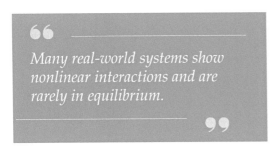

Many real-world systems show nonlinear interactions and are rarely in equilibrium.

In fact, many real-world systems show nonlinear interactions and are rarely in equilibrium. They show phenomena such as adaptation (e.g., markets, innovation), the formation of hierarchies (e.g., public and private organisations, discussions), self-organisation (e.g., collective decisions, public opinion formation), robustness and fault tolerance (e.g., many biological systems), resilience (e.g., ecosystems, some technological 'ecosystems'), lack of central control (e.g., collective decisions in social insects, bird flocks, fish swarms, task allocation in computer systems) and other features well known from complexity science (CS). None of these properties can be understood on the basis of the properties of the parts of the system alone. Instead, the relations and interactions between the parts are relevant and need to be studied.

Complex system behaviour also relates to the issue of reflexivity covering phenomena, e.g., the reflexive questioning of values, background assumptions and normative orientations, as well as the role of conscious reflection guiding individuals' behaviour and potentially making collective large-scale behaviour unpredictable.

Sound and fit-for-purpose scientific approaches are a necessary and minimal condition for effective and successful policymaking. The human nature and condition with its values, beliefs, drivers, emotions and other factors also need to be taken into account, and they are a source of complexity, too; hence, the issue of complexity relates also to the Enlightenment 2.0 discussion (EC, 2019b; Heath, 2014).

Reductionist approaches are useful for understanding the parts of a system, i.e., parts of the economy, the environment and society. Yet, when it comes to understanding the complex dynamics resulting from the interaction of these parts, it is necessary for both, scientists and policymakers, to shift the perspective from the parts to the system and to the interactions between the parts of the system. This is the realm of CS.

What Is Complexity Science?

Defining complex systems is a challenge, and there are different ways in which people have defined complex systems. As an example, complex systems (or CS) is defined by OECD (2009) as follows:

> *A complex system is composed of many parts that interact with and adapt to each other and, in so doing, affect their own individual environments and, hence, their own futures. The combined system-level behaviour arises from the interactions of parts that are, in turn, influenced by the overall state of the system. Global patterns emerge from the autonomous but interdependent mutual adjustments of the components.*

> *Neither reductionism nor holism presents the full picture, instead they are complementary.*

Complex systems exist in many domains of science, and many attempts have been made to grapple with them from within each domain (e.g., biology of ants and birds; computation with cellular automata; etc.). CS straddles many science fields, see Fig. 1.

Since CS deals with the relations between the parts of the system, it represents a holistic counterpart to reductionism.

Neither reductionism nor holism presents the full picture, instead they are complementary.

Complex systems research is also characterised by a change in the mathematical tools involved. This resulted in shifting from a focus on figures and the quantitative (in reductionism) to a focus on geometry and the qualitative (in holism), (see, e.g., several examples in Capra (1996)). This means that while it may be possible to predict the qualitative features of a system, quantitative predictions are rarely possible. A key output of CS methods is what one might refer to as complexity reduction. Often, the observed complex behaviour of a system may be related to one or a small number of equations or behavioural rules or a mathematical principle. The complexity is still there, but knowing what – simple – mechanisms are causing it, one appreciates and embraces the complexity – which is a great step forward towards a better understanding of a complex system. Some may want to say that CS provides methods for sense making.

The complex world around us is governed by many different forces, rules and boundary conditions, requiring different approaches for understanding them and for coping with them. The mathematician Lee Segel once said that it might be well imaginable that we need more than one theory for explaining complex systems such as the immune system. This may also be the case for the even more complex real world of human society. One may view these theories as models, grammars or even worldviews, depending on how encompassing they are. The crucial thing is one approach only focuses on some aspects of reality, whereas other phenomena remain disregarded, and these different approaches are needed for appreciating and coping with this complexity. The sciences of complexity and related methods based on discourse, inclusion, communication and others can contribute to this objective.

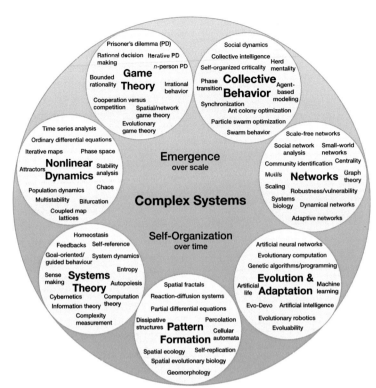

FIGURE 1 An organisational map of complex systems broken into seven subgroups. (Fig. 1: Created by Hiroki Sayama, D.Sc., Collective Dynamics of Complex Systems (CoCo), 2010, taken from https://en.wikipedia.org/wiki/Complex_system.)

What Are the Challenges that CS can Help to Tackle?

Communication

Policymakers are increasingly faced with the challenge of communicating about both, the complexity of reality and the policies addressing the issues arising from this complexity. CS methods provide powerful tools for addressing this challenge:

1. Since CS methods often involve a shift from a quantitative to a qualitative description, i.e., a shift from figures to geometry, visual concepts such as phase space, attractors, fitness landscapes and maps, they have the potential of being very powerful tools for understanding, describing and communicating complex issues – even to laypersons. For example, discussions on the transition from a fossil fuel–based energy system to a decarbonised one focus much on the technologies, markets, cost–benefits considerations and many other important aspects. Yet, for understanding lock-in phenomena such as technological and institutional, it helps to shift to CS methods. A fitness landscape perspective

allows understanding new aspects of these phenomena and thereby helps to focus the debate. In essence, it makes visible the trade-offs of, e.g., investing into marginal efficiency gains of combustion engines on the one hand or instead investing the same resources into renewable technologies on the other. The shift away from the quantitative to the qualitative is also illustrated by the use of the Economic Complexity Index (ECI) going beyond GDP. The ECI was developed by Hidalgo and Hausmann (2009) as a predictive tool for economic growth and income equality. The index is a 'holistic' measure of the productive capabilities of large economic systems, e.g., countries or regions. It aims to capture the knowledge accumulated in a population and which is expressed in the economic activities. The ECI covers information on the diversity of countries and the ubiquity of products. This information is used to produce a measure of economic complexity, containing information about both, the diversity of a country's export and their sophistication. Hence, highly developed countries with high ECIs and highly diversified economies export many goods of low ubiquity, whereas countries of a lower development degree with lower ECI and lower diversified economies export only a few products, which are of relatively high ubiquity (Cristelli et al., 2013, 2015; Hausmann et al., 2013).

2. CS methods also deliver powerful communication metaphors such as 'fitness landscapes', 'tipping points', 'critical points', 'point of no return', 'emergent properties', 'order on the edge of chaos', 'self-organised criticality' and 'multistationarity' to mention just a few. Due to the visual messages they bear, they lend themselves to be used as tools in communication between experts and nonexperts. For example, the notion of emergent property is related to hierarchical ontologies (i.e., system properties built up from the bottom to the top) as opposed to historical ontologies (i.e., properties result as a consequence of linear, consecutive steps). First, it is crucial to acknowledge such bottom-up processes. Second, awareness of emergent properties gives policymakers new levers for action. Examples of emergent properties include the appearance of resilience (in ecosystems (Peterson, 2000; Gunderson, 2000) and human society (Faulkner et al., 2018), collective decision-making, such as in public opinion formation (Weidlich and Haag, 1983), and the selection of technologies (Arthur, 1994)).

3. CS methods such as bifurcation theory, agent-based modelling and leverage point analysis (see more detail in Coping With Complexity section) as well as concepts such as fitness landscapes can help reducing complexity – in the sense described in What Is Complexity Science? section – and overcome mental lock-ins, thereby enabling powerful communication.

Coping With Complexity

CS methods can help to go beyond communication and allow coping with complexity. The following case distinction may illustrate this:

1. **Complexity reduction I**: Very often, complex behaviour can arise from very simple mechanisms or rules at the level of the interacting parts of the system (May, 1976). Whenever this is the case, developing models, followed by performing, e.g., *stability* and *bifurcation analysis* and an *analysis of the boundary conditions*, can help to reveal the simplicity underlying complexity. This way, policymakers find powerful places to intervene

in a complex system. This is used, e.g., for analysing technology lock-in (e.g., nonlinear Polya processes, i.e., a stochastic mechanism used for describing consumer choice in the case of increasing returns (Arthur, ditto)). Grandmont (1985) has shown how endogenous mechanisms can cause complex economic cycles. In ecological contexts, complex population dynamics, e.g., of insects can often be reduced to the logistic equation (Murray, 2008), and in fisheries, the Lotka–Volterra model is an important reference (Murray, ditto). Negative experiences like overfishing have been linked to using concepts such as 'maximal sustainable yield', possibly involving too simplistic and unrealistic assumptions regarding age structures of fish population (Walters and Maguire, 1996). The pattern of increasing fish catches followed by a sharp decline has been linked to phase transition behaviour (Pauly et al., 1998).

2. **Complexity reduction II**: Even if complex behaviour cannot be reduced to simple interactions at the level of the interacting subparts of the system, the method of *leverage point analysis* can provide a qualitative analysis of the relative importance of the system's parameters, feedback loops and boundary conditions, as well as about the assumptions made about the system, thereby delivering places for policymakers to intervene in a complex system (Meadows, 2008). Leverage point analysis facilitates identification of necessary and sufficient conditions with respect to the larger context. This way, important challenges such as reconciling micro- and macroeconomic objectives can be addressed, which is relevant in the sustainable development debate.

3. **Network analysis:** Not all complexity can be reduced and simplified as described before. There are cases, where the mere number of different interacting subcomponents of a system is entangled in such a way that the key to coping with a complex system lies in trying to figure out how strong and in which way parts are coupled to each other, using *network theoretical methods*. The behaviour of power grids, communication networks such as the Internet (a so-called 'small-world' net), as well as network-based infrastructures in general, the emergence of public opinion and many other phenomena can thus be analysed, possibly leading to increased understanding of such systems allowing analysis of stability and eventually coping with the system (see e.g., Garas and Lapatinas, 2017).

4. **Participatory approaches**: If none of the previous methods work, the minimum one would like to obtain is a description of the relevant factors of the complex system. Participatory approaches, such as *Living Labs* and *Maker Spaces*, are examples of participatory approaches where scientific and citizen knowledge is brought together to jointly account for the complexity of a system. The larger the amount of information added, the greater the knowledge. This way, parts, domains and rules of the system as well as parameters and boundary conditions become transparent through looking at and interacting with the system, thereby revealing powerful information for policymakers. Participatory approaches aiming at capturing a system understanding are also at play in *foresight* practice and the Joint Research Centre's *Policy Lab*. Participatory approaches are helpful to elaborate the scope of a complex situation. Modelling, which may follow in a next step to better understand a complex phenomenon, often focuses only on small parts of the entire scope. So, participatory approaches can help to appreciate what we know not.

Participatory approaches do not necessarily lead to one 'model' of a complex system. At best, one can obtain relevant 'models' that are jointly needed to describe the complex system. In the worst case, revealing ever more information about the complexity does not lead to actionable complexity reduction (see next point).

5. **Wicked problems:** There are systems in which nearly everything is connected to everything and where revealing more information does not lead to any complexity reduction. The complex behaviour of such systems is referred to as wicked problems (Rittel and Webber, 1973) – as opposed to tame systems, which may be tackled using reductionist methods. Such wicked systems are often encountered in social, urban and regional planning contexts (the domains in which the term was coined).

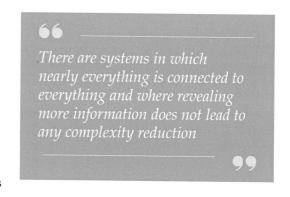

> *There are systems in which nearly everything is connected to everything and where revealing more information does not lead to any complexity reduction*

One very powerful approach for analysing such systems is to establish scaling laws. For example, the energy consumption of a town as a function of the number of inhabitants typically scales as a power law. Establishing such power laws does not reveal much about the underlying mechanisms as such – hence, more detailed models are needed – but it allows categorising towns and regions, thereby opening spaces for coping with complexity (see West (2018) for numerous examples). Scaling laws also help in other contexts, e.g., for categorising networks, such as (economic) issues related to internet traffic (e.g., Willinger et al., 2002).

6. **Sociological analysis:** There are questions, which can hardly be answered by any of the approaches above. For example, do modern societies create complexity by their very actions – and policies? Sociological analysis, i.e., stepping out of the system and taking a remote perspective, may propose answers to issues such as resilience of infrastructures, the occurrence of power blackouts, technology transitions like the shift to a decarbonised energy system, the shift towards a circular economy, the security of the internet and more generally (see, e.g., Labanca, 2017).

From a certain level of complexity onwards, it is very difficult to see effects, phenomena or even structures. Here, new modelling and quantification methods come into play. They can help to reveal structures in big data. Reductionist in essence, they make possible further analysis from a holistic perspective at a later stage. Hence, such methods help connecting the reductionist and holistic perspectives.

In essence, such new modelling and quantification methods contribute to bringing in new actors' perspectives in modelling (e.g., agent-based modelling (Bonabeau, 2002)) for tapping into new sources of (big) data or using modelling methods coming from the natural sciences for strengthening the economic modelling capacity.

Complex system methods span a wide range of scientific disciplines starting from the molecular level over the cellular to the societal level. It has been shown that similar phenomena and similar mechanisms apply to specific cases located at different levels and in different fields (Mikhailov and Calenbuhr, 2002). Hence, since many if not most policy issues are of an across-disciplinary nature, complex systems methods have great potential in supporting policymakers.

What Are the Implications for Policymakers?

Traditional equilibrium and linear cause and effect thinking and related models based on a reductionist mind set can neither cope with nor help managing complexity, since they do not address the interactions of system components.

Widening the concepts and tools including methods from CS will enable policymakers to deal with complex issues more appropriately. Yet, using CS methods will require from policymakers to widen their mind set, to be ready to give up concepts and expectations such as predictability, precision and control and replace them with thinking in terms of scenarios, fitness landscapes, connectivities, probabilities, etc.

The benefit of this can bring a critical support to policy coherence as focussing on the whole system will raise the profile of the interplay between policies, the possible synergies and trade-offs.

Complexity Science Initiatives at the JRC

Appreciating the fact that many complex system phenomena are of an across-disciplinary nature, the European Commission's Joint Research Centre is launching a series of projects addressing societal challenges. One project addresses the transition from a linear to a circular economy using the ECI, network theory and agent-based modelling. Another project analyses the social innovation dynamics emerging in the context of the transition towards a decarbonised energy system. Finally, dynamic aspects of hybrid threats are studied using game theory and learning algorithms. In order to overcome a too strong focus on mathematical methods, all projects contain four building blocks, i.e., a citizen engagement component for scoping the issue; a series of mutually supporting mathematical analysis and computer simulations to focus on specific constellations; sociological analysis to build on the citizen engagement and analytic results, and to put them into a wider picture, and finally advanced visualisation methods to support communication including with laypersons.

Conclusion

Complex systems methods have been applied in many domains, which are relevant for policymakers. In a next step, such methods could complement traditional reductionist approaches of scientific policy support.

In a wider context, there are also several discussion fora and initiatives with associated conferences addressing the question if and to what degree CS can be used in the policy context.

Amongst supportive opinions, there are also critical voices. One of the main criticisms expressed addresses the difficulty of defining a societal system in such a way that it can be analysed using a CS method. This is a justified criticism, and it also applies to all reductionist economic models currently used. After all, a model is only a reflection of reality and as such an idealisation.

Acknowledgements

The author would like to thank Nicola Labanca, Angela Guimaraes Pereira, Laurent Bontoux, Paul Smits, Giuseppe Munda and Nicole Ostländer for their valuable discussions.

Image: Andreanita - https://stock.adobe.com/be_en/images/a-pair-of-bonelli-s-eagle-aquila-fasciata-perched-on-a-branch/798926449?prev_url=detail
Icon in page corners: Eagle Icon by Erica Grau, from the Noun Project (https://thenounproject.com/search/?q=eagles&i=520372)

Foresight – Using Science and Evidence to Anticipate and Shape the Future

Authors: Eckhard Störmer, Laurent Bontoux, Maciej Krzysztofowicz, Elisabeta Florescu, Anne-Katrin Bock, Fabiana Scapolo

Key takeaways: Applications of foresight for policymaking

The fundamental premise of foresight is that while the future cannot be predicted, it can be actively influenced or created. Many tools and methods have been developed to achieve this. The Joint Research Centre (JRC) has applied its know-how in foresight specifically for the benefit of the European Union (EU) policymaking, but many of the tools and approaches it has developed have shown their usefulness in wider contexts. A special effort has also been made to make foresight practical and its results accessible. Foresight usually follows a step-by-step approach, covered in more detail in the chapter:

- Definition of scope.
- Detection of signals of change and trends (e.g., horizon scanning).
- Analysis of uncertainties, cross-impacts, actors, etc.
- Understanding possible evolutions of drivers, trends and many others; exploring implications (e.g., through scenario building).
- Generation and evaluation of strategies to deal with possible future developments.
- Communicating results (done in many ways, e.g., scenario reports, serious games, etc.).
- Monitoring of scenario assumptions, developments, trends, weak signals, etc.

Foresight helps creating anticipatory governance capacity and awareness about future-related issues. It enables policymakers to make prudent long-term decisions, helps revealing the need for policy action and channel evidence into policy discussions.

Key approaches developed and used at the JRC are as follows:

- *Horizon scanning:* for alert and detection of weak signals;
- *Megatrends monitoring and analysis:* to understand the implications of long-term trends;
- *Scenario building:* to develop a systemic understanding of complex issues;
- *Speculative design:* to illustrate specific future applications of technologies;
- *Serious games:* to help people experience the consequences of possible futures.

Copyright © 2020 European Union,
Published by Elsevier Limited.

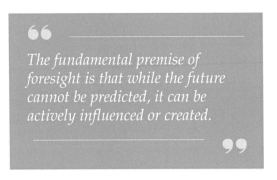

> *The fundamental premise of foresight is that while the future cannot be predicted, it can be actively influenced or created.*

The role of public policy is to create a desirable future. However, public policy is also about taking decisions as an authoritative response to a public issue to pursue specific government goals, considering the political priorities of the moment and being programmatic, as it expresses a proposed set of actions (Althaus et al., 2017). A question then arises about how to be authoritative when acting to shape a future that does not exist yet.

This is why public policy should take into account consciously a future time dimension even if its focus is on immediate public concerns. Often, the implementation of policy actions lies in the midterm future; electoral programmes, coalition agreements, Multiannual Financial Frameworks and others set targets and objectives for political decisions and actions in the next legislative time horizon. These actions then have a longer term impact as new regulations, funding or tax schemes are usually conceived with an open time frame. This requires taking a long-term perspective when they are developed.

However, there are strong political incentives to focus on immediate public concerns. In the words of Al Gore (1992, p. 170) *'the future whispers while the present shouts'*. Jonathan Boston (2016, p. 5) interprets this as follows: *'The future is politically muted for many reasons. Not only does it lack a strong voice, but it also lacks a vote'*. Debates around issues such as many environmental problems, climate change and social issues illustrate this 'presentist bias' (Boston, 2016). The problems of biodiversity losses, sea level rise or dysfunctionalities in the pension systems are often not recognised as relevant today; the effects of an irreversible loss of pollinators, mass destruction through extreme weather events or widespread old-age poverty resulting from a continuing business-as-usual policy might only be seen in the next decades.

Wicked Problems and Policymaking in a VUCA World

Few would disagree that the world of the 21st century is a VUCA world. Volatility, uncertainty, complexity and ambiguity (VUCA) surround us to a degree that has never before been faced by humankind. This creates an acute need to find ways to deal with them. Even if, by nature, VUCA elements are unpredictable, a well-prepared and resourced foresight approach can provide surprising levels of understanding about what could happen and how to deal with it (Da Costa et al., 2008). Short-sightedness, narrow-mindedness, simplistic lines of thought, linear thinking and lack of understanding of the past are probably the worst enemies of policymakers in a VUCA world.

Problems in a VUCA world are mostly complex, open-ended and intractable, or in other words *'wicked'*. Their nature, and therefore the solutions proposed to address them, is strongly contested. As a consequence, many policies and programmes developed to address wicked problems fail because of unforeseen side effects or difficulties in coordination and monitoring (Head, 2008). Sustainable development issues, very much in the limelight currently, are typically seen as wicked problems (Pryshlakivsky and Searcy, 2012).

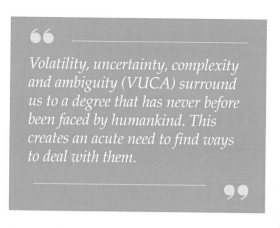

Volatility, uncertainty, complexity and ambiguity (VUCA) surround us to a degree that has never before been faced by humankind. This creates an acute need to find ways to deal with them.

The Call for Anticipatory Thinking in Policymaking

Examples from recent history show what a lack of anticipation can lead to. If Kodak, once a market leader in photography, had considered the then emerging digital photography in its business strategy, it might have been able to defend its strong market position, instead of filing for bankruptcy in 2012 (Lucas and Goh, 2009). In a similar fashion, a closer and open-minded look at emerging trends might have given an opportunity to preempt, counteract or better prepare for the economic crisis of 2008 or the EU migration wave in 2015. The size and urgency of the problems humankind is facing today call for overcoming the presentist bias to address the VUCA world in which we are living.

At the EU level, the European Commission has developed a '*Better Regulation Toolbox*' and '*Better Regulation Guidelines*' (SWD (2017)350) as a response to this challenge. They recognise the usefulness of foresight and forward-looking tools to generate 'evidence-based better regulation'[1] and, for the first time, foresight for EU policy is now officially one of the priorities of the von der Leyen Commission. While evidence is available for past and present developments (statistical data, scientific reports, etc.), there is no such thing as facts about the future as the future does not exist. The challenge is therefore to generate meaningful (and useful) knowledge about the future by interpreting facts about current developments and use imagination about the future (Duvka, 2020; EFFLA, no year). The ability to do that can make a significant difference to the impact of policies.

A Quick Methodological Overview of Foresight

What Is Foresight?

Foresight is a systematic participatory process, creating collective intelligence about the medium- to long-term future. It is aimed at informing present-day decisions and mobilising joint actions,[2] key features to support policymaking. Building on decades of experience shaping the field, Sardar & Masood (2006) defined foresight as '*the art of anticipation based on the science of exploration*'. Foresight helps to understand the possible future consequences of current trends, to detect new signals of change and to determine their potential developments. It facilitates the development of systemic understanding and generates plausible and coherent pictures of the future ranging from alternative scenarios (normative or exploratory) to vision building. Foresight also helps to understand both incremental and disruptive changes.

By being interdisciplinary and participatory, foresight facilitates the identification, analysis and understanding of the consequences of drivers of change from a 360° perspective, considering

---

[1] A similar call for forward thinking to achieve high quality of policymaking is part of the toolbox for public administration of European Member States (Hauser, 2017).
[2] Definition adapted from JRC-IPTS (2008).

societal, technological, environmental, economic and political drivers. It usually starts from a general perspective and zooms stepwise into the issue at stake. By design, it overcomes the limitations of selective sectorial perspectives ('tunnel thinking') and of limited data availability by relying on multiple perspectives and diversity of knowledge. As such, it is a powerful way to make use of all relevant sources of knowledge, in particular scientific evidence, to support decision-making.

Foresight sees the future as something to shape and gives actors knowledge to use when taking action. It is about making sense of the world to equip decision-makers to navigate the future and to shape it. Foresight works best not as a one-off exercise but as a regular practice across organisations. There is therefore value in institutionalising it, as some governments (e.g., Singapore, the UK, Finland, etc.) have done.[3]

The Main Functions of foresight for Policymaking

According to Boston (2016), there are five main intervention logics for governments to introduce strategic foresight activities and address the presentist bias.

1. **To create anticipatory governance capacity** to plan for the long-term and exercise foresight. An enduring linkage must be created to ensure the uptake and use of insights generated through foresight in day-to-day policymaking (Cuhls, 2015). This includes changing the motivations of policymakers (i.e., values, norms, preferences and priorities), activating future-oriented interests and concerns and incentivising policymakers to give greater weight to long-term considerations.

2. **To create awareness about future-related issues** that can be known to some but not to policymakers. The 360° perspective of foresight helps to open up the understanding of influences that arise from drivers not being in the focus of the daily work. To tackle particular long-term policy questions, policymakers need to have a safe space to think about future consequences and strategies, being for the time of the analysis insulated from short-term political questions.

3. **To enable policymakers to make prudent long-term decisions**. The deliberations held through inclusive participatory foresight processes bring together the relevant stakeholders and help build a shared understanding of possible long-term impacts of today's decisions. This includes establishing new coordinating mechanisms to enable decisions that would otherwise not be possible.

4. **To reveal the need for policy action.** The awareness of possible cumulative effects and disruptions that arise from the systemic perspective brought by foresight makes explicit the interactions of drivers and can bring to light looming policy problems.

5. **To channel (scientific) evidence into policy discussions.** The inclusive, interdisciplinary and participatory nature of foresight allows bringing all relevant experts and stakeholders together. An essential benefit of this practice is to make it possible for the experts to use and apply their knowledge in the most appropriate way to support the policymaking process.

---

[3] For an overview on strategic foresight capabilities in different countries, please see Boston (2016), Chapter 12.

Typical Implementation Steps of Foresight for Policymaking

Foresight uses a large toolbox of methods which can be applied in a step-by-step approach:

1. Definition of the scope. The objective and the scope of the foresight exercise need to be defined clearly. The objective is relevant for the development of the tailored approach and the structuring of the results as well as for the inclusion of participants in the process. The scope of the exercise clarifies the system boundaries of the issue to address. It needs to be defined and communicated clearly to guarantee that all participants have the same understanding and that the analysis and discussions stay focussed.

2. Detection of signals of change and trends (e.g., horizon scanning), identification of drivers. Defining the scope goes hand in hand with identifying relevant drivers of change. A 360° perspective, covering scientific, technological, economic, environmental and policy drivers, is important to be comprehensive and to shed light on possible blind spots on the issue. This reveals potentially important drivers to all participants from areas they are not familiar with. It is a key step to generate a systemic understanding of the issue by all.

3. Analysis of uncertainties, cross-impacts, actors, etc. A strong understanding of the system, including relevant actors and interlinkages in addition to drivers, is necessary in most foresight processes (e.g., economic factors need to be connected with social and environmental impacts). This generates some complexity and requires analytical thinking. Tools can help visualise the discussions and uncover underlying assumptions.

4. Understanding the possible evolution of the drivers, trends, etc., and exploring their implications. Scenario building in interactive workshops is an often used approach there.

5. Generation and evaluation of strategies to react to the possible future developments.

6. Communicating the results in scenario and trend reports, interactive workshops and explorative engagement exercises (e.g., serious games). To generate impact, foresight projects must provide results at the right time and their results need to be presented in a clear and attractive way. For this, an 'ambassador' can be useful to reach relevant potential users and launch a dialogue on necessary policy instruments (Rhisiart et al., 2017).

7. Monitoring of scenario assumptions, of developments of drivers and trends, or weak signals (Wiggert, 2014). This step has an alert function, raising awareness on development directions that were identified as important, resulting in increased preparedness.

In the participatory process, experienced facilitators are needed to help the participants share their knowledge, expectations and analyses. They must also keep the discussions focussed so as to remain within the scope of the project and deliver what is needed to achieve the objectives.

Many tools are available for the different steps, relying on one or more of the following approaches: literature reviews, scanning, extrapolation, modelling, elicitation of expertise through panels, interviews, surveys (e.g., real-time Delphi), participatory exercises (e.g., citizen panels, futures workshops) or creative speculative fictioning and design, gamified approaches, etc. (Popper, 2008).

Making Foresight Useful for Policymaking

Foresight is a rich field with a large toolbox that provides ample space to tailor forward-looking approaches to a wide range of policymaking needs and to generate genuinely novel knowledge about the future. The deliberative processes used in most foresight approaches are at the heart of future knowledge generation and of knowledge integration in policy processes.

Foresight is a rich field with a large toolbox that provides ample space to tailor forward-looking approaches to a wide range of policymaking needs and to generate genuinely novel knowledge about the future.

Prerequisites to Run a Good Foresight Exercise

Good foresight processes are participatory and require being run by a competent team to cover three important aspects.

1. **Methodological expertise**: This is needed to select the appropriate combination of tools, design the interfaces between the different tools, tailor the approach to the specific needs of the project and run the process successfully. As each foresight project has a different context, scope and objectives, the foresight approach has to be designed for purpose. Foresights for policy projects are most of the time transdisciplinary as policies rarely function in isolation and usually concern a wide variety of stakeholders.

2. **Recruitment skill:** As foresight is based on collective intelligence, it requires the know-how to define accurately the expertise/perspectives landscape required to cover the topic at stake, the capacity to identify the people needed to create this landscape and the capacity to effectively bring these people together. Foresight projects typically need expertise not only from the concrete issue at stake but also from connected sectors (e.g., upstream or downstream), as well as people who can influence the issue are influenced by it or understand well some of its key drivers.

3. **User involvement**: As the purpose of foresight is to influence decision-making in the present, the relevant policymakers need to participate in key steps of the process, gain ownership of the results and be able to use them in the policy process. As they are often under time pressure, ensuring their meaningful participation, even with limited time commitments, requires strong convincing power.

Practical Examples of Foresight Methods Applied for Informing Policymaking

- *Horizon Scanning: A Cross-Cutting Detection and Analysis of Weak Signals*

Horizon scanning is a systematic examination of information from a wide range of sources (e.g., news, scientific publications, conference proceedings, blogs, etc.) to identify early signs of future developments. It provides timely awareness of what is new or changing. It is used as a sort of radar to identify upcoming challenges and opportunities. Through collective sense-making of the scanned signals and validation through further research, issues that could lead to changes in behaviour, strategy or policy are identified. The added value of horizon scanning is to flag issues at the margins of current thinking that may have a large future impact. It helps organisations adapt and prepare for the future.

Horizon scanning can help bridge the gap between anticipatory thinking and evidence-based decision-making by drawing the attention of decision-makers to emerging issues of potential long-term importance (early warning). It requires credible results and the right type of communication, best achieved through an inclusive process, a clear purpose and a broad range of expertise. For optimum use, horizon scanning output must reach decision-makers at the right time: too early they are not recognised as a priority, too late they are not recognised as new (Krzysztofowicz et al., 2018).

The European Commission's JRC has set up a horizon scanning process to identify and monitor emerging issues and weak signals of change that might have significant future implications for the EU (Fig. 1).

- *Megatrends Monitoring and Analysis: A Systemic Look at the World*

Megatrends are long-term global driving forces that are observable in the present and are likely to continue to have a significant influence for a few decades. They are witness to large-scale transformations with a broad scope. Future developments of megatrends could affect not only their own fields (e.g., education, security, etc.) but also fields that do not seem to be affected at first sight. Because of their large scale, megatrends require monitoring and anticipatory thinking to be better prepared for the future. By their nature, their existence tends to be the object of a broad consensus and is well-documented. They are also considered in most foresight exercises.

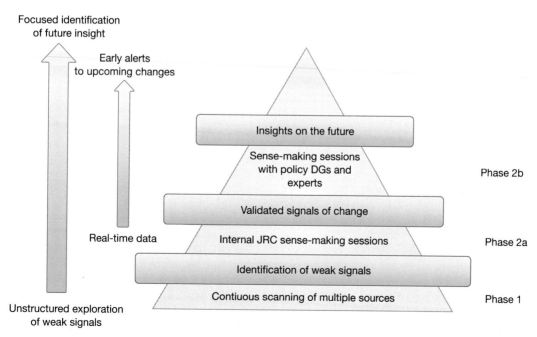

FIGURE 1 JRC horizon scanning process.

To use the power of megatrends analysis for policy fields, a structured approach is recommended. The systematic analysis of each megatrend's long-term impacts on a political issue allows a multidisciplinary 360° perspective, looking at the issue from societal, technological, economic, environmental and political perspectives (STEEP). A systemic view helps to avoid blind spots that might result from a thematic perspective. It is a form of anticipatory thinking useful to prepare and develop policies and strategies with a mid- to long-term perspective (Fig. 2).

JRC approach: Megatrends Hub

The lack of well-curated reference sources and the diversity of studies, perspectives, topics and users of megatrends resulted in a very inconsistent way of referring to them and required repeating their documentation every time a new study was started: a strong hurdle for their use in policymaking.

To address this situation, the JRC created the EC Megatrends Hub,[4] a publicly available reference repository of megatrends. The aim of this dynamic foresight knowledge management infrastructure is to foster the use of megatrends for long-range thinking. It presents a coherent set of megatrends defined by the JRC together with a group of foresight experts from around Europe, selected and framed to tackle a broad variety of global issues. Some focus is given to Europe to facilitate the understanding of their relevance for EU policy. The characterisation of these megatrends is systematically updated by the JRC Competence Centre for Foresight.

The Megatrends Hub covers 14 megatrends: (1) diversifying inequalities; (2) climate change and environmental degradation; (3) increasing significance of migration; (4) growing consumerism; (5) aggravating resource scarcity; (6) increasing demographic imbalances; (7) expanding influence of the East and South; (8) accelerating technological change and hyperconnectivity; (9) changing nature of work; (10) diversification of education and learning; (11) shifting health challenges; (12) continuing urbanisation; (13) increasing influence of new governing systems and (14) changing security paradigm.

For each megatrend, the hub provides concise information on current developments and forecasts, indicators to measure change, potential implications as well as European Commission and other resources for additional references. All the information is compiled using authoritative sources.

[4]https://ec.europa.eu/knowledge4policy/foresight_en.

JRC approach: Megatrends Workshop

To maximise the usability of the Megatrends Hub, the JRC Competence Centre on Foresight has developed the *'Megatrends Implications Assessment'* tool (EU Policy Lab, 2017). This tool allows anyone interested in an issue to assess quickly (half a day) the potential long-term impact of each megatrend on this issue in a systemic and multidisciplinary 360° perspective. The workshop format of the tool offers a short, easily accessible and user-friendly form of engagement useable by many in an EU policy context and beyond. Fig. 3 describes the steps of the workshop.

- *Scenarios: In-depth Systemic Analysis of Possible Future Worlds*

For policymaking, scenario building exercises are often requested when there is a need to define a long-term policy for a new domain, when there is a major reframing of a policy area or when there is a major review of a legislation or policy (e.g., an EU REFIT programme). In such a context, a scenario process generates a robust systemic understanding of changing conditions in the selected domain and puts in evidence the key domains of uncertainty. This builds a sound basis for the development of forward-looking political strategies.

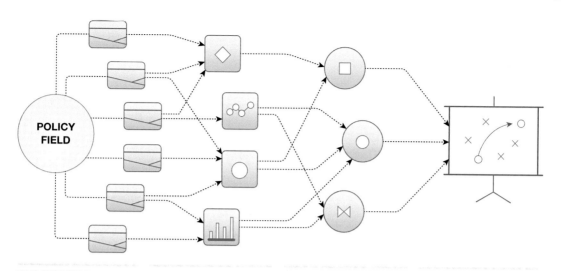

MEGATRENDS AFFECTING A POLICY FIELD

> **IMPLICATIONS**

> **POLICY IMPLICATIONS** > **STRATEGY**

All megatrends are assessed as of their potential impact—direct or indirect to the policy field addressed.

Example

Public health is influenced by climate change-related heat waves that mainly affect elderly people in urban areas. Demographic change and increasing urbanisation are reinforcing this issue.

Implications – opportunities or threats – are identified by assessing potential future changes.

Example

Urban heat islands are spreading and getting more severe; more elderly hospitalized; energy use increase.

The implications are affecting different policy areas. The policy implications are a call for coordinated action.

Example

Set standards for building insulation, regulation for urban micro climate planning, research for energy efficient cooling, etc.

Elaboration of policy actions that feed into a new or adapted strategy.

Example

Translate the implications into policy actions and develop a strategic action plan.

FIGURE 2 The megatrends implication analysis approach.

SET UP

Meet with representatives of participants before to understand their request and understand the policy field. Carry out a short research on the policy fields and a first megatrends analysis.

1. WELCOME & INTRO

Introduce foresight and anticipatory thinking; explain the megatrends concept and how they are used to analyze the policy field; aim and agenda of the meeting; icebreaker as first easy exercise.

2. PRIORITIZING TRENDS

Selection of relevent megatrends for the policy field using a matrix.

3. ANALYZING IMPLICATIONS

Implications of the the selected megatrends for the policy field are discussed and arranged in clusters. Policy implications are identified.

4. FINAL DICUSSION

Summary from main facilitator to make the outcome clear, questions and final comments from participants, next steps and potential follow-up initiatives.

FIGURE 3 Overview on the megatrends implication analysis workshop.

Scenario analysis is based on a systemic approach. It identifies the relevant drivers of change (see Fig. 4) of the system being considered and analyses the interplay between the respective drivers. This helps to develop a deep understanding of the logic of the various possible future developments. Scenarios are plausible and consistent with the combinations of developments that build multidimensional pictures of the future. They create the conditions to generate a

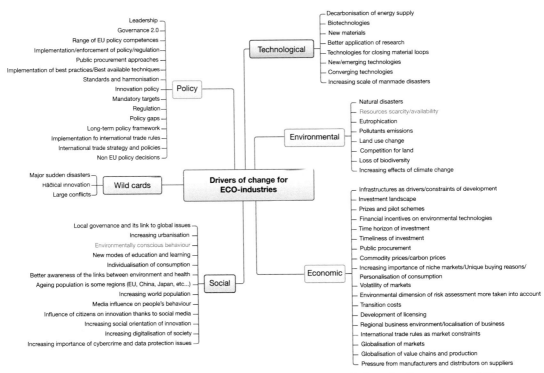

FIGURE 4 Drivers of change for eco-industries. (Source: JRC data for Bontoux and Bengtsson (2015))

deep understanding of the system of interest (e.g., the EU, the transport system, an institution, etc.). Future scenarios are often exploratory, laying out a variety of plausible developments to feed strategic reflections. They can also be used to generate visions and define a desirable future.

Future scenarios are a powerful means to deal with complexity by being analytical and focussing on the most relevant drivers of change. They are an approach of choice to deal with uncertainty; by creating a portfolio of clearly defined alternatives, they allow participants to build precise images of the diversity of opportunities and threats according to the evolution of key parameters that can be traced back to the present (Fig. 5). Scenarios provide a forward-looking knowledge base to derive implications for different stakeholders or policy fields. These implications are a basis for deriving possible options for action. Two important advantages of the scenario process are to overcome participants' preconceived ideas on an issue and to reveal trade-offs between options for political action and for different affected groups. The scenario process can take into account different system alternatives as possible solutions and diverging value considerations (Truffer et al., 2010).

One important success factor for a scenario process is the inclusion of relevant stakeholders (affected and involved) in addition to participants with diverse relevant expertise and futurists that can foster imagination and long-term thinking. The process generates a multidisciplinary

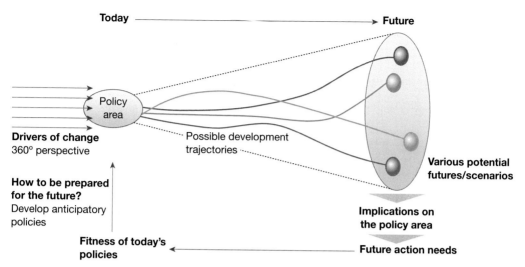

FIGURE 5 Process approach of a strategic scenario analysis (Eckhard Störmer (JRC)). (Adapted from Hancock and Bezold (1994).)

and multidimensional understanding of the field as well as a shared understanding of possible developments. Creative elements help to enrich the scenario narratives and to broaden the range of possible strategies to deal with upcoming challenges.

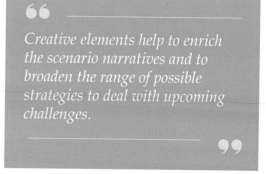

Creative elements help to enrich the scenario narratives and to broaden the range of possible strategies to deal with upcoming challenges.

- *Speculative Design: Experimenting With New Products, Services and Policy Instruments*

Even though foresight tools and approaches strive to create images of the future that are as concrete as possible, a certain degree of abstraction often remains, especially when dealing with very specific issues at the micro scale. There then is a strong need to make potential options and solutions visible. This calls for creative approaches.

Speculative design is one such approach. It enables speculation on how things could be and thus helps imagine possible futures. Like scenario building, it poses 'what if' questions to open a debate about the future in a tangible and concrete way (Dunne and Raby, 2013). Problems are explored by creating provisional solutions and participants act as co-researchers. New plausible but provisional insights are generated (Kimbell, 2015). In the JRC 'Blockchain4EU' project, for example, prototypes of potential blockchain applications for industrial transformations were used as core research components. They provided a critical space to expand the understanding of the blockchain and its potential, both through specific moments of co-creation and broad stakeholder engagement. The creation of fictional artefacts triggers forward-looking discussion (Nascimento et al., 2018). In the project on the 'Future of Government (2030)+', design schools were asked to provide prototypes of government concepts to generate innovative ideas unrestricted by path dependencies. Furthermore, the creation process can be seen as a 'futures dialogue' where young students apply their own future expectations and reflect their views as citizens on government (Vesnic-Alujevic et al., 2019).

- *Serious Games as a Way to Make Foresight More Applicable and More Concrete*

Foresight projects often run collective intelligence processes that help participants develop knowledge and systemic understanding about broad issues (e.g., mobility, water management, the EU, renewable energy, etc.) . This can end up being a set of scenarios describing alternative worlds functioning according to specific constraints. While such exercises are valuable in themselves, their usefulness can be limited by three main factors:

- While they clearly benefit the participants in the foresight process, their results can be difficult to share with others;
- Reading scenarios is often insufficient to help people answer concretely the specific questions that they are facing in their own contexts. Most people want to know *'and what does that mean for me?'*
- As the future does not exist today, experimentation upon its issues is often difficult.

However, participants in foresight processes can use their knowledge of the past and the present to develop intuitions about what could be possible. Can this then be used to test what would happen if certain events or circumstances were to appear? Serious gaming techniques can be a powerful way to address these questions. As explained by Sweeney (2017), serious games provide a practical way to experiment *with* (rather than upon) the futures created through foresight.

Foresight-oriented serious gaming is well-developed and growing. Dufva et al. (2015) propose a classification of foresight serious games within a space delimited by three key functions: to inform, to experience or to generate ideas. Recent experience seems to indicate that a greater engagement of participants is achieved through the use of physical games, which include card-based games, board games and role-playing, rather than digital games (Dufva et al., 2015). Recent examples of such games include the following:

- The '*SES*' (the *Scenario Exploration System*), a simulation/experience board game developed by the JRC's EU Policy Lab (Bontoux et al., 2016);
- '*IMPACT*', a foresight game focussing on emerging technologies and the future of society, developed by Idea Couture using content from the Canadian emerging technology scanning study (Policy Horizons Canada, 2014);
- '*The Thing from the Future*' offering a mind opening and fun experience developed by the Situation Lab (Candy and Dunagan, 2017) and
- The '*foresight eXplorer*', a board game to imagine a group's preferred future developed by the Centre for Postnormal Policy and Futures Studies (Sweeney, 2017).

Serious games apply many core characteristics and classic practices of future studies: systemic thinking, fun, exploration, engagement, collaboration, curiosity, anticipatory action and learning through experiential approaches (Sweeney, 2017). They can be applied as a final step of a foresight process or as a way to engage diverse publics, either with the outcomes from a foresight process or with self-generated future questions. In the latter case, people do not need to have any prior knowledge of foresight or of the specific topic of the foresight project. Rather, the experience often relies on the methods and skills of a moderator.

These characteristics make serious games very suitable to apply in a policy context. Indeed, the aim of policy is to create a desirable future. What better way to test before application whether a policy is likely to deliver the expected effects or whether some important implementation parameter has not been overlooked? The JRC has extensive experience in applying the Scenario Exploration System to explore policy-relevant issues as diverse as the sustainable transition, migration, food safety and nutrition, new technologies, etc., with policymakers and a wide range of other stakeholders (Bock and Bontoux, 2017).

Way Forward

Methodological Innovation to Make the Approach Fit for Purpose

Foresight can rely on a broad set of tried and tested methods and practices. However, foresight is also at the forefront of novel policymaking practices and is subjected to increasingly diverse demands. As the framings and contexts of foresight projects are evolving fast, the fact that foresight operates in a tailor-made fashion forces it to adapt its approaches constantly. Complexity in policies and other areas also increases and must be addressed. Therefore, looking towards the future using only conventional methods has become difficult (Kuribayashi et al., 2017) and new needs arise:

1. integration of new research methods and information processing tools, like automated semantic analysis tools, utilisation of crowd intelligence building platforms and new forms of interactive surveys, combination of quantitative modelling and qualitative analysis,

2. inclusion of new actor groups in the discourse, particularly citizens and lay people with their values and expectations (Wilhelmer, 2016),

3. innovations in the design of participatory exercises (Guimarães Pereira et al., 2018; Burmeister et al., 2018; Vesnic-Alujevic, 2019) and design of new tools (EU Policy Lab); see more in Chapters 8 and 13,

4. use of speculative design in the projection of futures (Nascimento et al., 2018),

5. innovations in deriving strategic implications and opening up the space for possible actions (Störmer et al., 2009),

6. new forms of communication of future stories using art and design, speculative fiction and other forms of storytelling and story visualisation,

7. new ways of engaging the audience with assumptions about the future to launch a reflection about needs for strategic action and start a dialogue (Bontoux et al., 2016).

The scope for methodological innovation is large, especially as foresight operates at the interface between numerous disciplines such as social sciences, economics, natural sciences, business administration, political sciences, modelling, design, arts, communication, etc.

JRC approach

Witness to this trend, the EU Competence Centre on Foresight (CC-Foresight) at the JRC is committed to the development and dissemination of new methods to address particular needs and constraints encountered in EU policymaking. It develops new approaches not for the sake of being innovative but to provide better anticipatory capacity to EU policymaking. To stimulate and facilitate this capacity to innovate, the CC-Foresight is embedded into the EU Policy Lab (see more in Chapter 13), whose remit is to experiment and to co-design tailor-made approaches to improve EU policymaking.

Mainstreaming of Anticipatory Thinking in Policymaking

The use of foresight and other futures approaches to inform policymaking has an extensive track record as testified by their long established practice in, e.g., the Finnish and Canadian governments, the European Commission and many others. However, moving from a few large strategically relevant foresight projects to mainstreaming forward-looking approaches in the daily routines of policymakers is still a challenge. Large continuous efforts are still needed to include basic elements of anticipatory and systemic thinking in the training curricula of policymakers and to overcome the presentism bias still dominating in the daily routines of policymaking work.

To introduce the long-term perspective that policymaking needs to deal with a VUCA world facing issues of sustainability, it is a strategic imperative to include foresight into policy development, ex-ante policy evaluations and REFIT exercises.

Image: New Africa - https://stock.adobe.com/be_en/images/cobweb-on-wild-meadow-closeup-view/225593129?prev_url=detail
Icon in page corners: Spider Web icon by Hawraa Alsalman, from the Noun Project (https://thenounproject.com/search/?q=spider%20web&i=1106831)

Design for Policy

Authors: Jennifer-Ellen Rudkin, Alessandro Rancati

Key takeaways:

- Design should be considered in its broader meaning, not just as a creative discipline or a tool. It needs to be understood as a culture with specific values and practices. Such culture can help facilitate culture change in your organisation.

- One-time 'policy lab' sessions are best avoided in favour of a set of coordinated actions that allows for exploration, sensemaking and prototyping.

- Design culture is about exploring a policy context in a collaborative way. Particularly useful is using visual approaches to support the sensemaking process, e.g., mapping complex contexts and concepts with colleagues and stakeholders.

- Carefully scripted choreographies create a space for open yet structured sensemaking conversations among people with different understanding of the matter at hand.

Copyright © 2020 European Union,
Published by Elsevier Limited

145

There has been, in the past years, a growing recognition of the value of design-based approaches in policymaking (Bailey and Lloyd, 2016). This success can be weighed by looking at the number of design-driven innovation labs that have invested governments around the world.

Design-based approaches are systemic in nature, explore complex context using visual methods, bring several disciplines together to make sense of the problem space and formulate proposals that focus on the quality of the experience from the point of view of the final beneficiaries.

In the context of policymaking, such approaches often result in multistakeholder, collaborative practices being used to understand and creatively address public and social issues, as well as organizational ones, with special interest and focus on the final beneficiaries, i.e., citizens and civil society.

The European Commission has also adopted design by setting up the EU Policy Lab, a creative and collaborative space for innovative policymaking. In this context, a unique fit-to-purpose design activity is being developed in order to respond to the EC policymaking needs.

The word 'design' has accumulated several different uses and its meanings shift according to the context in which it is used.

'It can refer to a process (the act or practice of designing); or to the result of that process (a design, sketch, plan or model); or to the products manufactured with the aid of a design (design goods); or to the look or overall pattern of a product ("I like the design of that dress")' (Walker, 1990). In a more open definition, design is the process of conceiving and planning a set of actions to reach a goal (Hevner et al., 2004; Papanek, 1971; Mau, 2007).

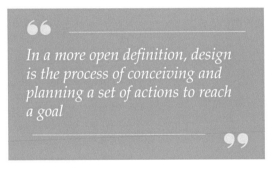

> In a more open definition, design is the process of conceiving and planning a set of actions to reach a goal

More recently, the adoption of design practices in business schools has also given popularity to the term 'design thinking', a way of perceiving, understanding and interacting with the world typical of designers, but that can also be acquired as a skill by nondesigners (Kimbell, 2012).

While the goal may be of different nature, for example, to improve the seating experience in private housings or to reimagine the delivery services in the age of big data, to design is to consciously modify the existent in order to improve it. Therefore, design may intervene in a wide range of areas and take on many shapes: a product, a system or an experience. In addition to its capacity to develop insights on any topic, and to find applications in many forms, design is by its nature a discipline that works in multidisciplinary settings. It looks into, relies on, and also pushes the limits of knowledge and expertise of diverse professions relevant to the project needs, with the purpose of building new solutions.

This chapter discusses the possible contributions of design to produce, and also to drive, evidence for policymaking. The intent is not to define a generic design for policy activity but rather to share a design for policy as it is pursued in the EU Policy Lab. Since its in-house integration, design has tackled many different topics and has played a role at different steps of the policy cycle. Design has been called upon to reach out to unsolicited stakeholders, to facilitate cocreation of problem definition and solution finding, to bring about novel and customised project approaches and to produce insights that contribute to other fields' research and analyses. This chapter starts with a presentation of the EU Policy Lab to then go into more detail on the added value of design for policymaking.

The EU Policy Lab

The EU Policy Lab has been created in 2016 at the Joint Research Centre Unit on Foresight, Modelling, Behavioural Insights and Design for Policy. The EU Policy Lab is a space for exploration (of the future), experimentation (in the present), openness (to citizen's voices) and understanding (of people's actions and reactions). With a people-centred approach, the lab acts all along the policy cycle: from ideation to implementation and evaluation.

The Lab is composed of a multidisciplinary team organized under four main competences: Foresight, Behavioural Insights, Design for Policy and most recently Modelling. By accessing diverse areas of knowledge, the EU Policy Lab team strives to cocreate, test and prototype ideas to address complex social problems and to enable collective change. The work undertaken can be as much targeted to specific project purposes or to improving internal capacities of the Joint Research Centre and the European Commission as a whole.

The Lab brings together various stakeholders and actors to explore issues and to jointly codesign solutions through experimental, i.e., custom-made processes. Thanks to the complementarity of its disciplines that comprise the EU Policy Lab, along with the specific backgrounds and areas of expertise of each member of the unit, a wide range of resources is made available. The diversity of competences and tools allows to produce an integrated set of insights for each EU Policy Lab intervention. With focus given to people and behaviours, to weak signals and innovation and to systems thinking and patterns, the Lab develops opportunities to respond to different types of policy needs.

By triggering recognition for our competences across Commission Services and building trust with our partners, the EU Policy Lab is in a unique position to support sensitive phases of the policymaking process and generate restricted open conversations.

The EU Policy Lab's physical space encourages novel activities to take place, all of which have as the underlying aim of raising awareness and providing hands on experience on new types of interfaces between policy, science and society. The EU Policy Lab is promoting new ways of working that combine more engagement and collaboration, innovation and experimentation, visual thinking, attention to people and behaviours, system thinking and anticipation. As a 'safe place', the EU Policy Lab allows to slow down, take a step back, unpack meanings and understandings and provide room for tests, trials and unknowns. For that purpose, a range of unconventional activities, from an EU policymaking perspective, are tapped into, such as public and bottom-up innovation, open and citizen science and Do-It-Yourself/ Do-It-Together trends, as well as other fiction and speculative practices. Design, by its nature, affords all of the above to take place, by ensuring a reflection on both the physical and the conceptual components of a project. The following part will describe in more detail the qualities of design applied to policymaking.

Design for Policy

Design is a creative practice commonly used in discussions around innovation: in management, organizational studies and social change fields of research. Recognized as a strategic tool, design is equipped with a creative tool set and mindset: 'As part of their education process, [designers] develop skills in creativity (i.e., original thinking), in idea generation, in problem solving creatively, and in innovation and design (i.e., taking ideas through to a finished product)' (Cooper and Press, 1995). Thus, not only can design bring creativity to the policymaking cycle but it can also contribute in a meaningful way to the production of knowledge and insights.

Design has increasingly been referenced in the management literature to describe both the expanding roles of designers, for example, 'facilitator of communication' (Press and Cooper, 2003), and the increasing acknowledgement of areas of application, such as design for social innovation (Manzini, 2013) or design for critical thinking (Dunne & Raby, 2013). Along these lines, the type of design practiced at the EU Policy Lab acts at different levels of the policy cycle and of the organisation itself. Focus is given to people's actions, means, knowledge and values; to scientific discoveries and new technologies and to the use of visual representations to exchange, create and think in systemic ways.

In Practice

The core services of the EU Policy Lab followed by a list of standardised services led by the Design for Policy team are described below, all of which have demonstrated the power to produce useful evidence, information and insights for policymaking.

Exploring issues by broadening people's vision of the present and providing a holistic view of policy challenges through multidisciplinary and collaborative observation and sensemaking; by bringing to the center of attention a panel of viewpoints and perspectives on a given topic or issue and by pushing people to become aware of their cognitive biases, design participates in thickening one's understanding of the present, what Fish and Scrivener have described as **'amplifying the mind's eye'** (Fish and Scrivener, 1990). For example, colleagues from the digital and business departments came to us to renew their perspective after a year of working on the issue on platform to business trading practices in the online platform. The support we provided allowed for both teams to take a step back from their 1-year endeavor. Two exploratory sessions were held, providing a whole new perspective to the issue. The focus shifted from a platform to business relation to a platform to business to user perspective. In doing so, the solution space expanded with the rise of new pain points and leverage points. In this sense, the exploration phase provides means for opening up one's perception, knowledge and possibilities for action. Design here is used to accompany a project team, an audience or a person, in being aware of the assumptions, i.e., the frames they use to construct meaning and to make sense of the world. 'Design can be understood as a practice of re-framing the real, not in absolute or oppositional terms but reinforcing the complexity and open-endedness of experience' (Mallol, 2012).

Experiencing lean and effective processes to inform policymaking and placing the experience of users and citizens at the centre of the policymaking process; this activity may be

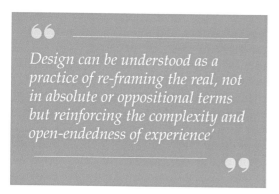

'Design can be understood as a practice of re-framing the real, not in absolute or oppositional terms but reinforcing the complexity and open-endedness of experience'

related to human-centred and social design, understood as the consideration, implication and translation of the explicit and tacit knowledge people carry with them on any given topics. The aim of design in bringing in the voice of the people is twofold; on the one hand it is about ensuring shared understanding within an internal team and on the other hand it is about gathering input from a large range of people, including ones external to the project. Including people (to not limit ourselves to a definition of citizens) can be done at different scales and in different formats depending on the project. The setting invites people to share input and generate knowledge and to experience an interactive process based on visual and manual activities. The design for Policy activity relies on this activity to ensure that all issues are tackled in line with people's needs, bearing an inclusive and open-minded approach. Creating bridges between European policy officers and decision-makers and the Europe-wide citizens who are affected by the laws ensures the effectiveness of the policy creation and implementation. More on this can be found in Chapter 8.

Experimenting and pretesting options and solutions, using prototyping; experimentation is a fundamental aspect of design-led processes. By producing processes that are fit to the specific needs of the project, design produces unique and novel approaches. The two main types of productions that have been tested and approved are service design and speculative design approaches. Service design may improve the competence of a policy team in delivering work, as well as ensuring effective crossing and binding of information across different commission departments. The aim is to improve the quality of a service in order to make its use more efficient and enjoyable. The transformation strategies used in service design focus on the relationships between service provider and the users of the service. Speculative design on the other hand operates transitions from the science and technology fields to our daily realities (Auger, 2013). Therefore, the possible applications and implications of advanced technologies such as blockchain, which in many aspects is very abstract to many, become more tangible through the materiality of an object. A project we worked on at the EU Policy Lab produced six design prototypes that illustrated possible applications of blockchain in our daily lives, from a traceable healthcare system that delivers blood by drone to a hair dryer regulating your energy consumption based on your cryptoactivity, all projects that served as prompts to analyse business opportunities and impacts of blockchain technology in the future. But the use of prototypes is not limited to testing new technologies, it may also be used to trigger in the audience new questions, relationships and behaviours with a topic or a product.

Explaining visually the underlying concepts, ideas, evidence and data behind policy options and adopting novel forms of sensemaking and reporting. **Visual thinking** serves the purpose of exploring (opening up possibilities), understanding (collectively or individually) and communicating (informing, disseminating and provoking dialogue). To think through shapes and representations in a nonlinear way is a designerly skill. 'Designing is intellectual arrangement, clarification of links, definition of dependencies, creation of weighing's, and requires a special ability in the head of the designer to be able to see and fix analogies, links and frames of reference'[1] (Aicher, 1991). During the creative process, experimental and iterative graphical and spatial representations are enabled to foster new meanings and allow shapes to emerge. At the EU Policy Lab, maps and other graphical representation are used in parallel with verbal and written exchanges in order to reveal and cover different levels of understanding. The use of visual communication (be it 2D or 3D) is a fundamental activity across all previously described EU Policy Lab services of exploring, experiencing and experimenting.

The Design for Policy activity plays a leading role in providing innovative types of evidence for policymaking by infusing transformation through design culture. Establishing a design culture within the organization is about infusing a way of doing that 'challenges the way in which people interact, the existing capabilities and how things are accomplished in daily activities' (Deserti and Rizzo, 2015). In order to do so, design uses insights, empathy, divergent thinking and visual representational tools such as drawing and form giving. Colleagues new to the design discipline have to go through a learning process to understand the benefits of a creative process for their daily work. In the following, services are listed the set of more specific services:

- **Exploratory sessions**: standardised half-day sessions with involved partners to explore and reframe specific policy challenges. The session should refine the understanding of defined problems and tackle ill-defined problems in order to open up the process to be implemented, to better identify gaps and enlarge the solution space.
- **State of the art research**: state of the art based on visual inputs, media, etc., to complement and better contextualize traditional literature reviews. Design develops cognitive capabilities that allow them to tap into different types of reference, cultural and scientific. Mixing the resources allows for making sense of relevant current trends that impact societies.
- **Stakeholder/user/citizen engagement workshops**: developing and maintaining a hybrid space where policymakers can interact and engage with members of the civil society in lab sessions, to gather experience of relevant communities and sense the state of play in civil society. This can be done in different ways, notably by mobilizing the EU Policy Lab design lab network across Europe.
- **Tailored project processes and formats:** fit-to-purpose, one-of-a-kind experimental project processes that comprise different levels of engagement with 'inside' and 'outside' participants. The aim is to produce innovative formats for solving issues in order to impact a targeted audience and spread research findings to a larger audience. Formats used may be custom-made workshops, speculative prototypes or serious games to cite a few.
- **Support to internal process development**: user-centred support services to oversee internal procedures and processes in order to improve the workplace experience and the quality of the end products. This activity is human centred and aims at producing transformational change.

To conclude, design contributes to the organisation by bringing in a culture that enables iterative and visual tools that make sense of explicit and tacit knowledge. This allows producing evidence that is reactive to ongoing emerging changes. The lateral mode of thinking

---

[1] Otl Aicher. Analogous and Digital (first published 1991), Ernst and Sohn, 2015.

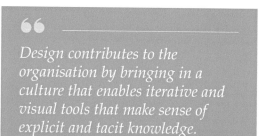

Design contributes to the organisation by bringing in a culture that enables iterative and visual tools that make sense of explicit and tacit knowledge.

of design enhances the options for tackling an issue while being solution oriented. The experience we have developed at the EU Policy Lab allows us to claim that scientific organisations can do more relevant science by systematically engaging in design with all policy actors. Design for Policy in this sense should not be treated as a side activity but integrated in the organisation to ensure qualitative, unique and inclusive scientific research that creates bridges across diverse disciplines and stakeholders.

Image: 2630ben - https://stock.adobe.com/be_en/images/low-angle-of-a-passing-elephant/256563137?prev_url=detail
Icon in page corners: Elephant icon by Tatiana Belkina, from the Noun Project (https://thenounproject.com/
search/?q=elephants&i=634963)

Monitoring the Impact of Science and Evidence on Policy

Authors: Daniel Neicu, Jonathan Cauchi, Jens Otto, Sari Lehto, Jorge Costa Dantas Faria

Key takeaways:

- Science for policy work is part of an ecosystem which includes policymakers and other stakeholders. It is therefore vitally important to envisage the possible effects of one's research on how policy is designed, implemented and evaluated.

- Project planning should include clear actions to achieve and increase the expected policy impact of science by informing on the pathway leading from activities to impact, or by describing how and when policies can be impacted by research.

- To do this, researchers need to understand the policymaking environment they operate in to achieve the impact they seek. With this in mind, this chapter identifies the ways in which the JRC monitors the impact of its activities and learns from this process for the benefit of policymakers and scientists working together at the science–policy interface.

Science for Policy Handbook
http://dx.doi.org/10.1016/B978-0-12-822596-7.00014-0

Copyright © 2020 European Union,
Published by Elsevier Limited

When a research organisation covers a wide range of topics and policy areas, capturing the impact of its activities presents a methodological challenge due to the multitude of different impact pathways which are not always easily traceable. In our experience, this can be overcome by employing a range of tools to measure impact, starting with documenting impact pathways, building impact inventories and case studies and performing portfolio analyses. The main lesson learnt from our experience with these approaches is that achieving impact requires constant interaction with policymakers not only as beneficiaries but also as co-creators of science for policy. Moreover, the desired impact on policy needs to be defined and traced throughout the scientific activity, rather than ex-post. Impact planning is done in the JRC as part of the ex-ante assessment. This creates a culture of sharing knowledge and learning from organisational memory, which enhances the take-up of scientific evidence and its impact on policy in the long run.

What Is Policy Impact and Why Monitor It?

Public research organisations need to demonstrate the impact of their research on policy-making or the society, and thus the value of public investment in research.[1] In the JRC's context, demonstrating policy impact is of paramount importance as it the JRC's mission to support policymaking with sound evidence.

In the scope of this handbook, the policy impact of scientific research refers to how research results influence the way policy is designed, implemented and followed-up. The broader impact evaluation literature often refers to it as 'outcome' or 'intermediate impact' (Joly et al., 2015), whereas impact is usually defined as a long-term effect at a larger scale, such as the economy or society. Policy impact is a process rather than a result, and it varies considerably across scientific fields, policy areas and environments.

However, besides accountability considerations, impact evaluation also promotes learning among researchers about the process of achieving impact (Bell et al., 2011), and leads to a better understanding of the relevance and importance of their work. Understanding the needs of both policymakers and scientists and finding a common denominator for the two is paramount to fostering an evidence-based policy environment and mitigating the 'two communities problem' – the view that scientists and policymakers live in separate worlds with different values, which results in a limited use of scientific evidence in policymaking (Caplan, 1979). Monitoring the pathways of impact from lab to plenary helps researchers understand where the critical points are and how to address them in their interaction with policymakers. This also serves the purpose of creating working relationships between the two sides. As discussed in most chapters of this handbook, close relationships and mutual understanding of the scientific evidence and the policy needs are paramount to co-creating the right research for evidence-based political decision-making. Moreover, regularly assessing policy impact helps create a culture of knowledge exchange where strengths can be replicated throughout the organisation.

Researchers should read this chapter both as a reminder that scientific advice for policymakers has to be designed in such a way as to have maximum impact and as a way to understand what the stages of achieving impact on policy are and where improvements can be made in

---

[1] The Research Excellence Framework (REF) in the United Kingdom is an example of a system for assessing the quality of research in higher education institutions.

their interaction with policymakers. There are significant parallels (including monitoring and learning) amongst the various impact assessment sources related to international development,[2] but the focus of this chapter is on the JRC as a public research organisation.

Overview of Monitoring Tools and Their Use

For public research organisations that collaborate closely with policymakers, there are ample opportunities to impact policies. The challenge is how to demonstrate it. Especially in a large research organisation spanning a wide spectrum of policy domains, impact pathways are very diverse. In some cases, evidence of research being used in the policy process is found in legal documents. In others, indirect evidence is required from other sources (policymakers, briefings, speeches, minutes of meetings, public fora or the media). However, the multitude of sources of scientific evidence used in policymaking can create attribution issues, in that it becomes difficult to track how research results are taken-up. Another complication is related to the time passed from when results are provided as input in the policy process and its final stages. Most of the time, and especially true for policy formulation, impact is only apparent once the policy process has reached its end. Complex policymaking environments can also complicate impact monitoring, usually by aggravating both timing and attribution issues.

More and more researchers close to the policy environment are following a codesign strategy, meaning that research projects are codesigned with policy stakeholders and beneficiaries. This implies that the role of research in policymaking changes from a research–results–deliverables style to a more interactive relationship. This also translates into a stronger role for researchers in engaging with partners throughout the policy process.

> "
> *More and more researchers close to the policy environment are following a codesign strategy, meaning that research projects are codesigned with policy stakeholders and beneficiaries.*
> "

Another issue with evaluating impact on policy is quantification. Measuring the scale or importance of impact is relevant for accountability and benchmarking across organisations, but the scale of impact can vary considerably.

To capture the impact of science on policymaking thus calls for a wide range of tools. Based on our experience, the most important ones are documenting impact pathways, building impact inventories, recording case studies and performing portfolio analyses of research projects. Fig. 1 illustrates these impact evaluation tools and their interdependencies. Although several approaches are plausible, recording a number of case studies allows drawing comprehensive impact pathways. These then help to build an impact inventory by defining what activities can lead to which outputs and types of policy impacts. Finally, the inventory can be used to select related activities and impacts and analyse the portfolio in a given research or policy area. The

---

[2] These include the World Bank and the Overseas Development Institute (ODI) amongst others.

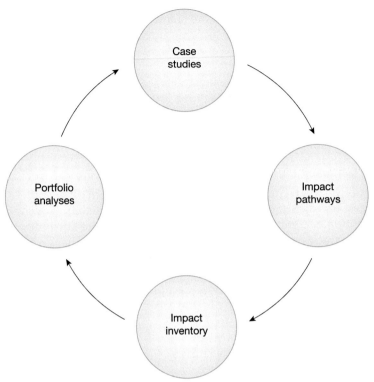

FIGURE 1 The impact evaluation cycle.

feedback loop is closed when portfolio analyses discover gaps to be addressed by analysing new case studies of an organisation's research activity.

Following this, Fig. 2 illustrates how different methods for impact evaluation and monitoring address the challenges of tracing policy impact and how they are affected by them.[3] The timing dimension refers to the time it takes for scientific activities to achieve policy impact. For example, impact pathway mapping can deal with longer time scales because the method links activities to outputs and then to impact irrespective of the time scales, whereas impact inventories are usually connected to reporting deadlines. On the other hand, quantification refers to the possibility to use indicators to objectively measure the scale of impact at an aggregated level (e.g., at organisation level). Although some case study–based methodologies do quantify impact, these usually involve subjective appreciations transformed to scales (Joly et al., 2015).

Case Studies

Case studies aim to answer a set of evaluation questions. While, for example, an impact inventory is useful for capturing large numbers and varieties of isolated instances of impact

---

[3] This is restricted to the evaluation of research in the specific fields that the JRC is involved in.

	Timing	Complexity	Attribution	Quantification
Case study	+	+	+	−
Impact pathway mapping	+	+	+	−
Impact inventory	−	−	−	+
Portfolio analysis	−	+	−	+

FIGURE 2 Impact monitoring tools and the challenges they address.

> **Box 1:** How case studies promote organisational learning
>
> Following consecutive recommendations from external evaluations of the Framework Programmes for Research and Innovation to better explain our impact, the Joint Research Centre has been regularly carrying out case studies and portfolio analyses. In order to assess our longer-term impact, we have worked with a number of external experts to select and analyse a series of case studies which, by themselves or by the portfolio they represent, span more than 10 years (three consecutive Framework Programmes). All types of impact were considered, and the cases were selected for their maturity, representativeness of impact and of activities. This kind of study allows analysing cases in which the R&D phase may be rather long, in which impact takes significant time to materialise, or in which specific individual cases of impact need time to accumulate to allow for a meaningful assessment. Working with external experts has a cost in terms of the process, but also clear benefits in terms of expert judgement, independence and credibility. In this particular case, the experts recommended to use such impact evaluations and cost–benefit analyses more systematically.

and for performing statistical analyses assisting management decisions, it lacks information of the magnitude of the impact a particular activity generates. Here, case studies bring a more balanced and deeper analysis, in particular because they aggregate impacts around a certain type of activity or body of legislation, and over a number of years.[4] They are also better suited for external evaluations by peer panels, although these come at a higher cost (Hill, 2016).

There have been recent attempts towards standardising information in case studies, based on methodologies such as the Socio-economic Analysis of Impacts of Public Agronomic Research – ASIRPA (Joly et al., 2015). However, as the number of research areas increases, so does the cost of developing comprehensive case studies. Moreover, the possibility of standardising case studies over various research areas is offset by the need for detailed information (Box 1).

---

[4] See also Gaunand et al. (2017).

Impact Pathways

An impact pathway is a method tracing the consecutive steps between activity and impact. Documenting impact pathways can be challenging due to the breadth of an organisation's portfolio of activities and beneficiaries, and its involvement in different phases of the policy cycle. An additional challenge is the lack of standardised referencing of scientific research in policy documents, which makes it difficult to trace contributions in an automated way (Topp et al., 2018).

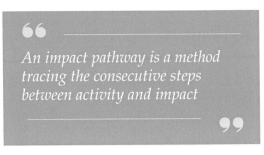

An impact pathway is a method tracing the consecutive steps between activity and impact

In some cases, the impact pathway is relatively straightforward when there is a specific request from policymakers to provide evidence for an agreed item on the legislative agenda. For example, during the policy preparation stage, policymakers may request researchers to model different policy options to be considered. One may then perform quantitative modelling of different options, or sensitivity analyses to establish the range of key parameters affecting the expected impact of the policy on society. The outcome of research usually manifests in this case as a set of policy options for policymakers, who will decide which one suits the needs that the policy addresses. The impact of research will thus be to refine the choice of policy options, or to provide evidence that helps policymakers choose the most suitable one. The attribution of impact may not be straightforward if, as in most cases, one can only provide part of the scientific evidence for the policy. As other chapters in this handbook note, strong interaction with policymakers leads to better-informed scientific work and policy development.

Another example is contributing to policy implementation, such as providing technical guidelines for European Union countries, monitoring the variables to be influenced by policy decisions (e.g., CO_2 emissions) or coordinating networks for the purpose of harmonisation and standardisation. In its remit, research can provide the tools and methods, as well as specific analyses for policy evaluation. In such cases, the impact pathway is fairly easy to trace if researchers act on an exclusive and specific mandate (Box 2). Other times, when researchers may be working with intermediaries or when there are many factors influencing a policy outcome, it is less clear how outcomes (e.g., implementation of smart specialisation or macroregional strategies) have an impact on policy implementation. For this reason, among others, there is a need to use complementary methods to capture impact, as was illustrated in Fig. 2.

Box 2: The INSPIRE Directive – an example of impact pathway analysis

The INSPIRE Directive (2007/2/EC) is one of the key pieces of legislation in European environmental policies. It provides the framework to collect, harmonise, organise the dissemination and use of spatial information in the European Union. Its origin goes back to the early 1990s, when public and private services started to use Geographic Information Systems (GIS). This opened up great possibilities to combine geographical data and maps into Spatial Data Infrastructures for urban planning, resource management, environmental impact assessment, location planning or crisis interventions. However, the lack of industry standards created problems with the quality, organisation, accessibility and sharing of the data. As Earth observation satellites created a rapid increase of geospatial data and digital maps, the European Commission launched the development of a policy framework for Geographic Information in Europe in the mid-1990s.

Role of the JRC and stakeholders

We were one of the early adopters of GIS satellite technology for earth observations and, based on our original mandate, for data harmonisation and validation. This technical competence, the position independent from special interests and networking with both research experts and national authorities, has led us to receive the mandate for the development of the Implementing Rules and the European Geoportal. We also followed developments and participate in the technical coordination with other international standardisation bodies.

The development of the INSPIRE Implementing Rules requires coordinating the work of hundreds of experts from European countries to ensure that the technical specifications are not only technically sound but also organisationally and financially feasible.

Output

The main output of our activity are the Implementing Rules proposed for the INSPIRE Directive.

Policy impact

The impact that our activity has on this policy is the take-up of technical specifications as Implementing Rules for the INSPIRE Directive and subsequent harmonisation of the geographical data.

The path from activity to impact described above is illustrated in Fig. 3.

Lesson learnt

This case is a prime example of how advanced scientific and networking capacity helps achieving policy impact. Our reputation allowed us to engage with a large number of policymakers, industry stakeholders and researchers. Combined with our position close to policymakers, it made us very successful as knowledge brokers.

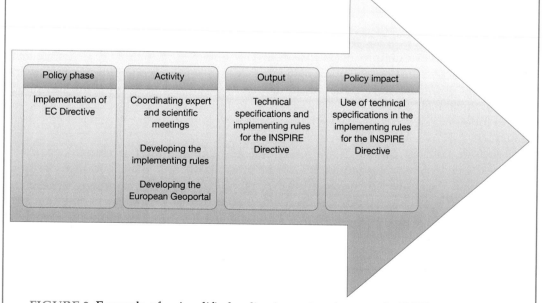

FIGURE 3 Example of a simplified policy impact pathway – the INSPIRE Directive.

Impact Inventories

An impact inventory comprises cases of policy impact reported by researchers (i.e., it is a self-assessment). It is an easy quantitative tool used to monitor impact on policy. Due to the difficulties with establishing a traceable causality, one often needs to focus on tangible impact, i.e., documented instances in which research results have been used in policymaking. In addition, researchers should explain in such exercise what is the nature and the level of their involvement in the policymaking process, including how they interact with stakeholders. In our case, these instances are tracked, recorded by the research teams and validated by internal peer review. The result is an inventory of impact cases that can be examined for patterns, drawing the organisation's impact profile. The inventory can provide statistical support to management decisions regarding research or customer portfolios, areas of improvement of scientific services and gap analyses, targeting specific beneficiaries, or improving links to political priorities.

The challenges of such a bottom-up process revolve around consistency issues. For example, due to a large number of reporters and validators and the breadth of portfolio activities, the scale of impact can vary considerably. Moreover, external validation, e.g., by end users, is difficult to achieve because of the large number and variety of impacts – in our case, we count, on average, over 350 cases of impact on policy each year (Box 3).

Maintaining an inventory of policy impact helps organisational learning in a number of different ways. First, it allows researchers to analyse the characteristics of successful activities which lead to impact. Then, the inventory can show what needs to be improved to increase the impact on policy. For example, one can analyse the reasons for rejecting impact claims made by scientific teams. This analysis sometimes contrasts with what researchers think their results are and how they are used by policymakers. The information can help focus researchers at the science–policy frontier on the fact that their science needs to respond to policy needs.

The organisation can track through the inventory the policy areas and stages where it has most impact. For example, Fig. 4 illustrates our impact profile in 2018, when we have had most impact on the implementation and monitoring of European policy. The following main groups of impact were policy formulation, agenda setting, evaluation and policy adoption. Such analyses can allow management to follow whether the organisation is on track in following its strategy or whether it needs adjustments in terms of the policy areas it covers.

These examples showcase the power of analysis residing in impact inventories. Yearly reports are disseminated to all colleagues. They help management to make informed decisions not only about the strategic orientation of the organisation but also about any operational changes needed to achieve strategic goals. Moreover, performance indicators based on such inventory support the organisation to show accountability for its resources in annual activity reviews and other documents required by decision-makers. And finally, they are an important feedback tool for researchers working at the science–policy interface, where showing impact on policy is required.

Box 3: Impact inventory

The JRC impact inventory contains individual impact claims made by our researchers each year. The process starts when a researcher (or a team) registers the impact of their work on a specific policy in a specialised IT system. This is then followed by reviews from hierarchy, and finally by a peer panel composed of staff from across our research centre.

The role of knowledge management is very important in this process. It needs to be able to broker the transfer of knowledge across the organisation and make the entire review process consistent. Knowledge management teams do so by ensuring that very specialised scientific information is translated in a way that can be easily interpreted by peers in their review.

To assist in clarifying the definitions and boundaries between what constitutes an output, an outcome and an impact, regular workshops are held across the JRC. Researchers are encouraged to think critically about how their intended stakeholders use their outputs, the short- and long-term consequences and the expected pathways. Guidelines are produced to communicate the best practices and examples to avoid common pitfalls when describing impacts. An internal forum is also maintained to encourage ongoing discussions on these matters.

Researchers should be very concise in describing the impact that their work has on policy. The high number of impacts recorded in the inventory requires a significant amount of time to evaluate; thus, information needs to be clear and concise to show how scientific activity impacted policy. The usual information that researchers need to record includes the description of scientific activities, of the interaction with stakeholders and of how their results affected the policy.

For analytical purposes, other information regarding the research and its output may be collected from project management platforms. Automation of such information collection ensures that scientists only need to focus on describing the impact they have on policy.

The inventory is essentially a database containing codified activities, outputs, beneficiaries and impacts. It can be analysed at different levels and for different needs. The inventory allows to analyse our overall impact either on specific policy priorities, by categories of research activity, or by policy area, among others. This makes it a versatile tool to quantify and analyse an organisation's impact profile.

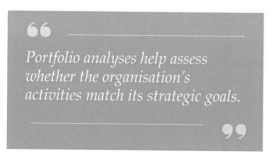

Portfolio analyses help assess whether the organisation's activities match its strategic goals.

Portfolio Analyses

Research portfolios are mostly used to manage private R&D projects, but they have also been taken-up by public research organisations as a way to manage and analyse subsets of research activities (Wallace and Rafols, 2015).

Portfolio analyses help assess whether the organisation's activities match its strategic goals, and they typically include benchmarking. They also help prioritisation, identifying gaps and redundancies. The term has been widely used in corporate finance to describe methods to manage portfolios of securities (Sharpe, 1963). Public research organisations use portfolio analyses to develop their strategy and analyse the cumulative impact of their projects (Bozeman and Rogers, 2001).

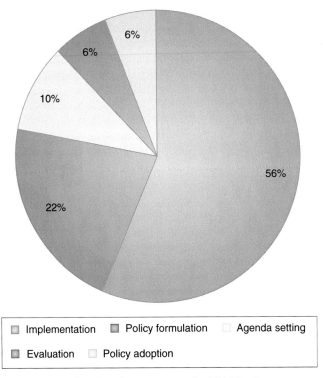

FIGURE 4   Share of JRC policy impacts in 2018 by impact category.

In general, these analyses are more relevant for the management of research organisations than for the researchers themselves, although important synergies between different activities can be proposed to scientific teams. Information about the broader context in which one's research is performed can help scientists understand how different activities can be connected to achieve impact. Using a formal intervention logic backed by portfolio analyses can enable the organisation to base its strategic and operational decision-making on a chain of expected effects (i.e., activities–outputs–outcomes–impacts). This might be further strengthened through the establishment of a priority-setting mechanism to support its development. A recent example of a portfolio analysis is an evaluation of our modelling support for the European Commission's policy impact assessments (European Commission, 2017) (Box 4).

There are a number of ways researchers can benefit from portfolio analyses. First, they can benefit from organisation-wide economies of scale. In the example above, we show how one type of portfolio – output portfolio[5] – can cover a very wide range of scientific activities and fields. The outputs of research are used in one type of policy document – impact assessment – which has a determined structure and research questions. This creates

---

[5]An output portfolio is one that is built on a type of scientific output, rather than similar activities or impacts (Bozeman and Rogers, 2001).

> **Box 4**: Example of a portfolio analysis
>
> In 2017, the JRC has performed an analysis of the portfolio of modelling techniques that had been used in the impact assessments of European policies. In a nutshell, impact assessments are carried out by the European Commission while preparing new policy initiatives expected to have significant economic, social or environmental impacts. We usually have a large role, especially in quantifying such impacts.
>
> The analysis was performed on 512 impact assessments for Commission initiatives between 2009 and 2014. Starting from information collected from case studies and impact inventories, corroborated with an analysis of the policy documents, we have found that we had contributed with models to 48% of the impact assessments. The organisation's most used tools were energy models, followed by environmental models, microeconomic models for financial markets, transport and agriculture models, respectively.
>
> This analysis provided a quantification of our modelling work and our impact by type of policy or beneficiaries and stakeholders. This quantification was then used to report to management on various issues, from the coverage of policy priorities to the effectiveness of the organisation's modelling activities in achieving policy impact.

the means for an organisation to reduce the cost of performing research in different areas by standardising its input into the science-for-policy process.

Then, portfolio analyses can help scientists to understand better the needs of the beneficiaries of their research. Research for policy is meant to support goals that are exogenous to science itself (Sarewitz and Pielke, 2007), and no one scientist or team of scientists can have a large impact by itself. Positioning oneself within an organisation's portfolio of research projects provides knowledge externalities that individual scientists or teams can use to improve their chances of having an impact on policymaking, as well as possibly improving their scientific knowledge.

Conclusion

The evaluation practices are evolving to respond to the growing demand to demonstrate the added value and impact of scientific work. We have shown in this chapter that one method alone is insufficient to capture the entire array of impact that a complex research organisation has on policymaking. Each of the tools described here has its strengths and weaknesses, and it is only by using them collectively that the organisation can learn and create the knowledge needed to improve. To be able to reap full benefits of impact evaluation, this set of basic tools will need to be extended to capture more diverse effects of scientific results on public debate and political behaviour, to include methods to weight impact, to capture customer feedback and modern alternative metrics information to better connect the different measurement methodologies and to better account for longer-term effects. These additions are necessary in a dynamic scientific and policy environment, where researchers find themselves at the science–policy frontier, needing to show how they can affect policymaking in an almost business-like way in which science becomes a service. In this sense, impact on policy needs not be thought of as a post-factum activity, but rather as one that needs to be proactively addressed even before research begins.

The key takeaway for researchers is that scientific work is part of an ecosystem which includes policymakers. It is thus paramount to imagine the possible effects of one's research on how policy is designed, implemented or evaluated, as this provides accountability for the public funds spent on research. To foster a 'think impact' mindset, project planning needs to include clear actions to achieving the expected policy impact. This exercise also offers insights on how to increase the policy impact of science, whether by informing on the pathway leading from activities to impact or by describing how and when policies can be impacted by research. Oftentimes, these paths are indirect, and researchers need to understand the policymaking environment they operate in to achieve the impact they seek. As Sarewitz and Pielke (2007: p.5) assert, '"better" science portfolios […] would be achieved if science policy decisions reflected knowledge about the supply of science, the demand for science, and the relationship between the two'.

Our experience and the analysis of the impact of our activities have given ample proof of the importance of working together with policymakers. The activities that are rated high in this respect have close contact with the demand side and often have a clear policy mandate. It is also important to note that many forward-looking, top-rated research activities have evolved to generate European-added value in the long run and uptake in the policy process, emphasising the importance of our role as an independent research body. This can be a lesson that we pass on to others at the science–policy interface, in an ever-changing environment that constantly brings with it new challenges.

Image: Artifirsov - https://stock.adobe.com/be_en/images/spinner-dolphins-underwater-in-ocean/293980607?prev_url=detail
Icon in page corners: Dolphins icon by Laymik, from the Noun Project (https://thenounproject.com/search/?q=dolphin&i=1078133)

Communicating Science in a Policy Context to a Broader Audience

Main authors: Marton Hajdu, Catherine Simoneau

Contributors: Anne-Mette Jensen-Foreman, Darren McGarry, Sofia Pereira Sá, Alexandre Gerez, Barbara Mortara

Key takeaways:

- Evidence does not speak for itself – it must be communicated.

- Communicating science for policy impact to non-scientific audiences requires a very different approach from communicating science to scientific audiences.

- Communication must be adapted to the desired objectives and audiences.

- To succeed, scientists and communicators must work hand in hand from the beginning to shape the message and narrative together, identify opportunities and prepare the right tools.

Science for Policy Handbook
http://dx.doi.org/10.1016/B978-0-12-822596-7.00015-2

Copyright © 2020 European Union,
Published by Elsevier Limited

Evidence does not speak for itself – it must be communicated. This much is already clear from other chapters of this book which discuss how policymakers and scientists communicate with each other about societal challenges and policy objectives, how they communicate about the role of science in policymaking and how they tap into diverse sources of knowledge and share it.

This chapter looks at the more institutionalised aspects of communication, in other words the processes and practices that may improve getting the message across to broader audiences affecting or affected by policymaking. Given the authors' background, there is an additional focus on political communication as practiced in the JRC, which is a scientific institution inside a political body, the European Commission. This unique setup means that its work must be aligned with the broader political and policy responsibilities of the Commission and its communication activities must be aligned with those of the Commission which ultimately serve political objectives. As evidence providers work closer and closer with policymakers, it is important they realise the importance of getting also the broader communication right in order to build trust with policymakers and politicians.

The Motivation to Communicate to a Broader Audience

Communication by a science for policy organisation will have multiple objectives. First and foremost, the objective is to provide evidence in an understandable, timely and contextualised form to policymakers, primarily those responsible for preparing decisions. This is the purpose of the organisation's existence.

Most organisations will also want to communicate their science more broadly to strengthen cooperation with and improve their image among their peers. Research shows that scientific articles featured in the media and on social media go further even among scientists, as opposed to research that stays within the confines of peer-reviewed journals, and this also increases their impact.

A third objective can be to inform more senior policymakers and politicians not merely to provide them with evidence tailored to their specific needs but also to demonstrate the value of 'science for policy' to them and their constituencies and thus advocate for evidence-informed policymaking.

> *Research shows that scientific articles featured in the media and on social media go further even among scientists, as opposed to research that stays within the confines of peer-reviewed journals, and this also increases their impact.*

Last but not least, in a democracy, a scientific organisation will also have to communicate directly with various segments of the general public, for example, to justify its funding to taxpayers, to inform people about how the science behind the policies impacts their life or simply to improve public understanding of science and fight the tide of fake news, among others. More often than not, these audiences will be very different from the traditional audience of science for policymaking organisations.

Some organisations will exclusively focus on the first two objectives. Others will do more, which in the current sociopolitical climate is a legitimate aim for scientific organisations wishing to become more closely involved in policymaking to help tackle the challenges our societies face. Given the JRC's specific situation, our communication activities also aim to highlight the importance of evidence-based policymaking to citizens and to policymakers. The ultimate objective of this is to demonstrate the value of EU policies, and the science they are based on, in the eyes of citizens and to strengthen the case for the use of science in policymaking in the eyes of politicians and policymakers.

Apart from these explicit objectives, nurturing and encouraging communication beyond the circle of policymakers and scientists can also support the transition to Science for Policy 2.0 by exposing researchers to novel ways of communicating and thinking about their research, for example, through questions from the media or the public. This promotes culture change in the organisation, helping scientists practice 'dialogue', requiring them to be proactive about and aware of the impact of their research from the beginning and also keeping them aware of the wider political and policy context that can impact the usability and value of their research.

Different Kinds of Audiences

The communication objective defines the audience to be reached. Again, beyond the traditional audiences of policymakers and scientists, many others can be considered, such as political parties and opinion leaders, members of parliament, regulators, religious bodies, donor organisations, businesses and civil society, the public at large in a given area (such as the host community of a research institute), etc. More on this can be found in Chapter 5.

Often these audiences, especially citizens, can only be reached indirectly, via multipliers like the media or social media influencers. Furthermore, the co-creation and continuous engagement approach that Science for Policy 2.0 calls for with policymakers is only possible to a lesser extent with broader audiences as those approaches rarely scale to the level needed to reach them, and even if they do, they can be very resource intensive and thus out of reach for most organisations. Communication activities will thus vary according to the objective, the intended audience and the resources available.

The following subsections provide a few examples.

Senior Policymakers, Members of Parliament and Other Politicians

High-level political communication should focus on the most sensitive and most valuable activities of the organisation. It should not merely focus on the science but also include narratives about how science plays a helpful role in resolving difficult

High-level political communication should focus on the most sensitive and most valuable activities of the organisation.

policy issues and improving the lives of citizens, as well about the most newsworthy, cutting edge research coming out of the organisation.

This communication will often be highly tailored and resource intensive and it may be channelled through policy briefs, case studies, conferences, high-level briefings or laboratory visits. It will aim to build trust and increase the credibility of the organisation as well as to drive coverage of the organisation in the media that senior decision-makers read.

Case Story: Science meets Parliaments

The JRC regularly organises 'Science meets Parliament' events to bring together JRC researchers and management with senior policymakers from the European Parliament, one of the key stakeholders and customers of the organisation. The multi day event includes not only lectures by senior experts and politicians, panel discussions, workshops but also demonstrations of some of the scientific achievements of the JRC and the services it offers to policymakers. It provides an opportunity to share knowledge and network and raise awareness of the value of the JRC's work for policymakers.

Local Communities

Research institutes do not exist in a vacuum and they interact in various ways with their host communities. In their everyday activities as well as under extraordinary circumstances (for example, an incident involving hazardous materials), they must rely on the cooperation of local authorities and the good will of local citizens. This can be promoted by engaging them regularly and offering them opportunities to interact with researchers and familiarise themselves with scientists' work in the interest of citizens.

Case Story: Open days and local media outreach

Spread across six sites across the European Union, the JRC has a unique opportunity to reach local citizens directly in a way that is difficult for other departments of the European Commission. In order to capitalise on this unique feature of the JRC and also to engage the host communities in a continuous dialogue, the JRC regularly organises open days when local citizens can visit laboratories and meet scientists. We also cooperate with local media, keeping them informed of our activities, providing them with interesting scientific and policy relevant news stories and organising regular media visits of our laboratories. Targeted online coverage of these events via web and social media allows the JRC to connect with local audiences who cannot attend the event in their region.

Journalists and Social Media Influencers

The knowledge that science for policy organisations create, manage and provide to policymakers is also valuable for journalists and the media. And while science organisations traditionally target science media, science for policy organisations can aim for a much broader reach because their work will have direct influence on legislative and regulatory outcomes that shape the economy and society. Beyond the traditional tools of press releases, laboratory visits and technical briefings, journalists can also be engaged in activities that help them better understand the role of science in policymaking and learn to use the tools and databases put at the disposal of policymakers to enhance their reporting.

Science and research 'gurus', well-known entrepreneurs and policymakers active on social media with many followers are important for the success of a digital communication campaign. Social media influencers can be multipliers of the knowledge produced by science for policy organisations; they can reach audiences that would not be reachable otherwise.

Case Story: European Commission tools for the media

The JRC regularly organises media visits to its laboratories and media seminars for interested journalists. Beyond talking about our research and its impact on EU policies, one of the objectives is to raise awareness of journalists of the tools and databases the JRC makes publicly available, and help them learn how to use them to find new stories and enrich their reporting. In the past, JRC tools mapping surface water on earth, population density or wildfires, among others, have been used by top tier media in their reporting.

Citizens

Publicly funded organisations are accountable to taxpayers, and even more so if they are involved in shaping the policies that affect people's life. They may also consider it their responsibility to educate the public about science in general and its role in policymaking in particular. Last but not least, as a public service, they can aim to popularise results and engage citizens with recent scientific findings that they can use to improve their lives or better understand certain important phenomena. While traditional and social media communication remains important for these audiences, in the case of a science for policy organisation, public engagement with a view to strengthening participatory democracy is equally important (see Chapter 8).

Case Story: ARTEFACTS exhibition coorganised with the Museum für Naturkunde in Berlin

The ARTEFACTS exhibition is coorganised with the Museum für Naturkunde in Berlin. It experiments with new ways of using art and science to bring facts to the hearts and minds of citizens. The exhibition aims to provoke a dialogue about environmental issues that connects politics, science and society by engaging citizens in key topics of public concern under the themes of food, energy, climate, air and water. The JRC worked with the Museum in developing the content, ensuring scientific accuracy and also providing 'meet the scientists' sessions, with JRC scientists engaging with visitors through live video link. The exhibition attracted 46,000 visitors in its first 3 weeks.

How to Do It?

A higher level of ambition in providing scientific advice to policymakers and the strengthened focus on communication that it inevitably entails will require changes in organisational culture, structure, procedures and skills. The key to understand about communication in this respect is that everyone has a responsibility to communicate, and communication should be the result of close cooperation and co-creation. While there is no silver bullet, there are a number of options to consider.

Structure and Procedures

The structure and procedures of the organisation will be determined and constrained by various factors, including its mandate, its governance and its history. Even when a complete restructuring is not feasible, steps should be taken to promote closer cooperation between scientists and communicators; to increase the feeling of ownership and responsibility for communication among scientists right from the beginning of their research and to ensure that senior management takes an active role in the strategic orientation of communication.

Case Story: Cross cutting projects to enhance cooperation

One way to promote closer cooperation of scientists and communicators is to involve them in cross cutting projects that do not entail changes in structures and procedures but require both sides for securing organisational objectives. Be it participation at science conferences, the organisation of outreach events or the creation of communication campaigns around specific deliverables, such activities build rapport between scientists and communicators and help each side appreciate the contribution of the other to shared goals.

Understanding Audiences

The characteristics of the various audiences, and their difference from traditional scientific audiences, must be clear to all participants when designing communication activities, right from the beginning. Politicians and senior policymakers require short, actionable information and a focus on what is in it for them in the given political and policy context. Experts and less senior policymakers are prepared to deal with more information to understand the wider context, but it must be conveyed in plain, non-scientific language, and offering a degree of certainty that may be difficult for a scientist to provide. The media looks for a hook or a story that makes sense for their readers and links to the issues of the day. Local authorities and citizens look for what is in a story for their immediate environment.

Case Story: The importance of timing and relevance for audiences

At the time of its publication in Nature, the media showed little interest in a JRC scientific article on the Mediterranean Sea. Later, in cooperation with the responsible policy department and the Commission's communication service, some of the key findings of the article – not necessarily the most relevant ones from a scientific perspective – were used to produce a Commission press release in time for a ministerial meeting addressing the Mediterranean fisheries crisis. Focussing on one specific aspect of the research with the title 'Saving our heritage, our future: The worrying state of Mediterranean fish stocks', it resulted in strong media coverage, including top tier media and tabloids that do not typically report on science and policy issues, thus increasing the visibility of the issue to citizens and policymakers.

Tailoring the Message

Depending on the objective, the audience and the medium, the same underlying evidence can provide the basis for different messages. In developing the messages, we must ensure that they do not contradict each other, but they are relevant and appropriate for the target audience.

Not all research will lend itself to creating messages for all audiences – in some cases we want to restrict communication to policymakers and experts, in others we may want to focus on various segments of the public.

Understandably, scientists are prone to keep their traditional audiences in mind when thinking about messages and they may be wary of focussing on other aspects of their research. Trust between scientists and communicators must be built up over time to put scientists at ease about using their research for communicating messages that they themselves may find irrelevant from a scientific perspective.

Not all research will lend itself to creating messages for all audiences – in some cases we want to restrict communication to policymakers and experts, in others we may want to focus on various segments of the public.

Case Story: JRC flagship reports

JRC flagship reports cover broad policy areas such as the future of transport or the role of AI, aiming to distil the current state of knowledge and present policy options from an EU perspective. With over a 100 pages in length, their primary audiences are policymakers and experts. For senior policymakers and politicians, the most relevant findings for policymaking purposes are repeated in short, easy to understand executive summaries or communicated in person. The findings most relevant for citizens and the media are summarised in an accompanying press release which focuses on real-life examples and the possible impacts on citizens' lives, while putting them in the context of existing EU legislation. Last but not least, the most eye catching insights, messages, etc., supported by easy to understand visualisation, are turned into social media content for attracting the attention of all potential audiences and inspiring them to read on.

Clear Writing

Science often has to be communicated in writing. Therefore, scientists must be able to write about their work in a way that non-scientists can understand without excessive mental effort. This is often a challenge even if they are highly experienced in writing articles for scientific journals.

Raising awareness of the importance of clear writing is a start. Clear writing trainings and regular cooperation with communicators provide learning opportunities and feedback to scientists. Organising communities of practice, creating opportunities to demonstrate the value of clear writing and recognising best performers in the organisation provide additional ways to strengthen this important skill among scientists.

Case Story: Clear writers' network

The JRC's clear writers' network focuses the challenges of communicating science clearly for various audiences. Its members are JRC scientists who dedicate up to 25% of their working time to the network and who benefit from specially designed training modules plus individual mentoring. The emphasis is on understanding the difference between writing for a scientific audience and writing for others. For example, whereas in a scientific article the methodology must be explained, this will only be of interest to policymakers if the methodology is questioned by certain stakeholders. The work of the network led to a noticeable improvement in the quality of briefings and other communication material from its members.

Visual Communication, Visual Identity

Just like clear writing, visualisation of knowledge is key for communicating it to various audiences. Visualisations are not just nice pages, they are about information, not decoration. The way in which a report or key results will be visualised and disseminated should be determined at the project planning stage – it is not an add-on outsourced to communicators at the end.

Furthermore, consistent use of visual communication and the creation of a visual identity provides an added value to the organisation by signalling that the communication comes from a reliable source. Visual identity must be recognised by managers and scientists alike as a key part of the communication strategy if we want our audiences to immediately recognise our brand and be inclined to engage with our products.

To prepare meaningful communications certain key questions have to be clarified in advance:

- Who is your target audience: the more specific you can be, the better you can focus the message, i.e., what is their environment, what are their interests, biases and communication habits.
- What do you want to achieve with this audience, and what can you produce with the available resources that help you get there? Assess the strengths, weakness, opportunities and threats (SWOT analysis) of using visual communication to achieve your goal.
- Which format serves the objective best? Digital, print, animation, motion graphics, etc.?
- What kind of interaction is desired with your target audience? What kind of interaction can you expect?

In order to get the message across, we need to leave out a vast amount of information. Condensing a 100 page scientific report into 2 pages is a major culture change. It goes against the principles of most scientists, and most often meets with resistance. However, getting rid of clutter is essential to pass the messages effectively. Clutter is every piece of information that distracts your audience and increases the cognitive load. Clutter can also mean visual elements that take up space but do not increase understanding. For a multiauthor report, there could be a need for compromise on the overriding key messages depending on the objective, target audience, the opportunity in the policy cycle and the timing of the communication.

Culture change will be reinforced through demonstration, such as when a one-pager lands on the desk of the decision-maker and is used. Smart workflow helps to achieve the desired objectives. First and foremost, all actors need to be involved: all key scientists, communication specialists, editors, graphical designers. They should work together in a well-planned process with many iterations.

A well-designed briefing template is key to save time. In it

- Keep asking the question 'what's it all about': what is your objective, what do you want your audience to learn or do?

- What is the communication environment like? Is my message relevant right now, or is there perhaps a better moment coming in the political, media cycle?
- Remember who you are talking to, why it matters, with three to five key issues or results, explained as if it were your next door neighbour.
- Create a story board: a visual outline of your story.
- Effective data visualisation is critical for your message; always mention the source of data.
- Consistent guidelines for style, colour palette, line thickness in graphs, a data base of icons help with coherence.

Your visual information should tell a story, one you should be able to explain in a few minutes. The beginning should give the context and the plot, bringing everyone on common ground. The end, a call to action. Test the infographic with a non-expert as well, to make sure it is read the way you intended.

Bear in mind that visualisation of knowledge can be just as resource intensive as the production of knowledge itself. Therefore, it is necessary to assess 'what works' and develop metrics to measure the impact. The benefits of knowledge visualisation and the processes behind it must be communicated clearly internally. Visualisation needs and processes must be defined clearly and effective team work for visualisation must be cultivated to enhance its communication potential.

Case Story: Translating complex messages about global supply and demand of cobalt in the transition to electric mobility

As a science for policy organisation, we aim to ensure that JRC knowledge and scientific evidence land on the desks of policymakers, can be easily understood and trigger policy thinking. Visual storytelling helped communicate key issues, results and prospective innovations related to global supply and demand of cobalt for the electric vehicle market today and in the future.

Key scientific evidence visualised within one page is a form that easily attracts attention and, hence, is more likely to achieve policy impact. The objective was to create an infographic and one page of a stylised synthesis of a detailed report (100 pages). The infographic had to tell a story literally within less than 2 minutes as our typical audience has to deal with an increasing number of very complex problems and often have very little time. Even when we have sound recommendations for them, the competition for attention is enormous.

Visual storytelling has been used to condense, edit and visualise this complex scientific report into two pages of 'bit-size' relevant knowledge. By following the principles discussed above, JRC achieved policy impact: our evidence was featured in the Commission Communication on the Implementation of the Strategic Action Plan on Batteries: Building a Strategic Battery Value Chain in Europe.

This was achieved primarily by involving all experts – scientists, communicators, designer, editors – in an interactive process from the first sketches to the final product. On top of the final product, we also prepared graphic elements for social media, to further disseminate the results (Figs. 1 and 2).

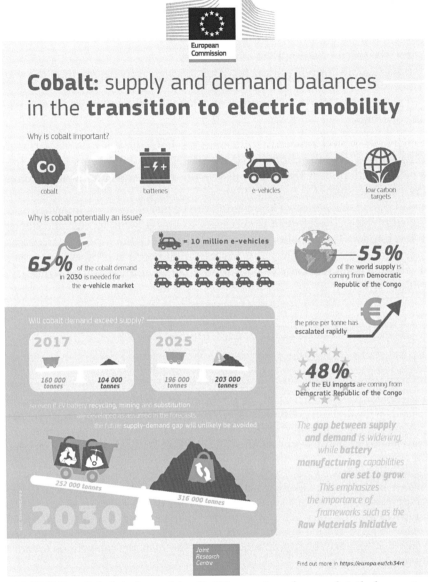

FIGURE 1 Cobalt infographic, distilling a story from a detailed report.

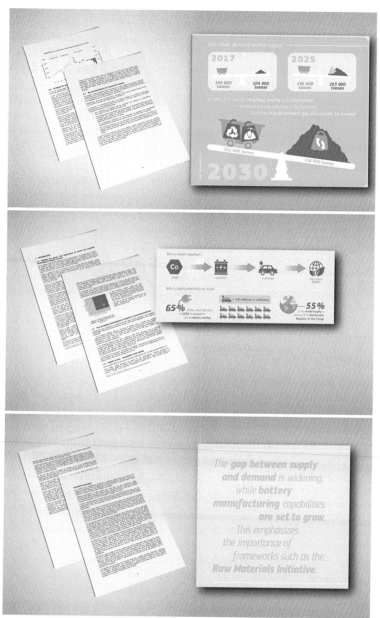

FIGURE 2 Condensing a scientific text into visual key messages.

Coordination, Co-creation

One of the most critical aspects in the culture change in communication is ensuring that it is seen by all as a joint effort between communicators and scientists right from the onset of a research project. In other words, communication must not be a mere afterthought but it must be mandated by management to be included already in the planning phase.

Procedurally, requiring a communication brief early on is the ideal approach. This brief can be used to address fundamental communication questions, such as 'what problem does our research intend to address', 'how does it fit into the policy landscape', 'why does it matter', 'to whom does it matter', 'who will be interested', 'who do we want to talk to', 'how does it make my neighbour's life better', etc.

Based on this brief, the content, narrative, visualisation and packaging can be developed in parallel with the project, leaving ample time for creative thinking and exploring various options for dissemination. It can also be used to flag high value communication opportunities to senior management and the political leadership, thus maximising the value of the work for political purposes.

From an organisational perspective, bringing scientists and communicators regularly together can help bring about this culture change and pairing scientists with communicators to work together on messages and communication products can lead to mutual learning and trust.

Skills

Chapter 4 deals more in depth with the skills scientists need for effective communication with policymakers. Many of the same skills are also necessary for effective communication with other audiences, such as talking with visitor groups, briefing journalists, drafting communication summaries or talking on stage at public events.

Traditional formal training opportunities play an important role in building those skills, for example, on public speaking, storytelling, visualisation, etc. Furthermore, the close involvement of communicators in research projects provides scientists with hands-on experience in communicating their work beyond their peers. Last but not least, involving scientists in 'cool', innovative communication activities can increase their motivation and provide them with opportunities to exercise their communication 'muscles'.

Case Story: Unlocking new communication powers in scientists

The JRC encourages its scientists to try novel communication methods and invests into their our colleagues training. For example, we regularly organise events around PechaKucha and TED-style talks, science coffees and live 'date a scientist' initiatives at large public events. Participation, which is voluntary, includes preparation with communication experts, and calls for expression of interest have brought forward not only scientists already recognised for their communication skills but it also allowed discovering hidden talents. In a virtuous cycle, the success of such events encourages more and more scientists to volunteer and showcase their work to various audiences, while gaining valuable communication experience. In parallel, we strongly encourage the scientists to be digital ambassadors. The concept of digital ambassadorship is based on our colleagues actively promoting their own work to their own networks with their own voice and expertise on the web and social media. The goal is to amplify the visibility, brand and reach for both them and the organisation itself. Therefore any JRC staff active on the web and social media can act as ambassadors.

Motivation

Ultimately, the culture change to engage in communication hinges on motivation. Motivation may be intrinsic, coming from the personality and drive of the scientist, or extrinsic, rooted in the desire to earn a reward or avoid punishment.

Communicating with non-scientific audiences is often challenging for scientists as it involves having to strip one's own science down and rewording it, peeling away the layers of scientific complexity and expressing it in layman's terms. It also means leaving one's comfort zone and doing things differently, through trial and error, to find the best approach.

Communicating with non-scientific audiences is often challenging for scientists. Therefore, management must make sure that the right incentives are in place to spur as many scientists as possible to engage in communication.

Therefore, management must make sure that the right incentives are in place to spur as many scientists as possible to engage in communication.

As an example of leveraging intrinsic motivations, cultivating a pool of scientists with an inclination and skills for communication and giving them high-value communication opportunities can provide an example for others to follow. For others, the mandatory inclusion of communication planning in research activities and setting aside a certain percentage of their working time for communication may be necessary.

Case Story: Measuring and recognising communication results

The wisdom of 'what gets measured gets done' is especially true in a scientific organisation. Measurement, reporting and public recognition of good results can be significant contributors to motivation. Using its expertise in indicators, the JRC is in the process of developing and deploying more sophisticated ways of measuring the results of its communication activities. At the same time, continuous recognition of and feedback on communication activities is required from managers to staff to signal the importance that management attaches to successful communication.

Science for Policy 2.0 in Specific Areas

Image: Evgeny Dubinchuk – https://stock.adobe.com/be_en/images/large-flames-of-forest-fire/24003771?prev_url=detail
Icon in page corners: Fire icon by Nicolas Vicent, from the Noun Project (https://thenounproject.com/search/?q=fire&i=91161)

Knowledge-Based Crisis and Emergency Management

Main author: Tom De Groeve

Contributor: Maurits van den Berg

Key takeaways:

- Science and knowledge enable a shift from reactive to proactive risk management.

- Scientists, policymakers and practitioners must work together. In particular, in the emergency management context, it is essential to create tight feedback loops between scientific developments and their application in the real world. Trust and transparency are crucial in this relationship.

- Scientists must learn what information to provide to whom at what time and in what format, so the information is directly relevant in the decision-making process of practitioners.

- In a disaster context, maps are essential communication tools. They can help build a narrative and can show evolution in time, historical background, thematic information and context information.

- No expert or single organisation can be sure to provide comprehensive science advice on everything alone. For a science for policy organisation, it is crucial to establish long-term partnerships with complementary organisations to leverage and exploit expertise and skills beyond the own organisation.

Please note that this chapter was drafted before the global COVID-19 outbreak. Some of the advice will inevitably benefit from further reflections from managing this crisis. Learning the lessons from COVID-19 response and the role of science in it is a crucial task to the wider science for policy community. The JRC is fully committed to it and will share the results in future publications.

Copyright © 2020 European Union,
Published by Elsevier Limited.

Starting from a situation where knowledge was used on an ad hoc basis, uncoordinated across hazards or sectors, and where emergency management was mainly reactive, without links to prevention and forward looking reconstruction, we have come a long way (UNISDR, 2015). Knowledge is now considered as part of the crisis response, rather than supporting it (IFRC, 2005). Two or three decades ago, the typical situation during a crisis was one of lack of information. Any piece of science-based information – be it a map, a satellite image or an analysis of press coverage – was welcome and used, but there were few mechanisms to deliver this information systematically and timely. Fast forward 20 years and we are in a situation of information overflow with new challenges of making sense of contradictory and volatile information for decisions that affect a reality with ever-more complex sociotechnical interdependencies, including ethical and legal considerations (Comes et al., 2017).

Being active for over 20 years not only at European Union (EU) level but also at global level, national level and local level, we have built an insight into roles and needs for science advice at each government level. Some of our key conclusions are described below.

Knowledge Is Enabling the Shift From Reactive to Proactive Risk Management

Emergencies are situations where a natural hazard, a technological accident, a disease outbreak, a violent conflict or another event shocks society and may become a disaster if not managed well. They are typically fast-changing situations with many stakeholders where decisions must be made based on incomplete information and in chaotic circumstances. In this context, scientific data, such as early warnings, real-time sensor observations, monitoring systems or predictive models, have the potential to fill an information vacuum and allow emergency responders to make more informed decisions. However, getting science advice to the right person at the right time in the right format remains an enormous challenge.

> *It is a huge challenge to bring science advice into a political process where it competes with vested and special interests, other policy priorities and short-term thinking.*

Science is equally useful in reducing disaster or conflict risk, such as taking mitigation measures for known risks, plan preparedness actions ahead and prevent the creation of new risk. In this context, science can offer a detailed understanding of current risk, future risk (with scenarios of demographic change, climate change, land use change or socioeconomic volatility), the expected impacts of disasters in multiple economic and social sectors and cost–benefit analyses of preventive measures. Also here, it is a huge challenge to bring science advice into a political process where it competes with vested and special interests, other policy priorities and short-term thinking. In addition, science advice faces the difficulties of communicating complex multidisciplinary science to a nonscientific and multisectoral audience.

The science–policy interface in the EU is quite diverse, with some models centralising the function through Chief Science Advisors and others with networks, partnerships or boundary organisations (Marin Ferrer et al., 2016). A golden rule in crisis and emergency management is to handle crises as local as possible and as global as necessary. Subsidiarity is essential not only as a principle of EU law but also as a crisis management principle. However, it makes the landscape of actors complex and multilayered, and, crucially, responsibilities for decision-making may escalate from one level to the next, involving coordination at EU level in extreme cases. Furthermore, as disaster risk reduction is a cross-sectoral policy, decisions on prevention involve many sectors of government simultaneously. It is therefore not surprising that the EU's Civil Protection legislation (Decision 1313/2013[1]) requires the Commission to 'take action to improve the knowledge base on disaster risks and facilitate the sharing of knowledge, best practices and information, including among Member States that share common risks'. A shared knowledge base across policy levels and sectors is essential to have coherent crisis management and risk reduction.

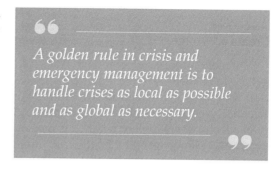

> A golden rule in crisis and emergency management is to handle crises as local as possible and as global as necessary.

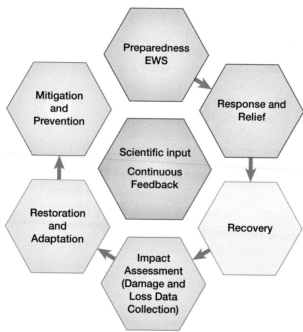

Crisis and emergency management are part of a disaster risk management cycle with six distinct phases. Sound risk assessment based on science and knowledge is essential for well-informed risk management.

---

[1] https://eur-lex.europa.eu/legal-content/EN/TXT/?uri=celex%3A32013D1313.

Five Lessons We Learnt

Create a Virtuous Feedback Loop Between Science, Policy and Practice

The most important lesson is that scientists, policymakers and practitioners must work together. In particular, in the emergency management context, it is essential to create tight feedback loops between scientific developments and their application in the real world. This allows scientists to see firsthand the strengths and weaknesses of their systems and focus further research and development where it is most needed. It allows practitioners to be involved in the design of systems from the beginning, understand possibilities and limitations, and therefore trust the information at time of crisis.

The codesign of our scientific work with policymakers and practitioners is now embedded in our corporate strategy. In practice, it requires an open and flexible approach from our scientists to work and deliver at the speed of crisis management practitioners or policy decision-makers. This is a mind shift that is well worth making as new research and solutions are continuously tested in the 'real world' (Box 1).

Our scientists frequently provide ad hoc scientific advice in crisis situations, including sectorial advice. For example, we sometimes provide rapid science-based response to requests from DG Agriculture and Rural Development concerning extreme agrometeorological conditions in specific regions of the EU. We can do this, thanks to a flexible organisation and expert staff that can be rapidly mobilised in addition to frequent communication with relevant policy stakeholders, anticipation and preparedness (e.g., prepare basic data on weather, agrometeorological indicators and crop model results readily available). This, in turn, is made possible because many of these elements are in place for regular non–crisis-related activities (for example, the **JRC MARS Bulletins Crop Monitoring in Europe** providing monthly yield forecasts, https://ec.europa.eu/jrc/en/mars/bulletins).

Furthermore, tight collaboration during the crisis management cycle led to a buildup of expertise in crisis rooms and crisis management support tools in the **European Crisis Management Laboratory**, which contributed to the launch of the Commission's Emergency Response

The European Commission's Emergency Response Coordination Centre was built in close collaboration with the Joint Research Centre.

Box 1: Global Disaster Alert and Coordination System

The JRC has worked since 2002 with the Commission's emergency response service (DG ECHO) to develop systems to forecast and monitor disasters for the European continent and globally. The Global Disaster Alert and Coordination System (GDACS, www.gdacs.org) was started in 2004 (De Groeve et al., 2006) and has been continuously developed in close synergy with DG ECHO and the UN Office for Coordination of Humanitarian Affairs, as well as emergency services of countries worldwide. Its development is driven largely by acute needs during disasters for which innovative solutions are built during the emergency and later integrated in the system. For example, a global tsunami calculation system was piloted during the 2004 tsunami in Indonesia and deployed in GDACS in 2005 (Annunziato, 2005, 2007). Similarly, GDACS was expanded to include global storm surge calculations associated with cyclones after the disasters of Katrina (2005, US), Nargis (2008, Myanmar) and Yasi (2011, Fuji and Australia). The in-house developed hydrodynamic model called Hyflux designed for dam break and nuclear accidents was adapted to model cyclone storm surges, with reliable and operational results (Probst and Franchello, 2012). Since then, it has been incrementally improved and radically redesigned based on operational experience (Probst and Annunziato, 2017).

Map of disaster alerts in the past 4 days. Last 24 hours events are highlighted in yellow. Small earthquakes are shown as green boxes. European Union, 2015. Map produced by EC-JRC. The boundaries and the names shown on this map do not imply official endorsement or acceptance by the European Union.

The Global Disaster Alert and Coordination System is the result of over 15 years of collaboration between scientists and practitioners

Coordination Centre in 2013 (European Commission, 2018). We continue to deliver and improve, including through a networked approach with academia and industry (Fonio and Annunziato, 2018), most of the crisis management systems though a virtuous feedback loop between new research and the challenging environment of real crisis management. Innovation requires a constant interaction among scientists, practitioners and, crucially, the **private sector**, which can turn experimental ideas into reliable knowledge services. The **Copernicus Emergency Management Service** must be considered a major success story of this trilateral partnership in the EU. Originating in research, in 2014, it became an operational service that is contracted out to an ecosystem of European industry.

Right Information, Right Time, Right Format, Right Place

In most cases, science advice is not a challenge of lack of knowledge but rather of abundance of knowledge (Boersma et al., 2017). Scientists must learn what information to provide to whom at what time and in what format, so the information is directly relevant in the decision-making process of practitioners. In crisis management, this is often a daily or ad hoc briefing where strategic and tactical challenges are discussed. We have provided such advice for over a decade and have learned some lessons on timeliness, clarity and uncertainty.

> *Scientists must learn what information to provide to whom at what time and in what format, so the information is directly relevant in the decision-making process of practitioners.*

Timeliness: For sudden-onset disasters, such as earthquake and tsunamis, speed is of the essence. The **Copernicus Emergency Mapping Rapid Mapping Service** (http://emergency.copernicus.eu/mapping/) is the operational outcome of years of research at JRC (Al Khudhairy et al., 2009; Corban et al., 2011) and in EU research programmes (e.g., SAFER project) on how to speed up the acquisition, processing and delivery of satellite-based mapping products. With delivery times less than 24 h, the Copernicus service now provides useful evidence during crises. Having access to science advice under predictable service level agreements is important.

Following this example, our ad hoc science advice during emergencies is now being turned into a similar service: the **European Natural Hazard Scientific Partnership**. This service aims to bundle competences from several Member States to provide an EU-wide science advice service and will ensure scientists are available 24/7 in case of need. It is a service that is complementary to the science advice mechanisms of Member States (De Groeve and Casajus Valles, 2015).

Clarity: There is no need to communicate the full scientific complexity of a situation to make a decision on how to manage the crisis. On the contrary, an overload of information can be counterproductive and lead to bad decisions. Science advice is most effective if translated into clear and concise bullet point style information. For example, together with DG ECHO, we provide a daily overview of the main disasters (**ECHO Daily Flash**, https://erccportal.jrc.ec.europa.eu/ECHO-Flash) as well as a daily map to illustrate the most important event of

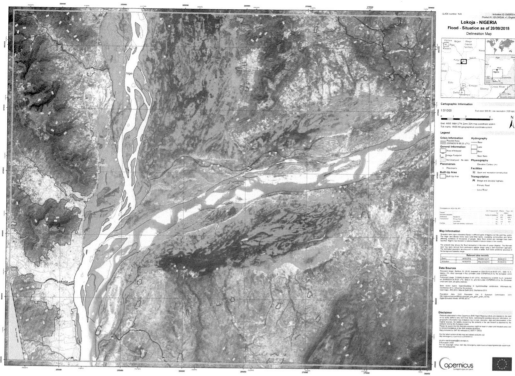

Example of a map produced by the Copernicus rapid mapping service during severe floods in Nigeria in September 2018.

the day (**ECHO Daily Map**). These products are the result of years of fine-tuning the translation of science into action-oriented briefs.

Uncertainty: Even with the best science, no model or expert can know the future completely. Communicating probabilities, degrees of certainty and gaps in knowledge is a challenging task as decision-makers prefer a world in black and white. A good practice on communicating uncertainty in clear and useful graphics is the **European Flood Awareness System** (EFAS, https://www.efas.eu). EFAS forecasts of extreme floods are complex. Uncertainty of an ensemble of meteorological forecasts, meteorological and hydrological observations and land surface information is propagated through a deterministic hydrological model to assess the likely impact. The uncertainty of the resulting flood forecasts is visualised in graphs that allow users to understand reliability and consistency of forecasts at a glance.

A Map Is a Thousand Words

Delivering science advice to a policymaker or a practitioner is a nontrivial task. Facts alone, without context or interpretation, are not enough to create meaning in the mind of the decision-maker. Instead, communication of science needs clear narrative (Allen et al., 2017): how does this disaster compare to the previous one? Is this the worst ever, and is there a trend? How likely is this disaster to be influenced by climate change? Where is this disaster happening? How will affected people cope?

We have built extensive expertise in building narratives using maps, in particular in the area of crisis and emergency mapping. Modern geographical information systems allow combining many different datasets in a single map, overlaying layer over layer. Maps not only present information geographically but also can show evolution in time, historical background, thematic information and context information. JRC teams collect and triangulate open-source data and subsequently represent them in maps. To facilitate map reading, it is important to use consistent templates, styles and symbology, preferably following **internationally agreed practice** (e.g., OCHA, 2012). We are defining mapping standards for the Copernicus Emergency Management Service (Broglia et al., 2010, 2013), and we are collaborating with UN organisations to develop good practices, including coordination mechanisms to **avoid duplication** of efforts when several organisations make the same map (IWG-SEM, 2015).

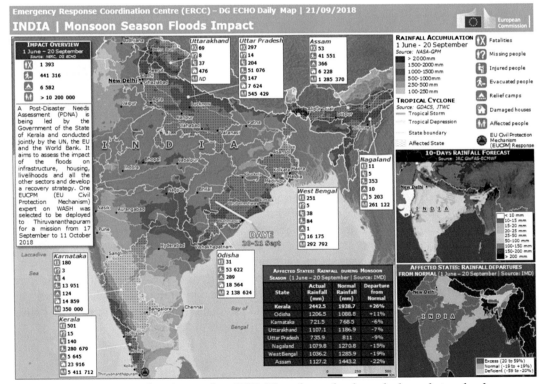

Example of Daily Map of 21 September 2018. Use of standard symbols and standard templates facilitates the integration of maps in standard operating procedures.

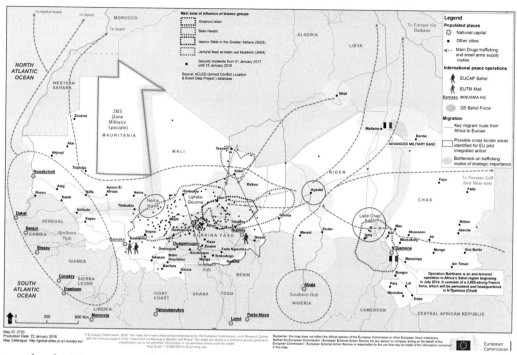

Example of crisis map over Sahel, part of the Science and Peace portal of the JRC.

Good Science Advice Is Built on a Foundation of Trust

No decision-maker will blindly trust advice. She or he will judge the value of the advice based on past experience of the advisor. **Trustworthiness** is built through frequent interaction and a history of good advice and met expectations. As disasters are rare events, such interaction can be forced through exercises or simulations. Tabletop exercises are excellent opportunities to introduce new science and tools in decision-making process at local, national or global level, as demonstrated recently in the Global Flood Partnership (Salamon et al., 2018), which led to the launch of the **GFP Support Service**. We are investing, together with research partners in the EU, in making such interactions more systematic (Fonio and Annunziato, 2018). In the DRIVER+ project, we lead the work on developing a **pan-European Testbed for crisis management** capability development enabling practitioners to create a space in which stakeholders can collaborate in testing and evaluating new products, tools, processes or organisational solutions.

Transparency is equally important, both for data and methods. Science advice should not be a black box, in particular for public policy where accountability towards the citizen is of primordial importance. On the contrary, science advice is best based on open data and open

Science advice should not be a black box, in particular for public policy where accountability towards the citizen is of primordial importance.

methods, which are reproducible and can be reviewed by peer scientists. One good example at JRC is advice based on the Global Human Settlement Layer (GHSL, https://ghsl.jrc.ec.europa.eu/), a **new open and free tool for assessing the human presence on the planet**. The data and methods were published early on (e.g., Pesaresi et al., 2016), its artificial intelligence algorithms produce explicit rules and a wide community of experts in the **Human Planet Initiative** (https://ghsl.jrc.ec.europa.eu/HPI.php) are vetting and developing the products. GHSL-derived information is now instrumental in urbanisation policy and also contributes to policies in sustainable development, disaster risk management and climate change.

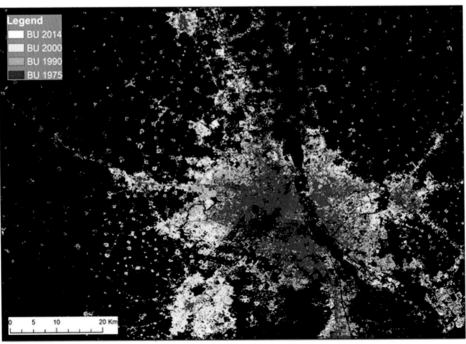

Example of the Global Human Settlement Layer for New Delhi, India, based on Landsat data. The colours illustrate the growth of the city from 1975 (red) to 2015 (white).

Transdisciplinary Learning Through Networking and Partnerships

No expert or single organisation can be sure to provide comprehensive science advice on everything. As a scientific organisation providing scientific advice, it is crucial to establish long-term partnerships with complementary organisations to leverage and exploit expertise and skills beyond the own organisation (UNISDR, 2016; Clark et al., 2017). For example, the Global Wildfire Information System (http://gwis.jrc.ec.europa.eu/) is a JRC-led initiative under the umbrella of the Group of Earth Observations that is bringing together existing information sources at regional and national level in order to have a comprehensive view and evaluation of fire regimes and fire effects at global level (San Miguel, 2017). We also champion the Global Flood Partnership (https://gfp.jrc.ec.europa.eu/), the Global Drought Observatory (http://edo.jrc.ec.europa.eu/gdo) and the Index for Risk Management (INFORM, http://www.inform-index.org/), each with a mix of scientific, practitioner and government members (De Groeve et al., 2015; Vogt et al., 2017; Marin Ferrer et al., 2017). These partnerships allow our scientists to learn efficiently from others and to build capacity of international partners by providing our own open-source tools and knowledge. Chapter 10 focuses on how to ensure that different interests common for partnerships do not jeopardise the quality of the science for policy work.

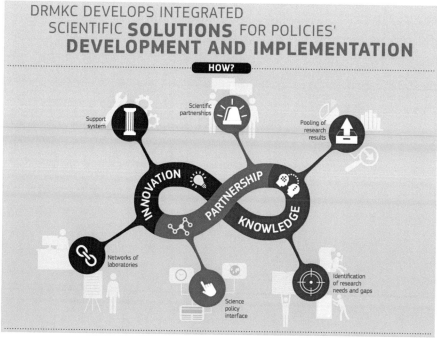

JRC's Disaster Risk Management Knowledge Centre (DRMKC) facilitates information and knowledge while enhancing the connection between science operational activities and policy

Even more important is to invest in building or participating in international and transdisciplinary networks to increase exposure to new knowledge and alternative views. This can start new conversations across boundaries of scientific disciplines, policy areas or international borders. The JRC's Disaster Risk Management Knowledge Centre (https://drmkc.jrc.ec.europa.eu/) is an excellent example of how this can work. The multifaceted Knowledge Centre enables thousands of participants in EU Member States to learn from each other and spread widely ideas, research results, good practices and opportunities for collaboration.

Whether it is for horizon scanning, foresight, long-term climate adaptation, mid-term disaster prevention or short-term emergency management, a broad understanding of the complex landscape of disaster risk management is the foundation for good science advice.

Image: Сергей Мироненко – https://stock.adobe.com/be_en/images/monkey-in-the-city-thinks-about-the-future-of-mankind/135973972?prev_url=detail
Icon in page corners: Monkey icon by parkjisun, from the Noun Project (https://thenounproject.com/search/?q=ape&i=912725)

Behavioural Insights for EU Policymaking

Author: René van Bavel

Key takeaways:

- Designing policies with the assumption that human behaviour is rational can lead to suboptimal results. Far better is to resort to a more nuanced understanding of behaviour, based on empirical evidence of how people actually behave.

- Behavioural insights can be applied throughout the policy cycle. They can help define a policy problem by identifying underlying causes of relevant behaviours, and

- Arriving at specific, relevant behavioural insights may require original empirical work. First, the research question will need to be defined tightly, followed by the choice of methodology (often randomised controlled trials (RCTs), experiments or qualitative research).

- Ultimately, behavioural insights are another tool for empirically based policymaking, complementary to existing tools. But they are also unique in that they can shed light on how decisions are taken in policymaking.

Science for Policy Handbook
http://dx.doi.org/10.1016/B978-0-12-822596-7.00017-6

Copyright © 2020 European Union,
Published by Elsevier Limited

Policymaking around the world has increased its attention to behavioural economics over the past decade. There is perhaps not one single cause for this, though there are a number of contributing factors. Disappointment with economics in the wake of the 2008 financial crisis, the publication of *Nudge* (Thaler and Sunstein, 2008), the subsequent appointment of its authors to top advisory positions in the US and UK government and the creation of the UK's Behavioural Insights Team all played a role. The European Union (EU) has also embraced behavioural economics, with its own approach to producing behavioural insights and embedding them in the EU policymaking process (Lourenço et al., 2016).

Behavioural *insights* are evidence-based conclusions about human behaviour in a given context. The behavioural *sciences* are all those disciplines that, through systematic observation and rigorous analysis, offer these insights. Most popular among them, in this behavioural turn in policymaking, is behavioural *economics*. This may have to do with the broader acceptance of economics in government circles. Psychology, which covers the same ground with a wider palette of methodological approaches, seems to have less policy appeal. As a result, it is sometimes branded as behavioural *science*. Anthropology, sociology, medicine, neuroscience and biology also contribute to our understanding of human behaviour.

This chapter outlines how behavioural insights can contribute to policy thinking generally and how they can be applied to the EU policymaking process specifically. They are not restricted to any particular policy area. As a general rule, wherever the effectiveness of a policy depends on human behaviour, behavioural insights will be relevant. Moreover, they are meant to complement – not compete with – other analyses. They simply contribute by adding a better understanding of behaviour. The chapter goes on to discuss the methodological options for arriving at these insights and what studies can be feasibly conducted to support EU policy.

Challenging the Assumption of Rationality

The best starting point for appreciating the contribution of behavioural insights is the assumption, explicit in economics and implicit in much of policy thinking, that human beings are rational. They maximise their well-being, or *utility* in the economics nomenclature, taking a number of variables into account and following a series of axioms. The assumption of rationality refers mainly to the outcome of decisions, not the process (i.e., a decision is considered rational if it maximises utility, regardless of how that decision was arrived at). Circumspect analysts might take this assumption with a grain of salt but will nevertheless adhere to it. It is useful for economic analysis.

However, as we know intuitively from observing our own behaviour and that of others, humans are far from rational. We exhibit consistent anomalies in our behaviour, oddities that cannot be properly explained by the assumption of rationality. These *biases and heuristics* have been identified through experimental studies and form the basis of behavioural economics (Kahneman and Tversky, 1979). They have been found to be consistent (i.e., they do not cancel each other out on aggregate) and widespread (i.e., the results have been replicated in different contexts). Formally recognising that we exhibit such biases and heuristics in our thinking invites further empirical exploration of how we actually behave.

The problem is that the literature is full of studies offering empirical evidence on behaviour. A quick search for cognitive biases on Wikipedia yields about 200 pages, from acquiescence bias to the well-travelled road effect. This includes popular biases in behavioural economics, such a loss aversion (losses loom larger than gains), as well as established findings in social psychology, such as the fundamental attribution error (other people's behaviour is attributed to dispositional factors, our own to situational factors). In the face of such a myriad of findings, what broad, reliable and useful insights can we apply to policymaking?

System 1 and System 2

The answer to this question may vary across disciplines. However, the distinction between System 1 and System 2 thinking is particularly helpful as a summary (Kahneman, 2011). People exhibit two ways of thinking. One (System 1) is characterised by being automatic, unconscious and frequent. It is prey to cognitive biases and strikingly prevalent in our everyday lives, accounting for about 95% of our thinking according to some estimates (Zaltman, 2003). For example, all the routine activities we do in the morning before arriving to work are governed by System 1. System 2, on the other hand, is reflective, slow, self-aware and infrequent. Solving a problem at work may require System 2 thinking. It calls for more effort than System 1.

In System 1 thinking, we rely on mental structures, or schemas, that select and process incoming information. These filter our perception of reality. We match the schema against incoming stimuli – if it is a good match, we impose the schema to have greater control over what we experience (Fiske and Taylor, 2013). If, on our way to work, we are approached by a stranger, we will quickly resort to our existing stock of schemas to evaluate him or her. Depending on how they look, the schema of 'commuter' or 'vagrant' may apply. Our schema-driven reaction to them will be largely preprogrammed and follow a certain behavioural script.

System 2, on the other hand, involves a much more data-driven process. The different elements of the incoming stimulus are evaluated afresh, without preconceived notions. We are generally reluctant to think in that way – it requires greater effort, and we have limited cognitive resources. We may resort to this kind of thinking only when needed, e.g., when the situation is new and there are no schemas to draw upon, and indeed, the distinction may not necessarily be discrete. It might not be the case of one or the other, but rather of thinking along a continuum, from more schema-driven to more data-driven.

Policy Implications

Why does the distinction between System 1 and System 2 matter and how is it relevant to policymaking? Because the design of many a policy initiative is based on the assumption that citizens routinely use System 2, whereas in fact, they may be using System 1. Take disclosure statements or product labelling: these assume that consumers will read and process and understand the implications of what they are buying or agreeing to. In fact, they are more likely to apply the shortcuts offered by System 1. This may explain why some of these policies have failed to meet their objectives.

What are some of the implications of designing policies expecting System 1 reactions? For one, we must challenge the assumption that more information is better. It is not about having *more* information, but *better* information, presented in a way that makes it easier for people to make a good decision. People are complicated, error-prone humans and not mindless information processing machines. Also we should not assume much 'rational' behaviour – in fact, we should not assume behaviour at all. There is no grand theory of behaviour (à la rational choice

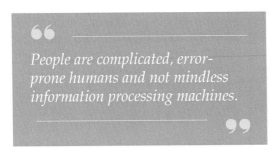

> *People are complicated, error-prone humans and not mindless information processing machines.*

theory). Rather, we should continuously rely on behavioural insights obtained by empirical observation.

The behavioural turn in policymaking has therefore two predominant characteristics. On the one hand, it is about applying a better understanding of the complexities of human behaviour into the policymaking process, rather than resorting to simplistic models. But it is also about systematically applying empirical methods to achieve this fuller understanding (Lunn, 2014). In other words, the key is not to assume behaviour, but to test it. It is a fundamental inversion, from a deductive, top-down approach to understanding human behaviour to an inductive, bottom-up approach.

How to Apply Behavioural Insights to Policymaking

Having introduced behavioural insights, the question arises: how can these be applied to policymaking in practice? What are the real-life implications for policymakers and for researchers seeking to produce policy-relevant results? In theory, behavioural insights can be applied to policymaking in any number of ways. For example, they can enrich the way citizens' behaviour is discussed in policy debates, which is already a significant contribution. However, for explicative purposes, it is useful to see how they contribute to different stages of the policy cycle (Troussard and van Bavel, 2018).

Problem Definition

Often human behaviour will lie at the core of a policy problem. It might be, for example, that farmers are not adopting new technologies (even if it is in their best interest to do so) or that social media users are failing to distinguish advertising from user-generated content (which might not be in their best interest). In these cases, behavioural insights can help de-

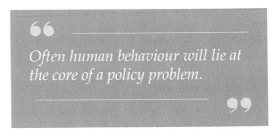

> *Often human behaviour will lie at the core of a policy problem.*

fine the problem by identifying possible underlying causes of behaviour. The solution might include some kind of behavioural insight or might just require straightforward regulation or economic incentives.

In the case of farmers, it might be that new technology leads to greater productivity on average over a number of years but makes bad years particularly bad. The principle of loss aversion suggests that losses loom larger than gains of equivalent value (e.g., the joy of winning €20 is less than the pain of losing €20). Therefore, farmers may be overweighing these potential losses when deciding whether to adopt the new technology. Policymakers might consider this explanation, test it and propose remedies which seek to address farmers' loss aversion specifically. They could, for example, combine programmes incentivising the uptake of new technology with risk management tools (Dessart et al., 2019).

Regarding social media users, they might be confused because advertisers are adept at concealing their products in user feeds. Ads no longer stand out and are disguised in posts that do not appear to be commercial (native advertising). Users who scroll down their user feeds in routine fashion are likely using their cognitively economical System 1 thinking, instead of their effortful System 2. This means that capturing users' attention and making them aware of the presence of advertising might require more sophisticated methods than simply informing them. Instead, regulatory action might be needed, such as updating the list of commercial practices that are explicitly prohibited (GfK Consortium, 2018).

Policy Design and Implementation

Behavioural insights can also be embedded in EU policy instruments. Take the case of energy labelling for electrical appliances, covered by an EU Regulation (European Union, 2017). A few years ago, technological advance in energy efficiency meant that some appliances reached energy efficiency levels of up to 'A+++' (previously the maximum rating was A). An experiment in a behavioural study showed that this scale was in fact suboptimal (London Economics, 2014). An 'A-to-G' scale, on the other hand, performed best among consumers, better than a numeric scale. The study also found that this kind of labelling was particularly important for products where energy efficiency was not the main concern for consumers.

Online gambling is another case in point. It became an important policy issue in Europe due to high levels of only gambling, the possible involvement of minors and indications of addictive behaviour. A behavioural study showed that trying to affect players' behaviour before they started playing was ineffective (Codagnone et al., 2014). Instead, measures needed to target players *while* they gambled, such as spending limits or alerts which interrupted the human–machine interaction. They were translated into principles to ensure the effective protection of consumers and were included in an EU Recommendation on on-line gambling (European Commission, 2014).

Policy initiatives that seek to influence behaviour through small changes to the environment in which people make a decision are *nudges* (Thaler and Sunstein, 2008). In the literature, these are often proposed as an alternative to more traditional approaches such as regulation, information provision or economic incentives. Depending on their jurisdiction, regional, national or supranational levels of governance will have different opportunities to nudge. In the case of the EU, these opportunities need to be sought out in collaboration with national and regional authorities.

An example of a highly effective nudge involves establishing the *default option*. The theory behind this is that, when presented with a choice, we are very likely to accept the default choice. This has been applied in areas such as pension plans and organ donation. If the default option is *not* to be enrolled in a private pensions plan or *not* to register as an organ donor, few people will. A simple change in the way the choice is presented, from opt-in to opt-out, has led to drastic increases in the number of people investing in a pension plan and registering as an organ donor.

Another very effective nudge is *simplification*. People have limited attention span and cognitive resources, especially in an age of information overload. Complexity creates confusion, increases costs and makes people reluctant to participate in important programmes (Sunstein, 2014). A very straightforward, often overlooked, nudge is to make programmes easy

> **Box 1:** Applying behavioural insights at the European Commission
>
> The European Commission has applied behavioural insights to a wide range of policy areas over the past 10 years. It began by recognising the power of default options in the Consumer Rights Directive in 2009, where it limited the use of prechecked boxes in consumer contracts. During that time, in a landmark case against Microsoft, the Commission relied on behavioural insights to arrive at a sensible solution for offering consumers a choice of Internet browser (the 'ballot box').
>
> These initial applications gave way to a more systematic approach, which included setting up a framework contract for the provision of behavioural studies. Over 30 large-scale behavioural studies have been conducted under this framework contract. Results from these studies have been integrated in a number of policy developments, in areas such as energy labelling, online gambling, packaged retail and insurance-based investment products, online marketing to children, consumer vulnerability, transparency of online platforms and online terms and conditions.
>
> Today, a behavioural approach is increasingly present in EU policymaking. For example, it is formally included in the better regulation guidelines and toolbox, for analysing the policy problem (Tool # 14), identifying policy options (Tool # 17) and assessing the impact on consumers (Tool # 32).[1] Informally, it is being incorporated into everyday policy discussions. This is partly not only because behavioural insights are appealing and make sense but also because the JRC has made a concerted effort to promote their application to policymaking (read more about the EU Policy Lab in Chapter 13). It routinely engages in dissemination activities, including a 2-day training course on behavioural insights offered to European Commission staff three times a year.
>
> [1] https://ec.europa.eu/info/law/law-making-process/planning-and-proposing-law/better-regulation-why-and-how/better-regulation-guidelines-and-toolbox/better-regulation-toolbox_en, accessed 05.05.20.

to understand and navigate. This should bring large rewards. Simplification has been applied, for example, in standardised forms for information on retail investment products, mandated by an EU Regulation (European Union, 2014). It has also been shown effective in a RCT looking at official communications from the Danish government to businesses (OECD, 2017).

Social norms complete the podium of examples of effective nudges. The premise behind this nudge is that people like to feel part of the majority. Highlighting what 'most people do', therefore, will lead people to behave accordingly. The more specific the behaviour and the more proximal the reference group, the more powerful the information will be. This nudge was proved effective getting people to reuse their towels in hotels (Goldstein et al., 2008) but has since been successfully applied to a number of policy areas, such as ensuring the prompt payment of taxes and combating overprescription of antibiotics by doctors (OECD, 2017).

Producing Behavioural Evidence

Having explained how behavioural insights can be applied to policymaking, the chapter now takes a methodological turn. From a research point of view, what are the methodological options available for producing and testing behavioural insights? The method will depend on the research question. Tightly defining the research question makes the choice of method straightforward and also increases the chances of having a successful behavioural study. A bad research question cannot lead to a good study (see more on this in Chapter 6).

Defining a Good Research Question

A necessary first step in defining a good research question is specifying the behaviour of interest. For example, a study which aims to identify the 'best way of communicating information about energy efficiency in a label' is too vague. Is the purpose of the label to increase comprehension of information or to attract attention? Perhaps, the intention is to persuade consumers to choose the most energy-efficient option, in which case their purchasing behaviour would be of interest, and not their immediate reaction to the label.

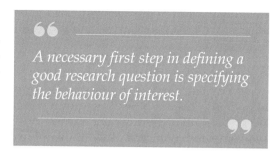

A necessary first step in defining a good research question is specifying the behaviour of interest.

The way in which results are expected to feed into the policymaking process is also a factor when formulating the research question. For example, 'why are minorities not motivated to apply to join the police force?' might invite a qualitative study where all the nuances of people's motivation are captured and described. But if results need to be immediately translated into policy remedies, a research question like 'what measures would increase the number of applications by minorities to the police force?' might be more appropriate. Notice here the presence of a measurable outcome (number of applications), inviting a quantitative analysis.

Methodological Options

In theory, a broad number of methodological approaches can be used to study behaviour. Following is a description of RCTs, experiments and qualitative research. Surveys are also a popular method and have been included in other accounts (van Bavel et al., 2013). But since they are a well-known method used across policymaking, they are not covered here.[2]

- *Randomised Controlled Trials*

In most countries where behavioural insights have taken hold, RCTs (or *field trials*) are the more popular method, as they offer demonstrable results from interventions in real-life settings among a sector of the population. However, policymaking at EU level has a number of characteristics that make lab and online *experiments* the method of choice. For one, there is the problem, mentioned earlier, that EU policy is often not at the front line of public service delivery. Public health and education, for example, are managed at the national or regional level in Europe. Implementing RCTs would therefore require collaboration with authorities at these levels of governance – feasible, but difficult.

Moreover, there is the problem of diversity. Unlike national or regional policies, EU policies have to be effective in 28 different member states. And results from RCTs are not necessarily transferable to other contexts (Cartwright, 2007). Interventions that work in Denmark might easily fail in Italy. Tackling this would imply running identical RCTs simultaneously in various countries and checking for differences. This is a tall order (which the JRC is nevertheless

---

[2] Also, surveys are not ideal for studying behaviour. They measure how people *talk* about behaviour (what they did or what they intend to do), but not actual behaviour. And they show what might correlate with this self-reported behaviour, but not necessarily what causes it.

attempting). Add to this the complication of running studies in a short time scale in order to dovetail with the policy cycle, and it becomes apparent that alternative methods needs to be relied upon.

- *Experiments*

Experiments are run in a laboratory or online, where two or more groups of people are compared with each other. One group is exposed to an intervention presumed to have an effect on behaviour, the other not (the 'control group'). The groups' behaviour is then measured and compared with each other. If there is a difference, it is attributed to the intervention, as everything else was kept exactly the same for both groups. In this way, the experiment can identify the variables that affect behaviour, going beyond correlation and establishing causality.

Experiments usually involve small samples. A mathematical procedure (i.e., a 'power analysis') will help determine the right sample size for each study. Although a balance is usually sought according to a couple of key sociodemographic characteristics, such as age and gender, these samples are not fully representative of the general population. Also, depending on the number of participants per group, the behaviour of some subgroups may or may not be analysed separately. First and foremost, experiments seek to uncover the existence of underlying psychological mechanisms that affect human behaviour. To know whether these are widespread in different contexts, the experiment would need to be replicated.

For supporting EU policy, experiments are useful. They do not require coordination with national or regional authorities, they can be conducted in a timely fashion to coincide with the policy cycle and they can take place in a number of countries to check for differences. The European Commission has been relying on such experiments for the past 10 years, covering a broad range of areas, from marketing practices in social media to the circular economy to warning labels in tobacco packages. Most experiments have been part of studies outsourced externally, but some have been conducted in-house by the JRC.

- *Qualitative Research*

Apart from experiments, qualitative methods have also proven useful. These include in-depth interviews, focus groups and participant observation, among others. They are different to experiments in their approach and fulfil a different purpose. For one, they do not seek to test hypotheses, but rather generate them. Their findings are not 'objective' (i.e., the perspective of the researcher must always be taken into account) or statistically generalisable. However, they offer a nuanced understanding of the meaning people associate to their actions, which is invaluable to understand why they behave in a certain way.

For example, taxes can be seen by citizens as their contribution to a state that offers public services in return, or they can be seen as a burden imposed by a corrupt and inefficient state. People's behaviour regarding taxes will likely be affected accordingly. Therefore, an intervention to make people pay their taxes might work on some people, but not others. Uncovering meaning is important, but not easy. It requires a rigorous, reflective and systematic process. Good qualitative evidence is not anecdotal.

Qualitative findings are complementary to experimental methods. By providing a richer description of behaviour and what lies behind it, they can help identify the interventions an experiment should test. This is particularly relevant in emerging areas of research where not much is known, such as children's behaviour on social media or reasons for consumers' willingness to buy new instead of repairing.

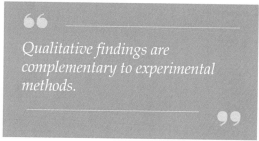

> Qualitative findings are complementary to experimental methods.

They can also follow-up on experimental results, providing explanations for unexpected or counterintuitive results.

Mainstreaming Behavioural Insights

What does the future hold for behavioural insights in a large public body institution like the European Commission? For one, they will continue to face scepticism by some and enthusiastic support by others. Sceptics will need to be reassured that behavioural insights do not pretend to replace traditional policy analysis tools – rather, they seek to complement them. Supporters, on the other hand, will need reminding that not all problems require a behavioural approach. Some just need decisive action based on tried-and-tested approaches like incentives and regulations. Behavioural scientists should be very clear when they believe a behavioural approach *should not* be applied to a problem.

Second, behavioural insights need to be applied introspectively to the policymaking process itself. Policymakers are also of flesh and bone and subject to biases and heuristics themselves. Take optimism bias, for example. When planning projects, there is a tendency to believe everything will go well, on time and within budget. In reality, things tend to work out rather differently. Applying behavioural insights to policy necessarily implies being reflexive about how people in government think and act, both individually and as part of a group.

Finally, the objective of integrating behavioural insights in policymaking will end when we stop talking about them as something distinct. Ideally, the analysis of any policy problem should include a reflection on behaviour, just as we now systematically consider cost, impact on well-being and whether these are equally distributed (for example). The behavioural turn in policymaking will be complete once behavioural insights are mainstreamed in the policy debate, to the degree that we may look back in wonder that they ever deserved special mention at all.

Image: DeCe - https://stock.adobe.com/be_en/images/group-of-different-pine-cones-isolated-on-white/238264138?prev_url=detail and cloud7days - https://stock.adobe.com/be_en/images/pine-cones-isolated-on-white-background/212650363?prev_url=detail
Icon in page corners: Conifer cone icon by arloenl evinniev, from the Noun Project (https://thenounproject.com/search/?q=pine%20cones&i=2213049)

The Use of Quantitative Methods in the Policy Cycle

Main authors: Giuseppe Munda, Daniel Albrecht, William Becker, Enkelejda Havari, Giulia Listorti, Nicole Ostlaender, Paolo Paruolo, Michaela Saisana

Contributors: Marcos-Dominguez-Torreiro, Leandro Elia, d'Artis Kancs, Sven Langedijk, Rossana Rosati, Eckehard Rosenbaum, Paul Smits, Daniel Vertesy, Ian Vollbracht

Key takeaways:

- The chapter presents a set of quantitative modelling approaches, connected to various steps of the policy cycle, that aim at being learning tools facilitating the dialogue among policymakers, scientists and different social actors.

- Quantitative policy modelling cannot provide exact answers, but it can help policymakers and all social actors involved by providing a scientific sound framework for a systematic, coherent and transparent analysis.

- Practical guidelines for structuring policy problems by using uncertainty and sensitivity analysis (SA), multicriteria decision analysis (MCDA), composite indicators and ex-post impact evaluation are provided.

- Uncertainty analysis (UA) and SA are quantitative 'Model Quality Assurance' techniques that provide information to understand uncertainty and ultimately enhance the quality of policy modelling.

- MCDA is the most widespread multidimensional approach to ex-ante impact assessment. The basic idea is that in comparing policy options, a plurality of technical dimensions and social perspectives is needed.

- Composite indicators are powerful practical tools that can help policymakers in summarizing complex and interdependent phenomena that are not directly observable and help the monitoring of their progress over time.

- Ex-post impact evaluation is used to measure the impact of policy changes on the ground. It is based on the 'what works?' approach to the policy cycle, in which the design of policy measures is guided by careful analysis that generates clear evidence of what has worked in the past.

Science for Policy Handbook
http://dx.doi.org/10.1016/B978-0-12-822596-7.00018-8

Copyright © 2020 European Union,
Published by Elsevier Limited.

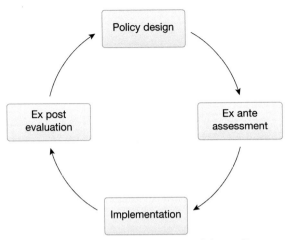

FIGURE 1 A simplified scheme of the policy cycle.

The real world is characterized by deep complexity. This apparently unremarkable observation has important implications for the manner in which policy problems are framed. A system is complex when the relevant aspects of a particular problem cannot be captured using one single perspective, thus any representation of a complex system reflects only a subset of its possible representations. This implies that for any policy modelling exercise,[1] there is a need to decide what is important for different social actors as well as what is relevant for the representation of the real-world entity described in the model (see, e.g., Frame and O'Connor, 2011; Jerrim and de Vries, 2017).

When a public administration wishes to implement policies, there is a previous need of comparing different options to assess their social attractiveness. This is the traditional scope of welfare economics and decision theory which is grounded in the use of theoretical models helping the definition of the intended effect of policy interventions in question (see, e.g., Dasgupta, 2001). However, theoretical models have their limits and can never *fully* capture reality in all of its complexity. Ultimately, policymaking is bounded by a reality check expressed by the simple question: *what worked and for whom?* To answer this question, the design of policy measures should be guided by careful analysis that generates clear evidence of what has worked in the past. Quantitative impact evaluation aims at measuring the impact of policy changes on the ground.

Of course, policy assessment and evaluation is not a one-shot activity. On the contrary, it takes place as a learning process that is usually highly dynamic, so that judgments regarding the political relevance of items, alternatives or impacts may present sudden changes, hence requiring a policy analysis to be flexible and adaptive in nature. This is the reason why assessment/evaluation processes have a cyclic nature. By this is meant the possible adaptation of elements of the process due to continuous feedback loops among the various steps and consultations among the actors involved. The policy cycle is usually described as the circular phases of policy design, ex-ante impact assessment, implementation and ex-post impact evaluation (see Fig. 1).

Obviously, the learning process that takes place while analyzing the issue and defining policies will itself influence perceptions and alter significantly the decisional space in which alternative strategies are chosen. At the other end, institutional and cultural representations of the same system, while also legitimate, are on their own insufficient to define what should be done in any particular case.

Funtowicz and Ravetz have shown that these concerns were not considered very relevant by scientific research as long as time was considered an infinite resource. On the other hand, the new nature of the problems faced in this third millennium implies that, when dealing with problems that may have long-term consequences, policy analysis and modelling is confronting issues 'where facts are uncertain, values in dispute, stakes high and decisions urgent'

---

[1] Throughout this chapter the term 'model' is referring to any quantitative approach to policy analysis.

(Funtowicz and Ravetz, 1990, 1991). Clearly ethical connotations are there; this implies that people, social scientists and governments differ significantly on what they consider to be an important policy issue, dimension, etc. As a consequence, values by which a society wishes to live cannot be relinquished to the preferences of an elite but need to be subject of extended dialogue with all constituencies (Benessia and Guimarães Pereira, 2015). Therefore, there is a need to invite the relevant constituencies into conversations about meanings and representations of policies, and the ethics and social practices that need to be fostered.

This chapter presents a set of quantitative modelling approaches that are designed and used within European Union (EU) policymaking processes, and beyond, with the objective of helping real-world policy processes without the ambition of being exhaustive; on the contrary, they aim at being learning tools to be used to facilitate the dialogue among policymakers, scientists and different social actors. Although they cover a wide spectrum of scientific approaches and can be used in different steps of the policy cycle, all of them have the common characteristic of being tools for boosting effectiveness, consistency and transparency of the policy process. Section 2 focuses on the issue of model transparency, Section 3 introduces quantitative approaches related to uncertainty and SA, Section 4 illustrates MCDA, Section 5 presents composite indicators, Section 6 is devoted to ex-post impact evaluation and finally in Section 7 some conclusions are drawn.

Model Transparency

Transparency is defined here as the extent to which external actors are afforded access to information about the way public organizations operate (Cucciniello et al., 2017: 36). The transparency and reproducibility of scientific evidence underpinning policy is crucial to build and retain trust. With respect to models, transparency serves to improve the understanding of the workings of a model and how it behaves in different contexts and for different policy measures. But it may also help to validate a model and test its behaviour. In addition, greater transparency of appropriately designed and tested models may also encourage a more widespread use of impact assessments at later stages of the policymaking process and thereby contribute to better regulation.

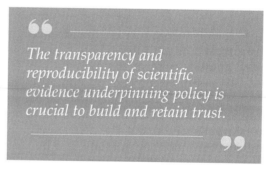

> " The transparency and reproducibility of scientific evidence underpinning policy is crucial to build and retain trust. "

Maintaining an overview of ongoing modelling activities is an elementary first step for a more transparent and coherent use of models in the policy cycle. It is, however, also a major challenge: For example, in the European Commission, more than 200 models are applied within various policy departments and services with hundreds of scientific and administrative users in various countries. The list of domains ranges from greenhouse gas (GHG) emissions, energy consumption and economy to structural integrity assessment, to name but a few. In addition, the majority of these models run in combination with other models. Thus, they form networks of interaction, further complicated by the related input datasets and assumptions. It is clear that capturing this knowledge, and communicating it in an understandable manner, will not only foster reproducibility and transparency of model use but also enable collaborative, interdisciplinary research that serves cross-policy issues.

In order to address some of these challenges, the corporate modelling inventory and knowledge management system, MIDAS contains descriptions of models previously or currently in use in support of the EU policy cycle (Ostlaender et al., 2015). One of the starting points of MIDAS was a particular case, where the question was raised whether models used in combination to answer a specific policy question were actually based on the same underlying datasets. As it turned out, answering this question was not that straightforward. In order to better understand how models are used, MIDAS therefore puts these models in their scientific and policy context, by asking the experts to link them to other models, to data, to domain experts, and publications, and to supported policies. In this manner, we are creating a network of thousands of relationships, documenting and preserving model knowledge and use.

To effectively communicate the resulting complex network to a nontechnical audience, MIDAS relies on 'the simple power of good visualization tools to help untangle complexity and just encourage you to ask questions you didn't think of before' (Berlow, 2010).[2] Especially the latter we frequently experienced over the last years: Scientists and policymakers that are confronted with MIDAS visual aids, start to ask questions about the bigger picture of model use, enquire on relationships between models and data and discover interesting facts that can be found in second or third order relationships, and that are usually hidden to the human eye (Fig. 2).

All of these enhance the transparency of models, the traceability of model results and our understanding of the ongoing support within and across different domains. This makes MIDAS an important corporate tool to use, reuse and document models in a proper way.

Uncertainty and Sensitivity Analysis

In the modelling process, the modellers generally use model assumptions and take input data, from different sources such as sound theory, experts and stakeholders opinions, experience, intuition surveys, measurements, rule of thumb or merely a guess (lack of knowledge). At each step of this process, uncertainty comes into play and may be very significant.[3] UA and SA are statistical analysis methods taking this uncertainty into account. Intrinsically, the UA and SA information are of quantitative nature; UA quantifies the uncertainty at the inputs and the output(s) of a model, while SA identifies the factors (assumptions, variables, data, etc.) that influence the most the output(s) and by how much (see e.g., Cacuci et al., 2005; Helton et al., 2006; Saltelli et al., 2008). The steps involved are the following ones:

1. The modellers, the experts, the stakeholders and the UA–SA practitioners identify which assumptions and parameters to vary, and from experiments, estimations, physical bounds, developers, expert and stakeholders opinion, characterise the uncertainty for each selected input by assigning a value, a range, a probability distribution etc.,

---

[2] Berlow, E. (2010).Simplifying Complexity, TEDGlobal 2010, at http://www.ted.com/talks/eric_berlow_how_complexity_leads_to_simplicity, accessed 12 November 2018.

[3] Recently, Silberzahn et al. (2018) showed a study where 61 analysts used the same dataset to address the same research question. The study concluded that a significant variation in the results of analyses of complex data may be difficult to avoid, even by experts with honest intentions; as a consequence, transparency of key assumptions used is always needed.

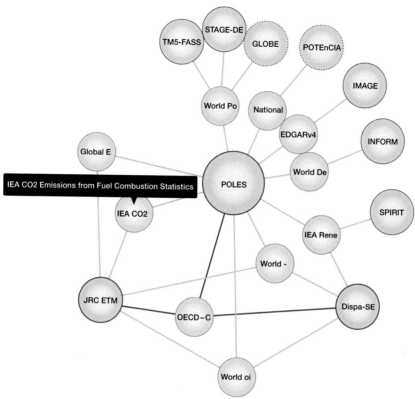

FIGURE 2 Example of datasets (in orange) which the model POLES (in the centre) shares with other models (in magenta).

2. The modellers, the experts, the stakeholders and the UA–SA practitioners define the output of interest of the model and the objectives of the SA,

3. SA practitioners generate randomly the input samples from the previously defined probability distributions (Monte Carlo[4]). The samples are generated so as to explore the whole space of uncertainty,

4. Modellers repeatedly run the model (Monte Carlo), using the values of the input variables dictated by the generated samples (scenario). For each run, they record the value of the output variable of interest,

5. SA practitioners calculate measures of uncertainty on the model output and the different sensitivity measures with respect to the input(s),

---

[4] Monte Carlo methods are based on reiterated random input generations. The random inputs are run through the model, and the associated output is recorded and analysed. From this uncertainty analysis, it is possible to infer valuable information about the behaviour of the model.

6. SA practitioners identify any major factor (assumption, variable, coefficient, etc.,) and examine the impact that these factors might have, namely their respective influence on the model output (ranking),

7. SA practitioners report the conclusions/inferences to the modellers, the experts and the stakeholders, for model improvement (model, data),

8. Together with the modellers, the experts, the stakeholders and the UA–SA practitioners will report to the policymaker on the quality of the model, and the credibility of the policy options and the related policy impact.

Overall, UA and SA give an increased understanding of the inner workings of the model, for example, the sensitivity measures can identify particularly sensitive assumptions and sometimes the uncertainty in these assumptions can be reduced, or an alternative model that does not rely on such assumptions can be built. However, in carrying out these practical steps, various caveats have to be considered, and above all, one has to remember that UA and SA concern with the internal validity of a model. Focusing on models' internal validity (e.g., the quality and quantity of the input parameters), they have little to say about the veracity of models. Veracity and validity are two different concepts; the former referring to the truth value of a model with reference to the real world and the latter referring to its logical consistency. A recent application of UA and SA to impact assessment modelling can be found in Pisoni et al. (2018).

At empirical level, UA and SA have proven to be essential when the quality of a model is an issue. Not only UA–SA techniques are strongly recommended by the Commission Better Regulations [SWD(2017), 350] as tools for modelling quality assurance but also the same techniques are adopted and included in the modelling guidelines of international agencies like the Intergovernmental Panel on Climate Change. The full potential of UA–SA is still little exploited by modellers and model users. This is often true in the field of impact assessment where the impact of uncertainty on the model output, the presumed impact of uncertainty on a policy option and thus its ranking may turn out to be significant particularly at the EU level.

Multicriteria Decision Analysis

The traditional welfare economics approach to ex-ante impact assessment is cost–benefit analysis that is grounded on market mechanisms; this implies that only the behaviour of individuals as consumers in one single institution, i.e., market, is considered. Is this fully acceptable in public policy? The Nobel Prize laureate A. Sen (2009, p. 239) gives the following answer: '... *there is such a long tradition in parts of economics and political philosophy of treating one allegedly homogeneous feature (such as income or utility) as the sole 'good thing' that could be effortlessly maximized (the more the merrier), that there is some nervousness in facing a problem of valuation involving heterogeneous objects, ... And yet any serious problem of social judgement can hardly escape accommodating pluralities of values, ... We cannot reduce all the things we have reason to value into one homogeneous magnitude'.*

The most widespread multidimensional approach to ex-ante impact assessment is MCDA (see, e.g., Arrow and Raynaud, 1986; Ishizaka and Nemery, 2013; Keeney and Raiffa, 1976; Roy, 1996). The basic methodological foundation of MCDA is incommensurability, i.e., the notion that in comparing options, a plurality of technical dimensions and social perspectives is needed

(Munda, 2016). MCDA builds on formal modelling techniques serving the purposes of decision and policymaking; its basic idea is that in assessment problems, one has to first establish objectives, i.e., the direction of the desired changes of the world (e.g., maximize profits, minimize environmental impact, minimize social exclusion, etc.) and then find useful practical criteria, which indicate the consistency between a policy option and a given objective. As a consequence, MCDA and in particular social multicriteria evaluation (SMCE), which has been explicitly designed for public policy, are very useful methodological and operational frameworks (Munda, 2008). In this framework, mathematical models aim at guaranteeing consistency between assumptions used and

FIGURE 3 Main characteristics of SMCE.

results obtained. This is a key success factor since multicriteria mathematics does answer to the standard objection that the aggregation of apples and oranges is impossible in a definitive way.

As a tool for policy assessment and conflict management, SMCE has demonstrated its usefulness in many real-world problems in various geographical and cultural contexts (see, e.g., Figueira et al., 2016). SMCE accomplishes the goals of being inter/multidisciplinary (with respect to the research team), participatory (with respect to the community) and transparent (since all criteria are presented in their original form without any transformations in money, energy or whatever common measurement rod) (see Fig. 3). In operational terms, the application of an SMCE framework involves the following main steps:

1. Description of the relevant social actors. For example, institutional analysis may be performed on historical, legislative and administrative documents to provide a map of the relevant social actors.

2. Definition of social actors' values, desires and preferences. In an SMCE framework, the pitfalls of the technocratic approach can be overcome by applying different methods of sociological research.

3. Generation of policy options and selection of assessment criteria as a process of cocreation resulting from a dialogue between analysts and social actors. In this way, criteria become a technical translation of social actors' needs, preferences and desires.

4. Construction of the multicriteria impact matrix synthesizing the scores of all criteria for all policy alternatives, i.e., the performance of each option according to each criterion.

5. Construction of an equity impact matrix, including all the distributional consequences of each single option on the various social actors.

6. Application of a mathematical procedure in order to aggregate criterion scores and obtain a final ranking of the available alternatives.

7. Finally, sensitivity and robustness analysis look at the sensitivity of results to the exclusion/inclusion of different criteria, criterion weights and dimensions. While such analysis may look very technical, in reality a social component is always present too. That is, inclusion/exclusion of a given dimension, or set of criteria, normally involves a long story of social, political and scientific controversy and involves social values and social actors.

These steps are not rigid; problem structuring may vary a lot across different real-world problems.

Monitoring Progress Through Composite Indicators and Scoreboards

Hardly any newspaper can resist the temptation of including a reference to an international country ranking. With the same 'apparent' ease and simplicity that football teams are ranked according to their performance, countries are ranked according to their ability to provide a high standard of living, competitiveness, and an attractive business environment. The rankings' use by global institutions (World Bank, EU, World Economic Forum, OECD, International Monetary Fund) has further captured the attention of the media and policymakers around the globe, and their number of applications has surged ever since. The appeal of the reported rankings lies in their simplicity and in their power to act as advocacy tools.

Composite indicators can be powerful practical tools that can help policymakers summarise complex and interdependent phenomena that are not directly observable, such as competitiveness, freedom of press or climate hazards. They provide the big picture, are easy to interpret, easy to communicate and attractive for the public. The resulting figures facilitate country, region or city comparisons and benchmarking. They help monitoring progress over time and evaluate ex-ante policy options based on multicriteria analysis. Scoreboards of indicators have, to some extent, similar objectives to composite indicators, yet they do not consist of a mathematical aggregation of data.

Indexes and scoreboards are also drivers of behaviour and of change by forcing institutions and governments to question their standards (Kelley and Simmons, 2015). The literature often describes the example of the Human Development Index (HDI), which has received a vast amount of criticism since its creation due to the arbitrariness of its methodological framework. However, it is the most well-known composite index to date. Moreover, it led the 1998 Nobel Prizewinning economist A. K. Sen, once one of the main opponents of aggregation, to change his position due to the attention that the HDI attracted and the debate that it fostered afterwards. A. K. Sen characterised it as a 'success' on drawing attention to human development, beyond looking at GDP alone, that would not have happened in the case of nonaggregation. Another similar example is the development of the Global Slavery Index by the Walk Free Foundation, which aims at drawing attention to a hidden and everyday problem: the confronting reality that even in the present day, men, women and children all over the world remain victims of modern slavery.

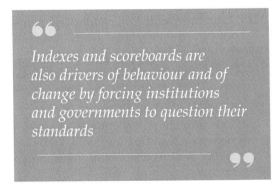

> *Indexes and scoreboards are also drivers of behaviour and of change by forcing institutions and governments to question their standards*

The increase of composite indicators over the past 20 years is exponential, and the number of yearly publications shows no sign of a decline. Nevertheless, this increase in the index popularity has underlined a key issue: the need for the index interpretation and consolidation. An example of the criticism surrounding the use of composite indicators comes from the Economist. Performance indicators are popular, influential and, if not flawed, then at least subjective and easy to manipulate: get rid of them. This was the main message of two articles in the Economist back in 2014.[5] The truth is that we are still far from settling the disputes and the criticism concerning the stages of the construction process. This is natural, as there are many stages in the development of a composite indicator and criticism could grow simultaneously regarding each of them. Moreover, if the procedure followed is not clear and not reasonably justified to everyone, there is considerable room for manipulation of the outcome.

One cannot disagree that there are composite indicators out there that are not of sufficient quality. But this should not imply that composite indicators should altogether be dropped from informing policy and public debates. Undoubtedly, the one-number-per country practice may send misleading or partial policy messages because of poor construction or misinterpretation (Hoyland and Moene, 2012). This is why it is important that one **systematically assesses the relevance, added-value and quality of existing (or new) composite indicators**. In this respect, there exist some principles of good practice that would allow the users of these 'statistical artefacts' to gauge their quality:

(a) a handbook on composite indicators (OECD/JRC, 2008) offering a ten-step process guide that aims to enhance the transparency and the soundness of the process; (b) SA offering tools to assess the extent to which a composite indicator is volatile to the specificities of its underlying assumptions (see e.g., Becker et al., 2017; Saisana et al., 2005); (c) sensitivity auditing assessing whether and to what extent models (including composite indicators) conform to the scientific standards of accessibility, transparency and reproducibility (Saltelli et al., 2013) and (d) a plethora of audits of international indices conducted upon request of the index developers, and many inspiring articles offering methodological advances in the field. Taken together, these tools, best practices and lessons learnt at least facilitate a public debate based on explicit reasoning in which composite indicators and scoreboards play a role.

The 10-step guide and checklist starts with the development of a conceptual framework that is relevant, easy to remember and apply. In steps 2 and 3, guidance is offered on how to select suitable indicators that meet key criteria and how to conduct analysis to inspect, clean, transform and model data. Step 5 is about normalization that aims at mapping data on a common scale. Steps 5 and 6 are about weighting indicators to allow for more balanced decisions and about aggregating data to reliably synthesize the maximum amount of information. Step 7 measures the statistical coherence of the framework through statistical control tests that help to ensure that information is not lost in aggregation. Step 8 relates to assessing the impact of the assumptions/decisions on the final outcome by means of robustness and SA. Step 9 zooms into the underlying data in order to help interpreting the final results. Finally, step 10 offers suggestions on how to visualise, interpret and communicate the results. Fig. 4 illustrates the 10 steps and an example regarding steps 7 and 8.

The main pros and cons of using composite indicators are the following (see Box 1).

---

[5] http://www.economist.com/news/international/21631039-international-comparisons-are-popular-influentialand-sometimes-flawed-ranking-rankings; http://www.economist.com/news/international/21631025-learn-ruses-international-country-rankings-how-lie-indices.

1. Framework

How to develop a conceptual framework that is relevant, easy to remember and apply

2. Data selection

How to select suitable indicators that meet key criteria

3. Data treatment

How to conduct analysis to inspect, clean, transform and model data

4. Normalisation

How to map data on a common scale

5. Weighting

How to weigh data to make more balanced decisions

6. Aggregation

How to aggregate data to reliably synthesise the maximum amount of information

7. Statistical coherence

How to use quality control tests to ensure that information is not lost in aggregation

8. Robustness and sensitivity

How to assess the impact of the assumptions

SSI categories	SSI Indicators	I	II	III
I. Basic Needs	Sufficient food	0.82	0.71	0.59
	Sufficient to drink	0.90	0.72	0.58
	Safe sanitation	0.97	0.79	0.64
II. Health	Healthy life	0.87	0.87	0.70
	Clean air	0.75	0.87	0.62
	Clean water	0.40	0.68	0.52
III. Personal & Social development	Education	0.80	0.82	0.71
	Gender equality	0.47	0.57	0.52
	Income distribution	0.35	0.37	0.81
	Good governance	0.62	0.76	0.76

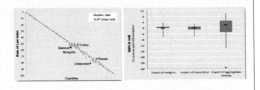

✓ Assess if an indicator dominates the framework [(correlation between indicator and index) > 0.95]

✓ Assess if an indicator behaves as "noise" in the framework [-0.3 < (correlation between indicator and aggregates) < 0.3]

✓ Assess if an indicator is lost in the aggregation [(correlation between indicator and index) < 0.3]

✓ Assess if indicators behave as trade-offs in the index [(correlation between indicator and index) < -0.3]

✓ Identify the sources of uncertainty in the index development and assess their impact to the index scores or ranks

✓ Complement aggregate scores/ranks with confidence intervals and consider policy guidance based on country groups than exact ranks

✓ Identify which uncertainties are more crucial in determining the results (why certain countries notably improve or deteriorate their performance given the assumptions)

✓ Do not confuse robustness with quality

9. Back to the data

How to make the most of an index by looking back at the data

10. Visualisation and Communication

How to visualise, interpret and communicate results

FIGURE 4 The 10-step guide for constructing a composite indicator.

Ex-Post Evaluation

Ex-post impact evaluation aims at answering questions of the type: 'What is the added value of the policy intervention?' This question cannot be fully answered by qualitative, process or monitoring evaluations because these approaches lack the ability to identify a causal effect; answering this type of question requires specific methods and data.

Box 1: Pros and Cons of Composite Indicators	
Pros	**Cons**
• Can summarise complex, multidimensional realities with a view to supporting decision-makers. • Are easier to interpret than a battery of many separate indicators. • Can assess progress of countries over time. • Reduce the visible size of a set of indicators without dropping the underlying information base. • Thus make it possible to include more information within the existing size limit. • Place issues of country performance and progress at the centre of the policy arena. • Facilitate communication with general public (i.e., citizens, media, etc.) and promote accountability. • Help to construct/underpin narratives for lay and literate audiences. • Enable users to compare complex dimensions effectively.	• May send misleading policy messages if poorly constructed or misinterpreted. • May invite simplistic policy conclusions. • May be misused, e.g., to support a desired policy, if the construction process is not transparent and/or lacks sound statistical or conceptual principles. • The selection of indicators and weights could be the subject of political dispute. • May disguise serious failings in some dimensions and increase the difficulty of identifying proper remedial action, if the construction process is not transparent. • May lead to inappropriate policies if dimensions of performance that are difficult to measure are ignored.

For instance, to quantify the impact of a training programme on employment, one can compare the employment status of participants to the training programme, the treated group, with the one of a group similar in all respects to the participants, but which was not exposed to the training, the so-called control group. In controlled experiments, units are either assigned to treatment or given a placebo at random. The comparison between treated and control groups is useful to disentangle the causal effect of the policy from additional factors that may occur in parallel and influence the outcome of interest, but in a manner that is not due to the policy.

The comparison with the control group is an example of how to construct a *counterfactual* outcome, which is defined as the outcome that *would have occurred without the policy intervention*. This type of evaluation, called counterfactual impact evaluation (CIE), is used to measure the causal effects of an intervention on a given outcome.

Causal evaluations require data of the appropriate granularity and appropriate methodology. In fact, in order to find a valid counterfactual, data on single individuals, firms or local level of government are usually needed; these data are called microdata, as opposed to macrodata. Data of different granularities are good for different policy evaluation purposes. Microdata are especially fit for finding evidence of policy impacts at the individual level, while aggregate data are useful for studying macroeconomic (or general equilibrium) effects.

Microdata can come from surveys or from other sources, like administrative records. These are usually collected for administrative purposes by governments or other public administration agencies in the course of their regular activities; examples include data on income collected in tax declarations, data on wages and employment collected by social security, data on education collected by Ministry of Education, etc. During the past 20 years, interest in administrative data for social research and policy evaluation has increased exponentially (see e.g., Poel et al., 2015; Card et al., 2010).

Microdata from different sources can be linked together; for instance, income data on a single individual can be linked to her/his education record coming from the registry in the Ministry of Education. Linked microdata offer several advantages: they are relatively inexpensive, they are typically of good quality and they usually provide information on large sets of individuals (units) for which statistical inference works well, see Crato and Paruolo (2019). Full respect for the legal safeguards for handling personal data is essential in this area of research and analysis. The General Data Protection Regulation, which came into force in May 2018, sets out the legal rules in force in the EU.

The major CIE techniques in current use are difference-in-differences (DiD), regression discontinuity design (RDD), instrumental variables (IVs) and propensity score matching. They are briefly reviewed below; see Imbens and Wooldridge (2009) and Imbens and Rubin (2015) for more details.

DiD: This CIE technique estimates the average treatment effect by comparing the changes in the outcome variable for the treated group with those for the control group, possibly controlling for other observable determinants of the outcome variables. Because it compares the changes and not the attained levels of the outcome variable, this technique eliminates the effect of the potentially different starting points of the two groups. A basic assumption of DiD is the common trends assumption, namely that treated and control groups would show the same trends across time in the absence of policy intervention. Hence, the change in the outcome variable for the control group can be used as an estimate of the counterfactual change in the outcome variable for the treated group (Box 2).

RDD: This CIE technique allows one to estimate the impact of a programme when participation in the programme depends on a rule or a threshold in any observed characteristics (e.g., age, income). Consider, for instance, a training programme that targets individuals below a given age. In this setting, to assess the impact of the programme on the employment status or wages, one can compare the outcomes of the marginal beneficiaries and nonbeneficiaries on either side of the threshold. RDD assumes that individuals on either side of the threshold but close to it are similar in terms of observed and unobserved characteristics. The size of the jump in the outcome of interest determines the impact of a programme. Since the observations that contribute to identifying the causal effect are those around the threshold, RDD may require large sample sizes, so it is not always easy to implement it. Furthermore, RDD identifies a local effect around the threshold, and in order to extrapolate the effect away from the threshold, stronger assumptions are needed to detect the effect (Box 3).

IVs: This CIE technique, known as IVs uses information from an observable variable, called the instrument, which predicts the assignment of units to the policy intervention (determines participation) but does not have other direct impacts on the outcome of interest, i.e., the instrument impacts the outcome variable only through its influence on the treatment status (Box 4).

Propensity score matching: This CIE technique has become a standard tool when evaluating the impact of participating in Active Labour Market Policies on participants' employment

---

Box 2: Example of an application of the DiD

Consider an impact evaluation of some regulations aimed at reducing the level of airport charges. Assume that for some reasons only one group of airports (treated group) was exposed to the regulation, while a second group of airports (control group) was not. One should not look at the average level of airport charges once the regulation is in place because the starting values for the airport charges in the two groups may be different. The DiD approach instead compares the magnitudes of the *changes* in the average level of airport charges in the two groups of firms. This gives an estimate of the impact of the regulation.

Fig. 5, taken from Conti et al. (2019), illustrates the effect of the implementation of the Airport Charges Directive. What emerges is that after the adoption, there is evidence of a significant decrease of the level of airport charges in treated airports compered to control ones.

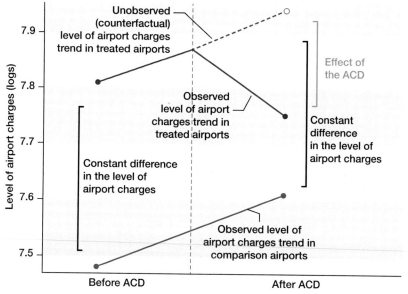

FIGURE 5 Illustration of the estimated Average Treatment Effect via DiD of the Airport Charges Directive in Conti et al. (2019).

---

prospect. The idea is to find a match for each participant in the programme (treated group) from the sample of individuals that did not participate in the programme. Matching occurs on basis of observed characteristics, such as age, gender, education, etc.

After creating all the matched couples, the effect is estimated by comparing the average of the outcome variable between the treated and control groups. Usually, individuals in the two groups are matched on the so called propensity score, which is the predicted probability of participation in the programme given the set of observed characteristics. This allows to reduce the complexity of the exercise, as one may run out of matches when increasing the number of observed characteristics used for the matching (Box 5).

Consider the Youth Guarantee (YG) programme in Europe, launched in 2014 to cope with the emergency of high unemployment rates among youth of age 15–29. For some programmes, priority to participation was given to registered unemployed youth aged below 25. In this setting, one can analyse the impact of a given programme financed under the YG by comparing the outcome (e.g., employment status) of the participants (those younger than 25) and nonparticipants (those older than 25).

For example, Bratti et al. (2018) evaluate the effectiveness of a vocational training (VT) programme on employment outcomes within the YG scheme in Latvia. Fig. 6, taken from this study, shows the estimated RDD impact of age on the probability to participate, with a clear discontinuity in the probability of participation at this training programme around age 25, normalised as age 0. RDD assumes a local randomisation around age 25. (Note that people cannot manipulate their age in order to participate in the programme.) The study then looks at the impact of participation in the VT programme on employment by comparing the employment status of individuals younger than 25 and those older than 25 exploiting rich administrative data.

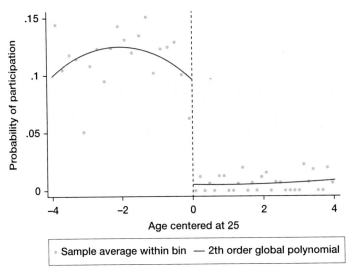

FIGURE 6 RDD estimate of the effect of age on the probability of participation to vocational training programme financed by the Youth Guarantee in Latvia, taken from Bratti et al. (2018). They study this effect as the first stage in the analysis of the effects of the programme on employment status.

In summary, counterfactual techniques typically provide causal inference by comparing a treated and a control group. When these groups are formed by random assignment or by other appropriate statistical techniques, the average impact of many extraneous factors, which might undermine the robustness of other assessment methodologies, is controlled for in the analysis. Counterfactual techniques provide a higher level of rigour to impact evaluation than other more descriptive analytical techniques. Counterfactual techniques can be combined with other econometric approaches to investigate which causal channels have been activated by the policy intervention, see Heckman (2010) and Heckman and Vytlacil (2007a,b).

> **Box 4**: Example of the application of instrumental variables
>
> A study by Martelli et al. (2018) uses IVs to understand whether the political commitment to reduce emissions at the municipal level undertaken by an incumbent mayor has an impact on the share of votes in the subsequent elections for the mayor's second term. In this study, political commitment is represented by the participation in the EU covenant of mayors (CoM), which is a mainstream European movement involving local authorities that decide to participate on a voluntary basis to meet the European target of GHG emissions under their mandate (−20% by 2020).
>
> Because participation in the CoM is voluntary, it is not possible to assume that participation to the programme is random, and one needs to deal with *selection bias* in programme participation. To solve this problem, the authors use an IV strategy and exploit the exogenous variation in the incentives to participate in the CoM given by the creation of a Covenant Territorial Coordinator (CTC), which is an entity offered by some provinces and regions. This is considered a good instrument because the creation of a CTC is expected to impact the probability to participate in the CoM by reducing its nonfinancial costs, but it should not affect the electoral outcomes in any other way. The authors find no reduction in the share of votes of the incumbent mayor who signed up for CoM.

> **Box 5**: Example of an application of the propensity score matching
>
> A recent study (Ghirelli et al., 2019) used this technique to evaluate the impact of an ESF-funded programme on employability and quality of the job (type of contract). The programme was a job training for registered unemployed graduates residing in the Italian region of Umbria. To estimate the impact of the programme, the study relies on matching graduates participating in the training with similar graduates that did not participate in the programme. To carry out the impact evaluation, the authors relied on administrative data on the whole population of registered unemployed graduates in the region.

The availability of data of a sufficiently granular level of detail is essential for the use of all of the counterfactual techniques described in this section. Where such data are not available, one may need to resort to other more aggregate (macro) techniques; however, this may render the effects of specific policies invisible to the analysis. On the other hand, macroanalysis may be useful to investigate general equilibrium effects.

Conclusions

In a recent Financial Times debate on the future of economics,[6] the main question was *'has economics failed?'* In general terms, everybody agreed that economics (and all quantitative policy analysis approaches) has developed many important tools to help real-world policymaking

---

[6] May 2018, more than 300 readers commented the initial debate between Tom Clark, editor of Prospect Magazine, and Chris Giles, the FT's economics editor.

although it is not an exact science, obviously. Quantitative modelling of policy problems cannot provide exact answers, but it can help policymakers and all social actors involved by providing a scientific sound framework for a systematic and transparent analysis.

In our opinion, in this context, 'evidence-based policy' does not mean that public policy is actually made on scientific evidence to the exclusion of all other considerations. It means that evidence from science and rigorous analysis should be used to the maximum extent possible, but of course within the wider constraints of legitimacy, politics and so on. Amartya Sen has raised the point that democracy to be effective in practice and needs a shared language of the public sphere, and this cannot be supplied by any specific single science.

Given that a complex real-world problem cannot be completely described by a model, since descriptive completeness and formal consistency are incompatible, it is essential to remember that a model always depends on the assumptions introduced to make the model relevant for a given policy problem, i.e., which representation of reality is used. Fairness in the policy process can be seen as an ethical obligation to take a plurality of social values, perspectives and interests into account in a coherent and transparent manner.

The responsible use of policy models requires some level of understanding of their limitations as well as their strengths. It is imperative that modellers devote efforts to explaining the assumptions underlying their work, margins of potential error and possible inconsistencies across different policy objectives. But it is also crucial that those formulating policy based on modelling inputs do so in an appropriate manner. Models and model results can of course be 'appropriated' by policymakers to support preordained objectives. In light of this, a two-way dialogue between modellers and model output users would seem to offer the greatest scope for responsible use of models in the policy process.

Image: BrunoWeltmann - https://stock.adobe.com/be_en/images/green-chameleon-on-bamboo/38526513?prev_url=detail
Icon in page corners: Chameleon icon by archivecto, from the adobe (https://stock.adobe.com/be_en/images/icon-chameleon-flat-symbol-chameleon-isolated-black-sign-chameleon-on-white-background-vector-illustration/200404411?prev_url=detailTerritorial policies)

19 Place-Based Solutions to Territorial Challenges: How Policy and Research Can Support Successful Ecosystems

Authors: Albane Demblans, Manuel Palazuelos Martínez, Carlo Lavalle

Key takeaways:

- 'One-size-fits-all' solutions cannot effectively grasp the complexity and the diversity of territories, which calls for deeper granularity of interventions at international, national and subnational level.

- Place-based approaches offer a relevant instrument to policymakers and researchers to address the challenges of an increasingly 'glocal' world, where globalisation is combined with a growing importance of local issues.

- Four main success factors stand at the core of place-based initiatives, as a way to impact on policymaking:

    - Smooth multiactor and multilevel governance;

    - Design of a strategic vision for the territory, building on its current capacities and forward-looking capabilities;

    - Cocreation, thanks to the mobilisation of all relevant actors from the public and private sector;

    - Use of participatory instruments as a facilitator and cement between the stakeholders involved.

- In the European Union (EU), Smart Specialisation and Territorial Impact Assessments exemplify the valuable role of place-based narratives to inform policies.

- Beyond the EU, localised practices are also gaining prominence, notably in relation to sustainable development.

Copyright © 2020 European Union,
Published by Elsevier Limited

Since their origin in the 1960s, place-based approaches have developed as a valuable tool for providing scientific evidence to policymaking. In a 21st century marked by a high degree of diversity, 'one-size-fits-all' policies cannot function effectively. Place-based logics are able to integrate territorial specificities, in order to formulate tailor-made solutions to challenges and thereby nurture policies. In this respect, initiatives in favour of territorial development in general, and the example of Smart Specialisation in particular, showcase to what extent a place-based logic can successfully inform policymaking, through a strong interaction between the universe of research and that of policy. The inspirational impact of Smart Specialisation, which increasingly fosters decentralised innovation policies in Europe, and even beyond, precisely shows the strong potential of place-based solutions to tackle territorial challenges.

In the endeavour towards providing scientific evidence to policymakers, place-based solutions to territorial challenges feature among promising tools to formulate relevant advice. Similarly to choosing the right lens for a camera, working with the proper territorial focus is a vital ingredient for a good understanding of to-day's and tomor-row's challenges, which is in turn crucial for designing relevant policies. The current context is that of a complex world, increasingly global but at the same time

PLACE-BASED SOLUTIONS ARE DESIGNED FROM THE TERRITORIES AND FOR THE TERRITORIES

> *In the endeavour towards providing scientific evidence to policymakers, place-based solutions to territorial challenges feature among promising tools to formulate relevant advice*

made up of a patchwork of territories where 'one-size-fits-all' answers are not optimal to address country-, region- or city-specific matters. The logic of intervention thus needs to respond to the motto of 'Think global, act local'. In this respect, place-based solutions, particularly subnational ones, have a role to play in reconciling regional and local distinctive features with the importance to make the most of globalisation and to integrate into global value chains.

This chapter will highlight the usefulness of place-based approaches for researchers desiring to influence policymaking. It will also provide a toolkit for scientists, highlighting the challenges and success factors of place-based initiatives. Finally, this chapter will explore opportunities for the way forward, by emphasising the steering potential of place-based approaches beyond the EU. On each of these dimensions, it includes dedicated advice for researchers and knowledge brokers, along with associated added value for policy-making (Table 1, Table 2 and Table 3).

Place-Based Approaches: A Promising Path Towards Evidence for Policy

Diversity is at the core of societies in the 21st **century**. While globalisation has shed some light on complementarities between various parts of the world and opened up opportunities for synergies, it has also brought to the fore a multitude of differences. This diversity observed at international level is further accentuated by interregional differences. Demographic, economic, labour market or sector-specific data reveal a diversity of patterns among the regions of a given country. For instance, analysing Employment in Science and Technology across European regions signals a strong heterogeneity, both across boundaries and inside national borders (see Chart 1[1]). For example, in Spain, with 57.1% of the active population employed in Science and Technology, the Basque Country distanced Extremadura by more than 24 percentage points in 2017. This gap is as much as the difference between the region of Paris in France and the region of Warminsko-Mazurskie in Poland.

It is important to move away from strictly national logics and to integrate subnational, regional or local dimensions. Living conditions as well as industrial structures, infrastructure endowment and geographical conditions vary substantially across the EU. The concepts of place and territory are therefore key to understanding the diversity and the specific local development matters of territorial units. These territorial units are mostly composed of subnational areas such as urban, metropolitan, regional or rural jurisdictions, but they can also include islands, coastal or mountainous areas. A better comprehension of territorial features might help policy measures directed at specific territorial areas or expected to have specific consequences concentrated in certain territories and hence increase the overall relevance and effectiveness of policies at all scales. Regions and cities are indeed pivotal actors for jobs, growth, competitiveness and investment. This is reflected in the latest evolution of the European Semester of economic governance, which includes a stronger focus on regional developments as of 2019. Generally, it is also visible in the changing nature of the country-specific recommendations under the European Semester, with 36% of the recommendations directly addressed to local and regional authorities in 2018, against only 24% in 2017 (Committee of the Regions, 2018). Since their genesis in the 1960s, place-based approaches provide an answer to diversity. Place-based approaches can help to grasp the complexity from bottom up, which more aggregated logics, for instance at national level, cannot capture. Indeed, place-based solutions capitalise on 'the identification and mobilisation of endogenous potential, that is, the ability of places to grow drawing on their own resources' (Tomaney, 2010). Therefore, they are not limited to a mere declination or adaptation of national policies. Place-based solutions have shown their added value to respect territorial specificities, while fostering territorial development. To achieve this, based on a comprehensive analysis of local features, they devise a consolidated

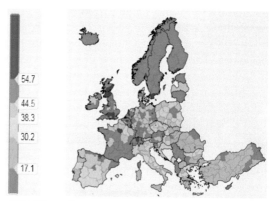

CHART 1 Human Resources in Science and Technology by NUTS 2 regions (% of active population), 2017 (Source: Eurostat (2017))

> *It is important to move away from strictly national logics and to integrate subnational, regional or local dimensions*

---

[1] The current NUTS 2016 classification has been in force since 1 January 2018. Eurostat distinguishes between NUTS 1 (major socioeconomic regions), NUTS 2 (basic regions for the application of regional policies) and NUTS 3 (small regions for specific diagnoses) – Source: Eurostat website, 2018

territorial vision and tailor support to the strengths and capabilities of a given territory. This is further reinforced by the bottom-up and inclusive governance associated to place-based approaches, which involves a rich patchwork of stakeholders – not only public authorities at national, regional or local level but also businesses, research institutions and the civil society, known as the 'quadruple helix'. This allows linking the world of policymakers and that of researchers and entrepreneurs, building cohesion between actors and making them feel associated from the design to the implementation of place-based solutions, which in turn boosts ownership. In a nutshell, place-based solutions are designed from the territories and for the territories, helping to formulate meaningful advice and solutions (Chart 2, Box 1).

CHART 2 Place-based solutions, roots in the territories.

Box 1: Smart Specialisation, an example of successful place-based solution informing regional innovation policies

Smart Specialisation exemplifies how the interaction between science and policy can impact on policymaking in a valuable way. In the light of the importance of policies tailored to the regional and local contexts, we have put place-based logics at the heart of territorial development activities, in particular through the channel of Smart Specialisation. Through its variety of features detailed below and mirroring the attributes of place-based approaches, Smart Specialisation epitomises the powerful role of the interface between science and policy and provides an inspiring example for scientists eager to feed into policymaking.

Smart Specialisation was conceived as an innovative, place-based approach to innovation. 'Smart specialisation describes the capacity of an economic system (a region for example) to generate new specialities through the discovery of new domains of opportunity and the local concentration and agglomeration of resources and competences in these domains' (Foray, 2015). As such, it aims not only at exploiting the main assets of a territory in terms of competitive advantages but also at developing them in a context of global challenges and rapid diffusion of knowledge. This new approach has been integrated as an essential part of the EU regional and cohesion policy over the programming period 2014–2020.

Smart Specialisation has demonstrated the benefits associated to place-based solutions for a strategic approach to policy. Smart Specialisation relies on the identification of strategic areas, 'based both on the analysis of the strengths and potential of the economy and on an Entrepreneurial Discovery Process (EDP) with wide stakeholder involvement […], supported by effective monitoring mechanisms' (European Commission, 2017a). The Entrepreneurial Discovery Process is at the heart of Smart Specialisation and stems from part of the New Industrial Policy literature, in particular the literature on 'self-discovery' and informational externalities (Hausmann and Rodrik, 2003; Rodrik, 2004). All along this process, all relevant public and private stakeholders explore current and new technoeconomic niches with potential for growth and excellence. This results in the choice of fields and technologies where the impact can be the greatest due to specialisation effects, returns on investment and critical mass (Henderson and Cockburn, 1996; Agrawal et al., 2011; Trajtenberg, 2002) and the empowerment of those actors most capable of realising the potential (Martínez-López and Palazuelos Martínez, 2019). In other words, if conducted properly, the Entrepreneurial Discovery Process confers stronger decision-making capacity through stakeholders' engagement (Periañez et al., 2015).

In less than a decade, Smart Specialisation has placed its stamp in the innovation ecosystems of the EU. Smart Specialisation has been widely endorsed at European, national, regional and local level. Up to now, European Member States and regions have developed over 120 Smart Specialisation Strategies. At the political level, the current first Vice-President (and former President) of the Committee of the Regions Markku Markkula stressed that 'Introducing a tailored innovation strategy on smart specialisation in each region has started an inclusive and bottom-up revolution pushing innovation-led growth policies all across Europe' (Committee of the Regions, 2017a).

The example of Navarra (Fig. 1) is representative of how Smart Specialisation has influenced policymaking by fostering the integration of policies. Departing from a silo approach, Navarra identified the range of priorities in the upper part of Fig. 1 and grouped them along three main clusters related to healthcare, environment and talent. The lower part of Fig. 1 describes the roots that have an effect on the competitiveness of the Smart Specialisation priorities. This was driven by a willingness to foster synergies and capitalise on the complementarities between several policies.

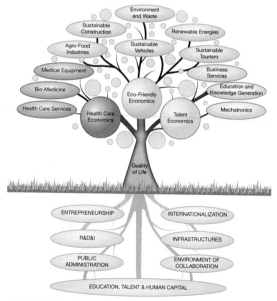

FIGURE 1 Smart Specialisation Strategy of Navarra.

Source: European Commission (2017b).

Table 1 Advice for researchers and knowledge brokers

	Advice for researchers and knowledge brokers	Possible impact on policymaking
Rationale behind place-based approaches	Take into consideration territorial diversity in order to get a full understanding of national/international complex pictures	Policies designed as more than a mere adaptation of national policies
Stages of the research and policy cycle	This 'territorial awareness' should take place at all stages of research, to anchor it into territorial realities	Territorial specificities to inform all steps of the policy cycle
Method and tools	• Liaise with all relevant actors (policymakers, businesses and the civil society) • Develop statistical data and evidence at territorial level	• Increase in ownership • Policies based on solid evidence • Better monitoring and evaluation of policies

Toolkit for Effective Place-Based Solutions

Challenges and Opportunities

To successfully inform policymaking, researchers and knowledge brokers need to anticipate four types of questions and challenges – in terms of governance, cultural changes, cocreation by actors and places and tools. In turn, these can become opportunities for scientists to feed into policymaking (Box 2). Governance, i.e., the architecture that governs the delivery of place-based solutions, is probably the most crucial and challenging aspect to be taken into consideration. It has the potential to foster – if properly designed – or impede – if it is not adapted to the context at stake – the implementation of policies. Finding the right governance framework means mobilising the right people around the right priority areas, through the right set of tools. In particular, a twofold challenge may emerge in the path towards advising policymaking: researchers and knowledge brokers need to find their place in the horizontal governance setting put in place and involving other actors; also, the question of vertical cooperation with other government levels to avoid fragmentation should not be neglected. The city of Bilbao offers a valuable illustration of the elaboration of a territorial Smart Specialisation initiative, coupled with the need to ensure synchronisation with the regional strategy of the Basque Country in Spain (Gianelle et al., 2016).

Against this background, a key ingredient for success lies in multiactor and multilevel governance. The former depicts the coordination between researchers and knowledge brokers, policymakers and all relevant actors from the business or civil society sphere, while the latter refers to the allocation of responsibilities between different layers of government. Robust multiscale governance practices need to be endowed with a number of features, such as (i) efficient coordination tools leading to integrated approaches, (ii) a clear allocation of roles to the different stakeholders to ensure fertile collaboration, (iii) solid and reliable data for evidence-based policymaking and (iv) the cocreation of policies by the actors involved, which refers to the inclusive dimension of place-based policies (OECD, 2018).

Obviously, moving from central or national policies to place-based ones entails deep changes linked to the vision of territories. A complete understanding of local assets is essential to customise tailor-made approaches rooted in the territory and leads to the definition of a strategic territorial vision relying on capacities, capabilities and potential. Shaping such an integrated vision often implies a cultural change from previous narrower logics focused on sectoral analyses. As such, place-based approaches may suffer from resistance to change, the difficulty to reach consensus on a common vision for the whole territory or the importance of involving the right actors. The Smart Specialisation process in Lapland, which led to the definition of 'Lapland's Arctic Specialisation Programme 2030', embodies a successful example of engaging the relevant actors towards the elaboration of a joint vision for the territory. In the case of Lapland, this took place by including all municipalities, as well as other organisations from industry, education and research (Gianelle et al., 2016).

In this context, the development of a comprehensive vision for the territory needs to be supported by thorough territorial analysis. The starting point needs to be a 360 degrees study of local characteristics. Such diagnosis would encompass the areas where the territory is stronger and weaker, and it would also have a forward-looking approach, by envisaging potential for further development and possible risks to take into account. In other words, this is about the internal and external factors that are likely to have an impact on the territory. The Strengths–Weaknesses–Opportunities–Threats tool, known as SWOT, provides a systematic way to present this analysis, which in turn paves the ground for defining an integrated and fully place-based vision (European Commission, 2012).

Researchers willing to provide input into the policymaking process should not see their contribution in an isolated way, but rather as part of a community of actors and places. In such a complex and connected world, shaping individual place-based approaches is not enough. The fruit of a collaborative work has higher chances of success for several reasons: it integrates the various dimensions at stake, it is enriched by the dialogue of stakeholders with different cultures and it benefits from greater support from a wide range of actors. However, the route towards it is not without obstacles. When it is about working and being engaged with numerous actors representing different interests, a difficulty may arise from preventing or solving possible conflicts and finding a way to collaborate smoothly. To this may be added a commonly flagged threat of capture of the place-based process by some actors to the detriment of the others, which necessitates careful management. Otherwise, the input from science to policy runs the risk of being underexploited, misunderstood or not taken into consideration.

Cocreation can make the difference to contribute to policymaking. Not only is it important to identify relevant stakeholders at an early stage but it is also vital to put in place a number of cooperation mechanisms between them (see Chapter 7 or the Sevilla process example in Chapter 10 for some insights). In particular, the collaboration between researchers, policymakers and other actors can benefit from the presence of 'boundary spanners', namely 'people or organisations with interdisciplinary knowledge or proven experience in interaction with different actors and who can hence help moderate the process' (European Commission, 2012). These people would have a key role in facilitating dialogue and acting as bridge-makers. Setting up spaces for exchanges, information sharing and networking between the different actors and places engaged, may also foster the building of links and eventually the cocreation of policies from the territories and for the territories. This contributes to empowering actors and places and thus increasing the feeling of ownership, which is crucial for the success of place-based solutions. In the Polish region of Wielkopolska, wide participation of actors was ensured through the setting up of a dedicated Smart Specialisation Forum, comprising 92 participants, including researchers and companies, in charge of steering dialogue. The Forum includes six Working Groups gathering 182 stakeholders, notably from the scientific and business sphere (Gianelle et al., 2016).

The questions of governance, territorial identity and mobilisation of actors do not exhaust the range of issues related to place-based approaches. Although the panorama of available statistical, quantitative, technical or qualitative tools is extremely vast, researchers and scientists need to cross the bridge between research and policy also in terms of tools. The objective is to make the outcome of their research accessible to policymakers and all relevant actors, to successfully influence policymaking. Bottlenecks inherent in the availability of tools for place-based solutions are at least twofold: first, in their analysis of territorial specificities and their attempts to formulate local diagnoses, researchers may face issues for obtaining data at the desired level of disaggregation. Second, the merits of place-based approaches are double-edged: on the one hand, their 'charm' is that they propose customised solutions to specific issues; on the other hand, their fundamental place-based nature limits their replicability to other territories.

By using participatory instruments, researchers have a key role to play in informing policymaking through place-based approaches. Instruments for place-based logics may not be accessible off the shelf among traditional ones and may require some ad hoc, innovative spirit. This can be achieved through a range of participatory instruments which, importantly, should not be deployed only in the first stages of the process, but throughout it to maintain the engagement of all actors and efficiently monitor and assess its impact. Channels such as consultations of actors, focus groups for generating ideas, peer reviews oriented towards mutual learning, benchmarking for getting inspiration from good practices or comparative studies to gain knowledge about others actors or places are worth exploring when putting in motion place-based solutions. As an illustration, in the Austrian region of Salzburg, the S3-4AlpClusters project relies on two innovative tools, namely Stress-Tests and Synergy-Diamonds, to identify opportunities for structural transformation within and across regions (Smart Specialisation Platform, 2018).

> *By using participatory instruments, researchers have a key role to play in informing policymaking through place-based approaches.*

Box 2: The partnership between science and policymaking in Smart Specialisation: the Smart Specialisation Platform

In less than a decade, Smart Specialisation managed to inform national and regional policymaking in the areas of research and innovation (see Box 1). In this endeavour, the Smart Specialisation Platform, which is the outcome of the collaboration between scientists and policymakers of the European Commission, has played a key role.

The Smart Specialisation Platform was established in 2011 to provide assistance and support to countries and regions in the design, implementation and monitoring of their Smart Specialisation Strategies. It is hosted by the Joint Research Centre of the European Commission, as the scientific arm of the European Commission, and runs in collaboration with the Directorate-General for Regional and Urban Policy. The work of the Smart Specialisation Platform has been further enriched by the establishment of three Thematic Smart Specialisation Platforms on energy, industrial modernisation and agri-food, which offer hands-on support to regions to promote interregional cooperation. They offer a forum where regions and relevant actors join forces and pool resources on the basis of matching Smart Specialisation priorities in high-added value sectors. Presently, more than 195 European regions and Member States are members of the Platform, while over 160 regions and countries are working together across the EU around areas of common interest.

Not only does the Smart Specialisation Platform represent an example of how scientists can usefully engage into policymaking, but it has also developed guidance for all actors, including researchers and knowledge brokers willing to interact with policymakers on innovation. For this purpose, two practical guides – 'Guide to Research and Innovation Strategies for Smart Specialisation (RIS3)' (European Commission, 2012) and 'Implementing Smart Specialisation Strategies – A Handbook' (Gianelle et al., 2016) – were prepared by the Smart Specialisation Platform. In addition, a number of tools – including guidance material, good practice examples, peer reviews or trainings to policymakers – were developed to reinforce the impact of Smart Specialisation. This helps to advise policymakers in an inclusive way, by involving them throughout the process instead of only placing them at the receiving end. A number of innovative policymaking instruments were also set in motion, building on participatory approaches. This is, in particular, the case of the innovation camps, driven by discussions around challenges, and Peer eXchange and Learning workshops, with regions and experts using peer reviews to debate around issues of mutual interest.

Overall, actors express their appreciation vis-à-vis this collaborative approach. According to a Fraunhofer study, national and regional policymakers expressed a 4.5 out of 5 satisfaction ranking about the Smart Specialisation Platform, thus strongly endorsing it (Fraunhofer, 2013).

Flanders provides a helpful example of how strong stakeholders' engagement can be decisive in policymaking. The Flanders Innovation Hub for Sustainable Chemistry (FISCH) was conceived under the umbrella of Smart Specialisation as an innovation hub aimed at influencing policymaking in the area of green chemistry. Its creation mobilised more than 300 stakeholders, with several research organisations represented. It showcases a model of cluster approach in industrial policy, based on Smart Specialisation. In 2017, FISCH transformed into the new spearhead cluster for Chemistry and Plastics, Catalisti (Department of Economy, Science and Innovation of Flanders, 2014).

Territorial Impact Assessments for Better Place-Based Solutions

The territorial dimension of policies is increasingly recognised in policymaking processes. It is, for example, fully embedded in the European Commission 'Better Regulation Guidelines' in assessing the impact of newly proposed initiatives and evaluating existing ones: '[the potential impacts of the options on] [...] different territories and regions (less developed or prosperous regions, cities, rural areas, border regions, overseas territories etc.)' (European Commission, 2015).

Territorial Impact Assessments strengthen the territorial dimension of European initiatives. A correct assessment of the territorial dimension of a problem will help to shape properly targeted policy options (Box 3). It can also avoid conducting policies in those areas and regions where no policy response is needed. Territorial Impact Assessments help to evaluate legal, compliance or administrative costs. The approach relies on addressing the following questions:

1. What is the issue at stake? Why is it important at European scale? Can it be quantified? Is there a territorial dimension?
2. Have EU policies the capacity to respond to the issue? What policy options can be considered? What is the impact/effectiveness of these options?
3. What are stakeholders' views? How would they react to policy proposals?

To tackle the abovementioned questions, the Territorial Impact Assessment process requires that a baseline be constructed to show how the problem is likely to evolve in the absence of policy intervention. A projection with a subnational component including demographic and economic projections can help to show the likely evolution of the issue at stake. Analytical and modelling tools can support an impact assessment, while visual and interactive instruments enhance the transparency of the process.

Box 3: The Knowledge Centre for Territorial Policies,
a vehicle towards territorial development

The Knowledge Centre for Territorial Policies was launched by the Joint Research Centre and the Directorate-General for Regional and Urban Policy in October 2016, in the frame of the Strategy on Data, Information and Knowledge Management of the European Commission. This Knowledge Centre was set up to strengthen overall support to territorial development and aims to be the point of reference on territorial and regional issues. In this capacity, the Knowledge Centre does not only provide a repository of relevant research and new initiatives but also serve as a place for analytical and networking activities.

The Knowledge Centre brings together a number of services in the form of data tools, platforms, models and dashboards such as LUISA, RHOMOLO, STRAT-Board, T-Board and the Urban Data Platform. Together, these services offer a vast amount of data and knowledge suitable for analysis, theoretical explorations, policy backing/development and scenario building, with one common denominator, i.e., a territorial outlook. This allows analysing the status and trends of European regions and cities, looking, for example, at their demographic or economic profile or at the provision of services for education and health.

The key element of the Knowledge Centre, in support to Territorial Impact Assessments, is the Territorial Reference Scenario. The scenario makes use of a solid knowledge base including past and future time series of socioeconomic variables and spatial information on housing, transport, energy and service infrastructures. It also includes existing European policies and legislation (such as the Common Agricultural Policy, the Renewable Energy Directive or the TEN-T) and serves as benchmark for policy options.

Table 2 Advice for researchers and knowledge brokers

	Advice for researchers and knowledge brokers	Possible impact on policymaking
Rationale behind the toolkit on place-based approaches	Anticipate recurrent challenges to ensure that scientific contribution adequately reaches policymaking	Create the conditions for well-informed, evidence-based policymaking
Stages of involvement	Ensure continuous researchers' engagement, not limited to the design phase	Efficient monitoring, assessment and follow-up
Method and tools: • Building governance • Defining a vision • Linking actors and places • Setting up tools	• Mobilise the right ingredients for good multiactor and multilevel governance • Carry out a comprehensive diagnosis of territorial strengths to achieve an integrated vision of the territory • Optimise participation in communities of experts involving different actors • Innovative instruments can enrich traditional research tools to design place-based solutions	• Move from top-down to bottom-up policymaking • Depart from sectoral approaches and shape a strategic vision anchored in the territory • Policymaking does not emerge from an isolated reflection at political level, but from the inclusive interaction with all relevant actors • Think out of the box to use innovative tools inspired by a participatory spirit

The Way Forward:
Place-Based Innovation Policies, an Approach 'Made in EU' Gaining Worldwide Interest

Place-based policies have a strong conceptual impact since they have been at the core of a new thinking on regional and territorial development. Although their starting point is the territories, the impact of place-based approaches goes far beyond the regional, national and European borders and has an international resonance. In particular, place-based approaches have been the source of what the OECD qualifies as a 'new paradigm' (OECD, 2009) in regional and local development. Previously 'negatively oriented' approaches focused on challenges and disparities are being replaced by 'positively axed' logics thinking in terms of strengths, capabilities and how to maximise them. The new reflection is more about tapping into possible pockets of growth, excellence and attractiveness than about managing weaknesses. Moreover, previously top-down, sectoral policies designed centrally are being replaced by bottom-up policies anchored in a global vision of the territories. Through this novel approach to territorial development, locally designed and owned strategies are conceived. This leads to the creation of true local ecosystems.

Place-based solutions have also triggered practical actions by researchers and policymakers at the international level in the area of innovation. Over the last years, based on European experiences and successes, place-based innovation policies inspired by Smart Specialisation have

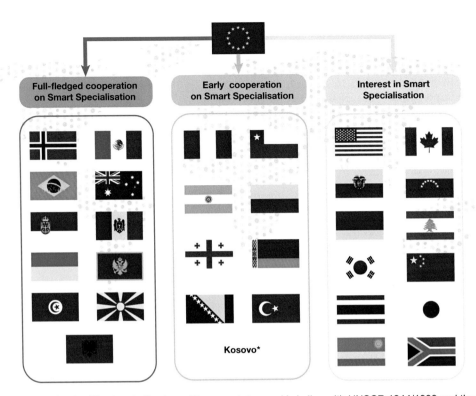

| Full-fledged cooperation on Smart Specialisation | Early cooperation on Smart Specialisation | Interest in Smart Specialisation |

Kosovo*

‡ This designation is without prejudice to positions on status, and is in line with UNSCR 1244/1999 and the ICJ Opinion on the Kosovo declaration of independence.

CHART 3 Worldwide cooperation on place-based innovation policies. (Source: all images © Wikimedia Commons under Creative Commons Attribution-ShareAlike 3.0, except: the European flag, © European Commission, 2018 and background image mimacz, © Adobe Stock, 2018.)

gained prominence beyond the EU. By attracting the attention and interest of researchers and policymakers on the five continents, they have become a possible gate to the world. Since they are by nature fitted to territorial specificities, place-based solutions can be applied to any part of the world, at all stages of development. So far, Smart Specialisation pockets, or elements of it, are present at different levels of implementation on the five continents. At this stage, the cooperation between the Smart Specialisation Platform and these countries has been genuinely place-based (see Chart 3), varying from early stage discussions (the United States, Canada, Ecuador, Venezuela, Armenia, Lebanon, South Korea, China, Thailand, Japan, Rwanda and South Africa), to first cooperation steps (Peru, Chile, Argentina, Colombia, Georgia, Belarus, Bosnia and Herzegovina, Kosovo[2] and Turkey) and full-fledged cooperation (at different levels, Norway, Mexico, Brazil, Australia, Serbia, Moldova, Ukraine, Montenegro, Tunisia, North Macedonia and Albania).

---

[2] This designation is without prejudice to positions on status and is in line with UNSCR 1244/1999 and the ICJ Opinion on the Kosovo declaration of independence.

Place-based approaches can serve as an enabler for the international agenda on sustainable development. The United Nations' 2030 Agenda for Sustainable Development encompasses 17 Sustainable Development Goals encompassing challenges of today and tomorrow. Although these goals have been agreed at international level, their delivery crucially depends on the mobilisation of national, regional and local levels. By helping to 'localise' the Sustainable Development Goals, the subnational levels embody a crucial nexus between the national and global levels (United Nations, 2018). The pertinence of the regional and local dimension of sustainable development has been corroborated by the Reflection Paper on a Sustainable Europe by 2030 (European Commission, 2019) and the Committee of the Regions, which portrayed regions and cities as vital partners able to find 'right answers to the big development issues' (Committee of the Regions, 2017b). Through their strong proximity to territorial concerns and their flexibility to local realities, place-based logics therefore appear as a fertile enabling methodology to nurture the achievement of the Sustainable Development Goals. In this respect, Smart Specialisation and its potential to foster place-based economic transformation have been identified by international organisations and countries as a promising vehicle for the fulfilment of the Sustainable Development Goals, notably as Science and Technology Roadmaps for these Goals.

Table 3 Advice for researchers and knowledge brokers

	Advice for researchers and knowledge brokers	Possible impact on policymaking
Theory and practice of place-based logics	• New paradigm on regional and territorial development, linked to the impulse from place-based solutions • Inspiring power at the global level, which can enrich academic work and knowledge	• The resonance of place-based solutions transcends territorial boundaries and has changed regional development policy • Inspire and steer policymaking in other territories, as well as foster possible partnerships and collaborations
Increasing trend	Place-based solutions related to innovation are gaining traction all around the world, which creates a momentum for research	Increasing influence of place-based solutions to challenges on policymaking
Method	Enrich the literature on place-based approaches worldwide	Policymaking could gain from international experiences in other territories

In conclusion, place-based approaches, which have developed as a game changer in the landscape of regional and territorial development policies, are endowed with valuable features to relevantly inform policy ecosystems through scientific evidence. Developing an overall strategic vision for the territory, which draws on a bottom-up, inclusive process involving all stakeholders and a thorough diagnosis of territorial strengths and challenges, is firmly anchored in the DNA of place-based logics. In turn, this makes them fully malleable to hugely diverse territorial realities. The potential of place-based approaches is not limited to policymaking at local, regional or national level, but can also impact on the international agenda. Looking forward, increasing attention ought to be paid to two important levels: at a lower territorial level, cities and, at a higher territorial level, the international dimension are both emerging as important to complete the picture of place-based approaches and further reinforce their contribution to policymaking. In a nutshell, this is about coming back to the idea that 'places matter' (Rodríguez-Pose, 2018) and reflecting it in the way policies are conceived and implemented.

References

Chapter 1

Andrews, L., 2017. How can we demonstrate the public value of evidence-based policy making when government ministers declare that the people 'have had enough of experts'? Palgrave Communications 3 (11), 1–9.

Ball, L., 2018. Explainer: What Is Evidence-Informed Policy-Making? Overseas Development Institute. https://www.odi.org/comment/10592-explainer-what-evidence-informed-policy-making. [Accessed 05 May 2020].

Boykoff, M.T., Boykoff, J.M., 2007. Climate change and journalistic norms: a case-study of US mass-media coverage. Geoforum 38 (6), 1190–1204.

Cairney, P., 2016. The Politics of Evidence-Based Policy Making. Palgrave Macmillan UK, London.

Cairney, P., Heikkila, T., Wood, M., 2019. Making Policy in a Complex World. Cambridge University Press, Cambridge.

Caplan, N., 1979. The two-communities theory and knowledge utilization. American Behavioral Scientist 22 (3), 459–470.

Chalmers, I., 2003. Trying to do more good than harm in policy and practice: the role of rigorous, transparent, up-to-date evaluations. The Annals of the American Academy of Political and Social Science 589 (1), 22–40.

Cook, J., van der Linden, S., Maibach, E., Lewandowsky, S., 2018. The Consensus Handbook.

Craig, C., 2019. How Does Government Listen to Scientists? Palgrave Macmillan, London.

Douglas, H., 2009. Science, Policy, and the Value-free Ideal. Pittsburgh University Press, Pittsburgh.

Gluckman, P., 2014. The art of science advice to government. Nature 507, 163–165.

Greenhalgh, T., Russell, J., 2006. Reframing evidence synthesis as rhetorical action in the policy making drama. Health Policy 1 (2), 34–42.

Hallsworth, M., Rutter, J., Egan, M., McCrae, J., 2018. Behavioural Government Using Behavioural Science to Improve How Governments Make Decisions. The Behavioural Insights Team, London.

Head, B., Ferguson, M., Cherney, A., Boreham, P., 2014. Are policy-makers interested in social research? Exploring the sources and uses of valued information among public servants in Australia. Policy and Society 33 (2), 89–101.

Institute for Government, 2016. Trust in Government Is Growing – But it Needs to Deliver. https://www.instituteforgovernment.org.uk/sites/default/files/publications/IfG_polling_note_WEB3.pdf. [Accessed 05 May 2020].

Jasanoff, S., Simmet, H.R., 2017. No funeral bells: public reason in a 'post-truth' age. Social Studies of Science 47 (5), 751–770.

Newman, J., 2017. Debating the politics of evidence-based policy. Public Administration 95 (4), 1107–1112.

Newman, J., Cherney, A., Head, B.W., 2016. Do policy makers use academic research? Reexamining the "two communities" theory of research utilization. Public Administration Review 76 (1), 24–32.

Oliver, K., Innvar, S., Lorenc, T., Woodman, J., Thomas, J., 2014. A systematic review of barriers to and facilitators of the use of evidence by policymakers. BMC Health Services Research 14, 2.

Oreskes, N., Conway, E.M., 2010. Merchants of Doubt: How a Handful of Scientists Obscured the Truth on Issues from Tobacco Smoke to Global Warming. Bloomsbury Press, New York.

Parkhurst, J., 2016. The Politics of Evidence: From Evidence-Based Policy to the Good Governance of Evidence. Routledge, New York.

Pielke Jr., R., 2007. The honest broker: making sense of science in policy and politics. Cambridge University Press, Cambridge.

Prewitt, K., Schwandt, T.A., Straf, M.L. (Eds.), 2012. Using Science as Evidence in Public Policy. The National Academies Press, Washington, D.C.

Ravetz, J.R., 1999. What is post-normal science. Futures 31, 647–653.

Rittel, H.W.J., Webber, M.M., 1973. Dilemmas in a general theory of planning. Policy Sciences 4 (2), 155–169.

Rutjens, B.T., Sutton, R.M., van der Lee, R., 2018. Not all skepticism is equal: exploring the ideological antecedents of science acceptance and rejection. Personality and Social Psychology Bulletin 44 (3), 384–405.

Schultz, D., 2013. American Politics in the Age of Ignorance: Why Lawmakers Choose Belief over Research. Palgrave Macmillan, New York.

Talbot, C., Talbot, C., 2014. Sir Humphrey and the Professors: What Does Whitehall Want from Academics? The University of Manchester, Manchester.

Chapter 2

Carson, R., 1962. Silent Spring. Houghton Mifflin Harcourt.

Funtowicz, S., Ravetz, J.R., 1990. Uncertainty and Quality in Science for Policy. Kluwer Academic Publishers, Dordrecht.

Funtowicz, S., Ravetz, J.R., 1993. Science for the post-normal age. Futures 25 (7), 739–755.

Gluckman, P., 2014. The art of science advice to government. Nature 507, 163–165.

PNS Symposium, 2016. New Currents in Science: The Challenges of Quality, Ispra. https://ec.europa.eu/jrc/en/event/workshop/challenges-quality.

Ravetz, J.R., 1971. Scientific Knowledge and Its Social Problems. Oxford University Press, Oxford.

Ravetz, J.R., 1977. The Acceptability of Risks. Council for Science and Society, London.

Weinberg, A.M., 1972. Science and trans-science. Minerva 10 (2), 209–222.

Chapter 3

Al Khudhairy, D., Campolongo, F., Langedijk, S. (Eds.), 2017. What Makes a Fair Society? Insights and Evidence. Publications Office of the European Union, Luxembourg.

Campolongo, F. (Ed.), 2018. The Resilience of EU Member States to the Financial and Economic Crisis. What Are the Characteristics of Resilient Behaviour?. Publications Office of the European Union, Luxembourg.

Craglia, M., 2018. In: Annoni, A., Benczur, P., Bertoldi, P., Delipetrev, B., De Prato, G., Feijoo, C., Fernandez Macias, E., Gomez, E., Iglesias, M., Junklewitz, H., Lopez Cobo, M., Martens, B., Nascimento, S., Nativi, S., Polvora, A., Sanchez Martin, J.I., Tolan, S., Tuomi, I., Vesnic Alujevic, L. (Eds.), Artificial Intelligence – A European Perspective. Publications Office of the European Union, Luxembourg.

Funtowicz, S., Ravetz, J.R., 1993. Science for the post-normal age. Futures 25 (7), 739–755.

Nascimento, S., Pólvora, A., Sousa Lourenço, J., 2018. Blockchain4EU: Blockchain for Industrial Transformations. Publications Office of the European Union, Luxembourg.

Saltelli, A., 2017. Science's Credibility Crisis: Why it Will Get Worse before it Can Get Better. The Conversation. https://theconversation.com/sciences-credibility-crisis-why-it-will-get-worse-before-it-can-get-better-86865. [Accessed 5 May 2020].

Saltelli, A., Giampietro, M., 2017. What is wrong with evidence based policy, and how can it be improved? Futures 91, 62–71.

Special Eurobarometer 401, 2013. Responsible Research and Innovation (RRI), Science and Technology. Conducted by TNS Opinion & Social at the Request of the European Commission. Directorate-General for Research & Innovation.

Special Eurobarometer 340, 2010. Science and Technology. Conducted by TNS Opinion & Social at the Request of the European Commission. Research Directorate-General.

Chapter 4

Alla, K., Hall, W.D., Whiteford, H.A., Head, B.W., Meurk, C.S., 2017. How do we define the policy impact of public health research? A systematic review. Health Research Policy and Systems 15 (1), 84.

Bastow, S., Dunleavy, P., Tinkler, J., 2013. The Impact of the Social Sciences: How Academics and Their Research Make a Difference. Sage, London.

Bedwell, W., Fiore, S., Salas, E., 2014. Developing the future workforce: an approach for integrating interpersonal skills into the MBA classroom. Academy of Management Learning and Education 13, 171–186.

Cairney, P., Kwiatkowski, R., 2017. How to communicate effectively with policymakers: combine insights from psychology and policy studies. Palgrave Communications. 3, 37. https://www.nature.com/articles/s41599-017-0046-8. [Accessed 5 May 2020].

Cairney, P., Oliver, K., 2017. Evidence-based policymaking is not like evidence-based medicine, so how far should you go to bridge the divide between evidence and policy? Health Research Policy and Systems 15, 35. https://doi.org/10.1186/s12961-017-0192-x.

Cairney, P., Weible, C., 2017. The new policy sciences. Policy Sciences. https://doi.org/10.1007/s11077-017-9304-2. [Accessed 5 May 2020].

Cairney, P., 2017. #EU4Facts: 3 take-home points from the JRC annual conference. Paul Cairney: Politics and Public Policy. https://paulcairney.wordpress.com/2017/09/29/eu4facts-3-take-home-points-from-the-jrc-annual-conference/. [Accessed 5 May 2020].

Cairney, P., 2016a. The Politics of Evidence-Based Policymaking. Palgrave Pivot, London.

Cairney, P., 2016b. Principles of science advice to government: key problems and feasible solutions. Paul Cairney: Politics and Policy. https://paulcairney.wordpress.com/2016/10/05/principles-of-science-advice-to-government-key-problems-and-feasible-solutions/. [Accessed 5 May 2020].

Cairney, P., Oliver, K., Wellstead, A., 2016. To bridge the divide between evidence and policy: reduce ambiguity as much as uncertainty. Public Administration Review. https://doi.org/10.1111/puar.12555. Early View . [Accessed 5 May 2020].

Chabal, P.M., 2003. Do ministers matter? The individual style of ministers in programmed policy change. International Review of Administrative Sciences 69 (1), 29–49.

Cook, B., Kesby, M., Fazey, I., Spray, C., 2013. The persistence of 'normal' catchment management despite the participatory turn: exploring the power effects of competing frames of reference. Social Studies of Science 43 (5), 754–779.

Damon, A., Lewis, J. (Eds.), 2015. Making Public Policy Decisions: Expertise, Skills and Experience. Routledge, London.

Davidson, B., 2017. Storytelling and evidence-based policy: lessons from the grey literature. Palgrave Communications 3, 201793.

Davies, P., 2006. What is needed from research synthesis from a policy-making perspective? In: Popay, J. (Ed.), Moving beyond Effectiveness in Evidence Synthesis–Methodological Issues in the Synthesis of Diverse Sources of Evidence. National institute for Health and Clinical Excellence, London, pp. 97–105.

Estrada, F.C.R., David, L.S., 2015. Improving visual communication of science through the incorporation of graphic design theories and practices into science communication. Science Communication 37 (I), 140–148.

European Commission, Joint Research Centre, DDG.01 Econometrics and Applied Statistics, 2015. Dialogues: Public Engagement in Science, Technology and Innovation. Publication Office of the European Union, Luxembourg.

European Commission, 2017. Communication from the Commission to the European Parliament, the Council, the European Economic and Social Committee and the Committee of the Regions, Completing the Better Regulation Agenda: Better Solutions for Better Results. SWD (2017) 675 final, 24.10.2017 https://ec.europa.eu/info/sites/info/files/completing-the-better-regulation-agenda-better-solutions-for-better-results_en.pdf. [Accessed 5 May 2020].

Fox, D., Bero, L., 2014. Systematic Reviews: Perhaps "the answers to policy makers' prayers"? In: Environmental Health Perspectives, Vol. 22, Issue 10.

Greenhalgh, T., Malterud, K., 2016. Systematic review for policymaking: muddling through. The American Journal of Public Health 107 (1) January 2017.

Hart, P.S., Nisbet, E.C., 2012. Boomerang effects in science communication: how motivated reasoning and identity cues amplify opinion polarization about climate mitigation policies. Communication Research 39, 701–723.

Jasanoff, S., Simmet, H., 2017. No funeral bells: public reason in a 'post-truth' age. Social Studies of Science 47 (5), 751–770.

Jones, M., Crow, D., 2017. How can we use the 'science of stories' to produce persuasive scientific stories? Palgrave Communications. 3, 53. https://doi.org/10.1057/s41599-017-0047-7. [Accessed 5 May 2020].

Klein, C., DeRouin, R., Salas, E., 2006. Uncovering workplace interpersonal skills: a review, framework, and research agenda. International Review of Industrial and Organizational Psychology 21, 79.

Larrick, R.P., 2016. The social context of decisions. Annual Review of Organizational Psychology and Organizational Behavior 3, 441–467.

Nascimento, S., Guimaraes Pereira, A., Ghezzi, A., 2014. From Citizens Science to Do It Yourself Science. An Annotated Account of an Ongoing Movement. Publications Office of the European Union. EUR 27095.

Oliver, K., Innvar, S., Lorenc, T., Woodman, J., Thomas, J., 2014. A systematic review of barriers to and facilitators of the use of evidence by policymakers. BMC Health Services Research 14 (1), 2.

Pielke Jr., R., 2007. The Honest Broker: Making Sense of Science in Policy and Politics. Cambridge University Press, Cambridge.

Reiss, K., 2015. Leadership Coaching for Educators–Bringing Out the Best in School Administrators, second ed. Corwin Press, Thousand Oaks, CA.

Smith, K.E., Stewart, E.A., 2017. Academic advocacy in public health: disciplinary 'duty'or political 'propaganda'? Social Science & Medicine 189, 35–43.

Sloman, S., Fernbach, P., 2017. The Knowledge Illusion: Why We Never Think Alone. Riverhead books, New York.

Stoker, G., 2010. Translating experiments into policy. The ANNALS of the American Academy of Political and Social Science 628, 47–58.

Stone, D., Maxwell, S., Keating, M., 2001. Proceedings from an International Workshop Funded by the UK Department for International Development: Bridging Research and Policy. Warwick University, Coventry, England.

Warira, D., Mueni, E., Gay, E., Lee, M., 2017. Achieving and sustaining evidence-informed policy making. Science Communication 39 (3), 382–394.

Weible, C., Heikkila, T., deLeon, P., Sabatier, P., 2012. Understanding and influencing the policy process. Policy Sciences 45 (1), 1–21.

Wilcox, C., 2012. It's time to evolve: taking responsibility for science communication in a digital age. In: Biological Bulletin, Guest Editorial, Vol. 222, No 2. The University of Chicago Press Journals.

Chapter 5

Badgett, M.V.L., 2015. The Public Professor: How to Use Your Research to Change the World. New York University Press, New York and London.

Banuri, S., Dercon, S., Gauri, V., 2017. Biased Policy Professionals. Policy Research Working Paper. World Bank Group, Washington, D.C.

Cook, J., Lewandowsky, S., 2011. The Debunking Handbook. University of Queensland, St. Lucia, Australia.

Hallsworth, M., Rutter, J., Egan, M., McCrae, J., 2018. Behavioural Government Using Behavioural Science to Improve How Governments Make Decisions. The Behavioural Insights Team, London.

Lakoff, G., 2004. Don't Think of an Elephant: Know Your Values and Frame the Debate. Chelsea Green Publishing, White River Junction.

O'Connor, C., Weatherall, J.O., 2019. The Misinformation Age: How False Beliefs Spread. Yale University Press, New Haven.

Oliver, K., Cairney, P., 2019. The dos and don'ts of influencing policy: a systematic review of advice to academics. Palgrave Communications 5, 21.

Pielke Jr., R.,A., 2007. The Honest Broker: Making Sense of Science in Policy and Politics. Cambridge University Press, Cambridge.

Sarewitz, D., 2011. Looking for quality in all the wrong places, or: the technological origins of quality in scientific policy advice. In: Lentsch, J., Weingart, P. (Eds.), The Politics of Scientific Advice: Institutional Design for Quality Assurance. Cambridge University Press, Cambridge.

Tversky, A., Kahneman, D., 1981. The framing of decisions and the psychology of choice. Science 211 (4481), 453–458.

Chapter 6

Cairney, P., 2016. The Politics of Evidence-Based Policy Making. Palgrave Macmillan, UK, London.

Cairney, P., Oliver, K., 2017. Evidence-based policymaking is not like evidence-based medicine, so how far should you go to bridge the divide between evidence and policy? Health Research Policy and Systems 15, 35.

Dewulf, A., Bouwen, R., 2012. Issue framing in conversations for change: discursive interaction strategies for 'doing differences'. The Journal of Applied Behavioral Science 48 (2), 168–193.

Douglas, H., 2009. Science, Policy, and the Value-Free Ideal. Pittsburgh University Press, Pittsburgh.

Hallsworth, M., Rutter, J., Egan, M., McCrae, J., 2018. Behavioural Government Using Behavioural Science to Improve How Governments Make Decisions. The Behavioural Insights Team, London.

Langer, L., Tripney, J., Gough, D., 2016. The Science of Using Science: Researching the Use of Research Evidence in Decision-Making. EPPI-Centre, Social Science Research Unit, UCL Institute of Education, University College London, London.

Oliver, K., Cairney, P., 2019. The dos and don'ts of influencing policy: a systematic review of advice to academics. Palgrave Communications 5, 21.

Oliver, K., Innvar, S., Lorenc, T., Woodman, J., Thomas, J., 2014. A systematic review of barriers to and facilitators of the use of evidence by policymakers. BMC Health Services Research 14, 2.

Rittel, H.W.J., Webber, M.M., 1973. Dilemmas in a general theory of planning. Policy Sciences 4 (2), 155–169.

Chapter 7

Bonabeau, E., 2009. Decisions 2.0: the power of collective intelligence. MIT Sloan Management Review 50 (2), 45–52.

Collison, C., 2014. When Collect and Connect is not Enough. Chris Collison's blog. http://www.chriscollison.com/blog/2014/11/10/when-collect-and-connect-is-not-enough. [Accessed 5 May 2020].

Gray, D., Brown, S., Macanufo, J., 2010. Gamestorming: A Playbook for Innovators, Rulebreakers, and Changemakers. O'Reilly Media. gamestorming.com.

Ingham, J., 2017. The Social Organization: Developing Enmployee Connections and Relationships for Improved Business Performance. Kogan Page Ltd., New York.

Kienle, A., Wessner, M., 2005. Principles for cultivating scientific communities of practice. In: van den Besselaar, P., et al. (Ed.), Communities and Technologies 2005. Springer, pp. 283–299.

Malone, T., Laubacher, R., Dellarocas, C., 2010. The collective intelligence genome. MIT Sloan Management Review 51 (3), 21–31.

McDermott, R., Archibald, D., 2013. Harnessing your staff's informal networks. HBR's 10 must reads on collaboration. Harvard Business Review.

Mulgan, G., 2017. Big Mind: How Collective Intelligence Can Change Our World. Princeton University Press, Princeton.

Sloman, S., Fernbach, P., 2017. The Knowledge Illusion: Why We Never Think Alone. Riverhead Books, New York.

Weber, E., 2016. Building Successful Communities of Practice. Drew London Ltd.

Wenger, E., McDermott, R., Snyder, W., 2002. Cultivating Communities of Practice: A Guide to Managing Knowledge. Harvard Business School Press.

Wenger, E., Trayner, B., de Laat, M., 2011. Promoting and Assessing Value Creation in Communities and Networks: A Conceptual Framework. Rapport 18. Ruud de Moor Centrum, Open University of the Netherlands.

Wenger-Trayner, E., Wenger-Trayner, B., 2015. Introduction to Communities of Practice. http://wenger-trayner.com/introduction-to-communities-of-practice/.

Web References

EU4Facts – Evidence for Policy Community. https://ec.europa.eu/jrc/communities/community/76/about.

Gartner IT Glossary. https://www.gartner.com/it-glossary/knowledge-community [Accessed 5 May 2020].

Knowledge for Policy – Audience Research. Knowledge4Policy: Audience Research | Knowledge for policy.

Chapter 8

Andersen, I.E., Jæger, B., 1999. Scenario workshops and consensus conferences: towards more democratic decision-making. Science and Public Policy 26 (5), 331–340.

Arnstein, S., 1969. A ladder of citizen participation. Journal of the American Institute of Planners 35 (4), 216–224.

Bio Innovation Service, 2018. Citizen Science for Environmental Policy: Development of an EU-wide Inventory and Analysis of Selected Practices. Final report for the European Commission, DG Environment under the contract 070203/2017/768879/ETU/ENV.A.3, in collaboration with Fundacion Ibercivis and The Natural History Museum, November 2018.

Blomkamp, E., 2018. The promise of Co-design for public policy. In: Routledge Handbook of Policy Design. Routledge, London and New York, pp. 77–92. https://doi.org/10.1111/1467-8500.12310.

Bloor, M. (Ed.), 2001. Focus Groups in Social Research. Sage.

Boyce, C., Neale, P., 2006. Conduction In-Depth Interviews: A Guide for Designing and Conducting In-Depth Interviews for Evaluation Input. Pathfinder International, Watertown. http://www.cpc.unc.edu/measure/training/materials/data-quality-portuguese/m_e_tool_series_indepth_interviews.pdf.

Burgess, J., 1996. Focusing on fear: the use of focus groups in a project for the Community Forest Unit, Countryside Commission. Area 28 (2), 130–135.

Chilvers, J., Kearnes, M., 2015. Remaking Participation: Science, Environment and Emergent Publics. Routledge, London and New York.

Darier, É., Gough, C., De Marchi, B., Funtowicz, S., Grove–White, R., Kitchener, D., Guimarães Pereira, Â., Shackley, S., Wynne, B., 1999. Between democracy and expertise? Citizens' participation and environmental integrated assessment in Venice (Italy) and St. Helens (UK). Journal of Environmental Policy and Planning 1 (2), 103–120.

Davies, S.R., Selin, C., Gano, G., Guimarães Pereira, Â., 2012. Citizen engagement and urban change: three case studies of material deliberation. Cities 29 (6), 351–357.

Elam, M., Bertilsson, M., 2003. Consuming, engaging and confronting science: The emerging dimensions of scientific citizenship. European Journal of Social Theory 6 (2), 233–251.

Felt, U., Fochler, M., Müller, A., Strassnig, M., 2009. Unruly ethics: on the difficulties of a bottom-up approach to ethics in the field of genomics. Public Understanding of Science 18 (3), 354–371.

Funtowicz, S., 2006. Why knowledge assessment? In: Guimarães Pereira, A., Guedes Vaz, S., Tognetti, S. (Eds.), Interfaces between Science and Society. Greenleaf Publishing, Sheffield, pp. 138–145.

Funtowicz, S., Ravetz, J., 1990. Uncertainty and Quality in Science for Policy. Springer, Dordrecht.

Gibbs, A., 1997. Focus groups. Social Research Update 19 (8), 1–8.

Gilbert, J.K., Stocklmayer, S.M., Garnett, R., 1999. Mental modeling in science and technology centres: What are visitors really doing. In: International Conference on Learning Science in Informal Contexts, Canberra, pp. 16–32.

Goodin, R.E., Dryzek, J.S., 2006. Deliberative impacts: the macro-political uptake of mini-publics. Politics & Society 34 (2), 219–244.

Guimarães Pereira, Â., Corral Quintana, S., Funtowicz, S., 2005. GOUVERNe: new trends in decision support for groundwater governance issues. Environmental Modelling & Software 20 (2), 111–118.

Guimarães Pereira, Â., L'Astorina, A., Ghezzi, A., Tomasoni, I., 2018. Dialoghi sul Cibo: Food Futuring Tours ad #expo2015/Dialogues on food: Food Futuring Tours at the #expo2015. EUR 28213. European Commission, Luxembourg. https://doi.org/10.2788/254857; https://doi.org/10.2788/684250.

Herivaux, C., Vinatier, F., Sabir, M., Guillot, F., Rinaudo, J.D., 2018. Combining scenario workshops, quantitative approaches and land use change modeling to design plausible future land use scenarios in the Tleta catchment (Morocco). In: Vulnerability of the Mediterranean Soils to Water Erosion: State of Knowledge and Adaptation Strategies in the Face of Global Change. http://shalarchives-ouvertesfr/hal-01755112/.

House of Lords Select Committee on Science and Technology, 2000. Science and Society. The Stationery Office, London.

Irwin, A., 1995. Citizen Science: A Study of People, Expertise and Sustainable Development. Routledge, London and New York.

Irwin, A., Michael, M., 2003. Science, Social Theory &Public Knowledge. McGraw-Hill Education, Philadelphia.

Jasanoff, S., 2003. Technologies of humility: citizen participation in governing science. Minerva 41 (3), 223–244.

Joss, S., Durant, J. (Eds.), 1995. Public Participation in Science: The Role of Consensus Conferences in Europe. NMSI Trading Ltd., London.

Kimbell, K., 2015. Applying Design Approaches to Policy Making:Discovering Policy Lab. University of Brighton, Brighton.

Kitzinger, J., 1994. The methodology of focus groups: the importance of interaction between research participants. Sociology of Health & Illness 16 (1), 103–121.

Kliiver, L., 1995. Consensus conferences at the Danish board of technology. In: Public Participation in Science: The Role of Consensus Conferences in Europe. Science Museum, London.

Kvale, S., 2008. Doing Interviews. Sage, London.

Lassiter, L.E., 2005. The Chicago Guide to Collaborative Ethnography. Chicago Univ. Press, Chicago.

Lezaun, J., Soneryd, L., 2007. Consulting citizens: technologies of elicitation and the mobility of publics. Public Understanding of Science 16 (3), 279–297. https://doi.org/10.1177/0963662507079371.

Mega, V., 2000. Cities inventing the civilisation of sustainability: an odyssey in the urban archipelago of the European Union. Cities 17 (3), 227–236.

Michael, M., 2012. "What are we busy doing?" Engaging the idiot. Science, Technology &Human Values 37 (5), 528–554.

Morgan, D.L., 1996. Focus groups. Annual Review of Sociology 22 (1), 129–152.

Morgan, D.L., Krueger, R.A., Scannell, A.U., 1993. Planning Focus Groups. Sage.

Nascimento, S., Guimarães Pereira, Â., Ghezzi, A., 2014. From Citizen Science to DIY Science. EUR 27095 EN European Commission. https://publications.europa.eu/en/publication-detail/-/publication/1baaa4aa-d199-49fd-8166-c4d9648bcb80/language-en.

Nascimento, S., Pólvora, A., 2016. Social sciences in the transdisciplinary making of sustainable artefacts. Social Science Information 55 (1), 28–42.

Nascimento, S., Pólvora, A., Paio, A., Oliveira, S., Rato, V., Oliveira, M.J., Varela, B., Sousa, J.P., 2016. Sustainable technologies and transdisciplinary futures: from collaborative design to digital fabrication. Science As Culture 25 (4), 520–537. https://doi.org/10.1080/09505431.2016.1193131.

Roy, H., Groom, Q., Adriaens, T., et al., 2018. Increasing understanding of alien species through citizen science (alien-csi). Research Ideas and Outcomes 4, e31412. https://doi.org/10.3897/rio.4.e31412.

Salgado, P.P., Corral Quintana, S., Guimarães Pereira, Â., del Moral Ituarte, L., Mateos, B.P., 2009. Participative multi-criteria analysis for the evaluation of water governance alternatives. A case in the Costa del Sol (Malaga). Ecological Economics 68 (4), 990–1005.

Stappers, P.J., Sanders, E.B.–N., 2012. Convivial Toolbox: Generative Tools for the Front End of Design. BIS Publishers, Amsterdam.

Sawyer, B., 2003. Serious Games: Improving Public Policy through Game-Based Learning and Simulation. Woodrow Wilson International Center for Scholars. https://www.wilsoncenter.org/publication/executive-summary-serious-games-improving-public-policy-through-game-based-learning-and.

Schade, S., Herding, W., Fellermann, A., Kotsev, A., 2019. Joint Statement on new opportunities for air quality sensing - lower-cost sensors for public authorities and citizen science initiatives. Research Ideas and Outcomes 5, e34059. https://doi.org/10.3897/rio.5.e34059.

Selin, C., Pillen Banks, J., 2014. Futurescape City Tours: A Novel Method for Civic Engagement. The Center for Nanotechnology in Society at Arizona State University (CNS-ASU), Tempe, AZ, U.S.A.

Selin, C., Rawlings, K.C., de Ridder-Vignone, K., Sadowski, J., Altamirano Allende, C., Gano, G., Davies, S.R., Guston, D.H., 2017. Experiments in engagement: designing public engagement with science and technology for capacity building. Public Understanding of Science 26 (6), 634–649. https://doi.org/10.1177/0963662515620970.

Singh, J., 2008. The UK Nanojury as 'upstream'public engagement. Participatory Learning and Action 58 (1), 27–32.

Soneryd, L., 2015. Technologies of participation and the making of technologized futures. In: Chilvers, J., Kearnes, M. (Eds.), Remaking Participation: Science, Environment and Emergent Publics. Routledge, London and New York, pp. 144–161.

Stirling, A., 2008. "Opening up" and "closing down": power, participation, and pluralism in the social appraisal of technology. Science, Technology &Human Values 33 (2), 262–294. https://doi.org/10.1177/0162243907311265.

Van Asselt, M.B.A., Rotmans, J., Rothman, D.S., 2005. Scenario Innovation: Experiences from a European Experimental Garden. Taylor& Francis, London.

Videira, N., Antunes, P., Santos, R., Gamito, S., 2003. Participatory modelling in environmental decision-making: the ria Formosa natural park case study. Journal of Environmental Assessment Policy and Management 5 (3), 421–447.

Wakeford, T., 2002. Citizens Juries: a radical alternative for social research. Social Research Update 37 (1), 1–4.

Wynne, B., 1993. Public uptake of science: a case for institutional reflexivity. Public Understanding of Science 2 (4), 321–337.

Chapter 9

European Commission, 2007. Directive2007/2/EC of the European Parliament and of the Council establishing an infrastructure for spatial information in the Community (INSPIRE). Official Journal of the European UnionL .108/1 to 14 25/4/2007. Publication Office, Luxembourg.

Harari, Y.N., 2015. Homo Deus: A Brief History of Tomorrow. Harvill Secker, London.

Kambatla, K., Kollias, G., Kumar, V., Grama, A., 2014. Trends in big data analytics. Journal of Parallel and Distributed Computing 74 (7), 2561–2573.

Krumm, J., 2011. Ubiquitous advertising: the killer application for the 21st century. IEEE Pervasive Computing 10, 66–73.

Laney, D., 2001. 3D Data Management: Controlling Data Volume, Velocity, and Variety. META Group. https://blogs.gartner.com/doug-laney/files/2012/01/ad949-3D-Data-Management-Controlling-Data-Volume-Velocity-and-Variety.pdf. [Accessed 5 May 2020].

Mayer-Schoenberger, V., Cukier, K., 2013. Big Data. A Revolution that Will Transform How We Live, Work, and Think. John Murray Publishers, London.

Nativi, S., Mazzetti, P., Santoro, M., et al., 2015. Big data challenges in building the global earth observaiton system of systems. Environmental Modelling & Software 6, 1–26.

Van Dijck, J., 2014. Datafication, dataism, and dataveillance: big Data between scientific paradigm and ideology. Surveillance and Society 12 (2), 197–208.

Vesnic-Alujevic, L., Stoemer, E., Rudkin, J.E., et al., 2019. The Future of Government 2030+: A Citizen-Centric Perspective on New Government Models. Publication Office, Luxembourg.

Zuboff, S., 2015. Big Other: surveillance capitalism and the prospects of an information civilization. Journal of Information Technology 30, 75–98.

Chapter 10

Bramoullé, Y., Orset, C., 2018. Manufacturing doubt. Journal of Environmental Economics and Management 90, 119–133.

de Melo-Martín, I., Intemann, K., 2014. Who's afraid of dissent? addressing concerns about undermining scientific consensus in public policy developments. Perspectives on Science 22 (4), 593–615.

de Rijcke, S., Wouters, P.F., Rushforth, A.D., Franssen, T.P., Hammarfelt, B., 2016. Evaluation practices and effects of indicator use—a literature review. Research Evaluation 25 (2), 161–169.

Douglas, H., 2009. Science, Policy, and the Value-Free Ideal. Pittsburgh University Press, Pittsburgh.

Elliott, K.C., 2017. A Tapestry of Values: An Introduction to Values in Science. Oxford University Press, Oxford.

Fanelli, D., 2009. How many scientists fabricate and falsify research? A systematic review and meta-analysis of survey data. PLoS One 4 (5), e5738.

Group of Chief Scientific Advisors, 2019. Research and innovation scientific advice mechanism (SAM). In: Scientific Advice to European Policy in a Complex World, Scientific Opinion No.7.

Hoggan, J., Littlemore, R., 2009. Climate Cover-up: The Crusade to Deny Global Warming. Greystone Books, Vancouver.

Kuhn, T.S., 1962. The Structure of Scientific Revolutions. University of Chicago Press, Chicago.

Latour, B., Woolgar, S., 1979. Laboratory Life: The Construction of Scientific Facts. Sage Publications, Beverly Hills.

Martinson, B.C., Anderson, M.S., de Vries, R., 2005. Scientists behaving badly. Nature 435, 737–738.

Merton, R.K., 1942. The normative structure of science. In: Merton, R.K. (Ed.), The Sociology of Science: Theoretical and Empirical Investigations. University of Chicago Press, Chicago.

OECD, 2005. Managing Conflict of Interest in the Public Sector: A Toolkit. OECD Publishing, Paris. https://doi.org/10.1787/9789264018242-en.

Oliver, K., Cairney, P., 2019. The dos and don'ts of influencing policy: a systematic review of advice to academics. Palgrave Communications 5, 21.

Oreskes, N., Conway, E.M., 2010. Merchants of Doubt: How a Handful of Scientists Obscured the Truth on Issues from Tobacco Smoke to Global Warming. Bloomsbury Press, New York.

Pielke Jr., R., 2007. The Honest Broker: Making Sense of Science in Policy and Politics. Cambridge University Press, Cambridge.

Proctor, R.N., 2012. The history of the discovery of the cigarette–lung cancer link: evidentiary traditions, corporate denial, global toll. Tobacco Control 21, 87–91.

Ravetz, J.R., 1999. What is post-normal science. Futures 31, 647–653.

Siegel, E.H., Wormwood, J.B., Quigley, K.S., Barrett, L.F., 2018. Seeing what you feel: affect drives visual perception of structurally neutral faces. Psychological Science 29 (4), 496–503.

Steele, S., Ruskin, G., et al., 2019. "Always read the small print": a case study of commercial research funding, disclosure and agreements with Coca-Cola. Journal of Public Health Policy 40 (3), 273–285.

Thagard, P., 2007. The moral psychology of conflicts of interest: insights from affective neuroscience. Journal of Applied Philosophy 24 (4), 367–380.

Van 't Wout, M., Chang, L.J., Sanfey, A.G., 2010. The influence of emotion regulation on social interactive decision-making. Emotion 10 (6), 815–821.

Chapter 11

Arthur, B., 1994. Increasing Returns and Path Dependence in the Economy. Ann Arbor.

Bonabeau, E., May 14, 2002. Agent-based modeling: methods and techniques for simulating human systems. Proceedings of the National Academy of Sciences 99 (Suppl. 3), 7280–7287.

Capra, F., 1996. The Web of Life. Anchor Books, New York (Chapter 6).

Cristelli, M., Gabrielli, A., Tacchella, A., Caldarelli, G., Pietronero, L., 2013. Measuring the intangibles: a metrics for the economic complexity of countries and products. PLoS One 8 (8), e70726. https://doi.org/10.1371/journal.pone.0070726.

Cristelli, M., Tacchella, A., Pietronero, L., 2015. The heterogeneous dynamics of economic complexity. PLoS One 10 (2), e0117174. https://doi.org/10.1371/journal.pone.0117174.

EC, 2013. In: Capros, P., Van Regemorter, D., Paroussos, L., Karkatsulis, P., (Eds.). GEM-E3 Model Documentation. JRC Technical Reports European Commission. EUR 26034 EN; ISBN 978-92-79-31463-6 (pdf); ISSN 1831-9424 (online) https://ec.europa.eu/jrc/en/gem-e3/publications.

EC, 2019a. EU Science Hub. Website of the General Equilibrium Model for Economy-Energy-Environment (GEM-E 3) Listing Publications and Policy Documents Based on the Model. https://ec.europa.eu/jrc/en/gem-e3/publications.

EC, 2019b. European Commission: Enlightenment 2.0 Research Programme. Available from: https://ec.europa.eu/jrc/en/enlightenment-research-programme.

Faulkner, L., Brown, K., Quinn, T., 2018. Analyzing community resilience as an emergent property of dynamic social-ecological systems. Ecology and Society 23 (1), 24. https://doi.org/10.5751/ES-09784-230124.

Garas, A., Lapatinas, A., 2017. The role of consumer networks in firms' multi-characteristics competition and market share inequality. Structural Change and Economic Dynamics 43, 76–86.

Grandmont, J.M., 1985. On endogenous competitive business cycles. Econometrica 50, 1345–1370.

Gunderson, L., 2000. Ecological resilience - In theory and application. Annual Review of Ecology and Systematics 31, 425–439.

Hausmann, R., Hidalgo, C., Bustos, S., Coscia, M., Chung, S., Jimenez, J., Simoes, A., Yildirim, M., 2013. The Atlas of Economic Complexity. MIT Press, Cambridge, MA. The Growth Lab at Harvard University. The Atlas of Economic Complexity. Available from: http://www.atlas.cid.harvard.edu.

Heath, J., 2014. Enlightenment 2.0. Harper Collins, New York.

Hidalgo, C.A., Hausmann, R., June 30, 2009. The building blocks of economic complexity. Proceedings of the National Academy of Sciences 106 (26), 10570–10575.

Labanca, N., 2017. Complex systems: the latest human artefact. In: Allen, T.F.H., Arrobbio, O., Bartiaux, F., Bauwens, T., Bertoldi, P., Byrne, D.S., Ellegård, K., Fath, B.D., Giampietro, M., Kovacic, Z., Labanca, N., Maschio, I., Moezzi, M., Paci, D., Padovan, D., Palm, J., Ruzzenenti, F., Shaw, D., Shove, E., Tainter, J. (Eds.), Complex Systems and Social Practices in Energy Transitions, Springer International Publishing, Switzerland, pp. 3–28.

May, R.M., 1976. Simple mathematical models with very complicated dynamics. Nature 261 (5560), 459–467.

Meadows, D., 2008. In: Wright, D. (Ed.), Thinking in Systems: A Primer. Chelsea Green Publishing, Chelsea, VT.

Mikhailov, A.S., Calenbuhr, V., 2002. From Cells to Societies – Models of Complex Coherent Action. Springer, Heidelberg, Berlin.

Murray, J.D., 2008. Mathematical Biology – An Introduction. Springer, Berlin, Heidelberg.

OECD, September 2009. Applications of complexity science for public policy. OECD Global Science Forum 5.

Pauly, D., Christensen, V., Dalsgaard, J., Froese, R., Torres jr., F., February 6, 1998. Fishing down marine food webs. Science 279 (5352), 860–863.

Peterson, G., February 2000. Scaling ecological dynamics: self-organization, hierarchical structure, and ecological resilience. Climatic Change 44 (3), 291–309.

Rittel, H.W.J., Webber, M.M., 1973. Dilemmas in a general theory of planning. Policy Sciences 4 (2), 155–169.

Sayama, H., 2010. Collective Dynamics of Complex Systems Taken from. https://en.wikipedia.org/wiki/Complex_system.

Walters, C., Maguire, J., 1996. Lessons for stock assessment from the northern cod collapse. Reviews in Fish Biology and Fisheries 6, 125–137.

Weidlich, W., Haag, G., 1983. Concepts and Models of a Quantitative Sociology. The Dynamics of Interacting Populations. Springer Series in Synergetics, Vol. 14. Springer, Berlin, Heidelberg.

West, G., 2018. Scale – The Universal Laws of Life, Growth and Death in Organisms, Cities and Companies. Penguin Books, New York.

Willinger, W., Govindan, R., Jamin, S., Paxson, V., Shenker, S., February 19, 2002. Critically examining criticality. Proceedings of the National Academy of Sciences 99 (Suppl. 1), 2573–2580.

Chapter 12

Althaus, C., Bridgman, P., Davis, G., 2017. The Australian Policy Handbook. A Practical Guide to the Policy Making Process, sixth ed. Allen & Unwin.

Bock, A.-K., Bontoux, L., 2017. Food safety and nutrition – how to prepare for a challenging future? New approaches for using scenarios for policy-making. European Journal of Futures Research 5, 10. https://doi.org/10.1007/s40309-017-0119-3.

Bontoux, L., Bengtsson, D., 2015. 2035 Paths towards a sustainable EU economy, JRC science for policy report. EUR 27376 EN. https://doi.org/10.2760/8029. Luxembourg, Publications Office of the European Union.

Bontoux, L., Bengtsson, D., Rosa, A.B., Sweeney, J.A., 2016. The JRC scenario exploration system – From study to serious game. Journal of Futures Studies 20 (3), 93–108.

Boston, J., 2016. Governing for the Future: Designing Democratic Institutions for a Better Tomorrow. https://doi.org/10.1108/S2053-769720160000025001. Published online: 01 Nov 2016; 3-43. Permanent link to this document.

Burmeister, K., Fink, A., Steinmüller, K., Schulz-Montag, B., 2018. Deutschland neu denken. Acht Szenarien für unsere Zukunft. oekom verlag München.

Candy, S., Dunagan, J., 2017. Designing an experiential scenario: the people who vanished. Futures 86, 136–153.

Da Costa, O., Warnke, P., Cagnin, C., Scapolo, F., 2008. The impact of foresight on policy-making: insights from the FORLEARN mutual learning process. Technology Analysis & Strategic Management 20 (3), 369–387.

Cuhls, K., 2015. Bringing Foresight to Decision-Making - Lessons for Policy-making from Selected Non-European countries. Policy Brief by the Research, Innovation, and Science Policy Experts (RISE). Publications Office of the European Union, Luxembourg.

Dufva, M., 2020. How was the Megatrends update 2020 compiled? https://www.sitra.fi/en/articles/how-was-the-megatrends-2020-update-compiled/.

Dufva, M., Kettunen, O., Aminoff, A., Antikainen, M., Sundqvist-Andberg, H., Tuomisto, T., 2015. Approaches to Gaming the Future: Planning a Foresight Game on Circular Economy. Games and Learning Alliance. Springer, Cham, pp. 560–571. https://doi.org/10.1007/978-3- 319-40216-1_60.

Dunne, A., Raby, F., 2013. Speculative Everything. Design, Fiction and Social Dreaming. MIT Press Cambridge, MA and London, UK.

EFFLA - EUROPEAN FORUM ON FORWARD LOOKING ACTIVITIES (no year): Policy Brief No 13. Strategic Intelligence Methodology. URL: https://ec.europa.eu/research/innovation-union/pdf/expert-groups/effla-reports/effla_pb_13_-_strategic_intelligence_methodology.pdf.

EU Policy Lab, 2017. Megatrends Implications Assessment. A Workshop On Anticipatory Thinking and Foresight for Policy Makers. European Union, Brussels. https://ec.europa.eu/knowledge4policy/sites/know4pol/files/megatrendsbooklet_20171221.pdf.

European Commission, 2017a. Better Regulation Guidelines. SWD (2017)350.

European Commission, 2017b. Better Regulation Toolbox. Complement to SWD (2017)350.

Gore, A., 1992. Earth in the Balance: Ecology and the Human Spirit. Houghton Mifflin, New York, NY.

Guimarães Pereira, Â., L'Astorina, A., Ghezzi, A., Tomasoni, I., 2018. Dialoghi sul Cibo: Food Futuring Tours ad #expo2015/Dialogues on Food: Food Futuring Tours at the #expo2015. EUR 28213, Publications Office of the European Union, Luxembourg. https://doi.org/10.2788/684250. JRC103583.

Hancock, T., Bezold, C., 1994. Possible futures, preferable futures. Healthcare Forum Journal 37 (2), 23–29.

Hauser, F. (Ed.), 2017. Quality of Public Administration. A Toolbox for Practitioners, 2017 edition. European Commission.

Head, B., 2008. Wicked problems in public policy. Public Policy 3 (2), 101–118.

JRC-IPTS, 2008. FOR-LEARN Online Foresight Guide. http://forlearn.jrc.ec.europa.eu/index.htm.

Kimbell, L., 2015. Applying Design Approaches to Policy Making: Discovering Policy Lab. Discussion Paper. University of Brighton, Brighton. http://ualresearchonline.arts.ac.uk/9111/.

Krzysztofowicz, M., Goudeseune, L., Bontoux, L., Balian, E., 2018. Workshop on Horizon Scanning: From Interesting to Useful, from Practice to Impact. JRC. JRC112992.

Kuribayashi, M., Hayashi, K., Akaike, S., 2017. A proposal of a new foresight platform considering of sustainable development goals. European Journal of Futures Research 6, 4. https://doi.org/10.1007/s40309-017-0130-8.

Lucas, H.C., Goh, J.M., 2009. Disruptive technology: how Kodak missed the digital photography revolution. The Journal of Strategic Information Systems 18, 46–55.

Nascimento, S., Pólvora, A., Sousa Lourenço, J., 2018. Blockchain4EU: Blockchain for Industrial Transformations. Publications Office of the European Union, Luxembourg. ISBN: 978-92-79-85719-5. https://doi.org/10.2760/204920. JRC111095.

Policy Horizons Canada, 2014. MetaScan 3 Emerging Technologies. Government of Canada, Ottawa.

Popper, R., 2008. Foresight methodology. In: Georghiou, L., Cassingena, J., Keenan, M., Miles, I., Popper, R. (Eds.), The Handbook of Technology Foresight. Edward Elgar, Cheltenham, pp. 44–88.

Pryshlakivsky, J., Searcy, C., 2012. Sustainable development as a wicked problem. In: Kovacic, S.F., Sousa-Poza, A. (Eds.), Managing and Engineering in Complex Situations. Springer Netherlands.

Rhisiart, M., Störmer, E., Daheim, C., 2017. From foresight to impact? The 2030 Future of Work scenarios. Technological Forecasting and Social Change 124, 203–213.

Sardar, Z., Masood, E., 2006. How Do You Know? Reading Ziauddin Sardar on Islam, Science and Cultural Relations. Pluto Press, London.

Störmer, E., Truffer, B., Dominguez, D., Gujer, W., Herlyn, A., Hiessl, H., Kastenholz, H., Klinke, A., Markard, J., Maurer, M., Ruef, A., 2009. The exploratory analysis of trade-offs in strategic planning: Lessons from Regional Infrastructure Foresight. Technological Forecasting and Social Change 76, 1150–1162.

Sweeney, J., 2017. Game on: foresight at play with the United Nations. Journal of Futures Studies 22 (2), 27–40. https://doi.org/10.6531/JFS.2017.22(2).A27.

Truffer, B., Störmer, E., Maurer, M., Ruef, A., 2010. Local strategic planning processes and sustainability transitions in infrastructure sectors. Environmental Policy and Governance 20, 258–269. https://doi.org/10.1002/eet.550.

Vesnic-Alujevic, L., Stoermer, E., Rudkin, J., Scapolo, F., Kimbell, L., 2019. The Future of Government 2030+: A Citizen-Centric Perspective on New Government Models. EUR 29664 EN Publications Office of the European Union, Luxembourg.

Wiggert, M., 2014. Der Zukunft ein Stück näher. Bundeswehr entwickelt Analyse-Tool. Behörden Spiegel, p. 54.

Wilhelmer, D., 2016. Society in need of transformation. Citizen-Foresight as a method to co-create urban future. Public Philosophy & Democratic Education 5 (2), 51–72. https://doi.org/10.14746/fped.2016.5.2.21.

Chapter 13

Alexander, C.W., 1964. Notes on the Synthesis of Form. Harvard University Press.

Aicher, O., 1991. Analog and Digital. John Wiley & Sons, p. 100.

Auger, J., 2013. Speculative Design: Crafting the Speculation, Digital Creativity.

Bailey, J., Lloyd, P., 2016. The introduction of design to policy-making and the UK government. Design Research Society Conference.

Buchanan, R., 2001. Design research and the new learning. Design Issues 17 (4), 3–23.

Cooper, R., Press, M., 1995. The Design Agenda: A Guide to Successful Design Management. John Wiley and Sons, Chichester & New York.

Deserti, A., Rizzo, F., 2015. Design and organizational change in the public sector. Design Management Journal.

Dunne, A., Raby, F., 2013. Speculative Everything: Design, Fiction, and Social Dreaming. MIT Press.

Fish, J., Scrivener, S., 1990. Amplifying the mind's eye: sketching and visual cognition. Leonardo 117–126. https://doi.org/10.2307/1578475.

Gropius, W., 1956. Scope of Total Architecture. Allen and Unwin, London.

Hevner, A.R., March, S.T., Park, J., Ram, S., 2004. Design science in information systems research. MIS Quarterly 28 (1), 75–105.

International Council of Graphic Design Associations, 2007. Defining the Professions. ICOGRADA. http://www.icograda.org/about/about/articles836.htm. [Accessed 8 March 2011].

Jungkind, W., Roussell, Y., 2006. Graphic Design – Definition. Society of Graphic Designers Canada. http://www.gdc.net/designers/features/articles122.php. [Accessed 3 May 2009].

Kimbell, L., 2012. Rethinking design thinking: Part II. Design and Culture 4 (2), 129–148. https://doi.org/10.2752/175470812X13281948975413.

Krippendorff, K., 2006. The Semantic Turn; A New Foundation for Design. Taylor&Francis, CRC Press, Boca Raton, London, New York.

Love, T., 2002. Constructing a coherent body of theory about designing and designs: some philosophical issues. Design Studies 23 (3), 345–361.

Mallol, G.M., 2012. In: "F(r)ictions. Design as Cultural Form of Dissent." Design History Society Annual Conference, Barcelona, 7–10 September 2011.

Manzini, E., 2013. Making Things Happen: Social Innovation and Design. Design Issues, volume 30, Number 1. Winter 2014.

Mau, B., 2007. What is massive change? Massive Change. http://www.massivechange.com/about/. [Accessed 12 February 2007].

Papanek, V.J., 1971. Design for the Real World: Human Ecology and Social Change. Chicago, Ill.

Press, M., Cooper, R., 2003. The Design Experience: The Role of Design and Designers in the Twenty-First Century. Ashgate Publishing Company, Burlington, UK.

Ralph, P., Wand, Y., 2009. A proposal for a formal definition of the design concept. In: Lyytinen, K., Loucopoulos, P., Mylopoulos, J., Robinson, B. (Eds.), Design Requirements Engineering: A Ten-Year Perspective, vol. 14. Springer Berlin Heidelberg, Berlin, Heidelberg, pp. 103–136.

Rand, P., 2001. In: Maeda, J. (Ed.), Maeda@Media. Universe Press.

Simon, H.A., 1969. The Sciences of the Artificial. M.I.T. Press, Cambridge.

Walker, J.A., 1990. Design History and the History of Design. Pluto Press.

Chapter 14

Bell, S., Shaw, B., Boaz, A., 2011. Real-world approaches to assessing the impact of environmental research on policy. Research Evaluation 20 (3), 227–237.

Bozeman, B., Rogers, J., 2001. Strategic management of government-sponsored R&D portfolios. Environment and Planning C: Government and Policy 19 (3), 413–442.

Caplan, N., 1979. The two-communities theory and knowledge utilization. American Behavioral Scientist 22 (3), 459–470.

European Commission, 2017. Analysis of the Use of Models by the European Commission in Its Impact Assessments for the Period 2009–2014. EUR 28628 EN. Publications Office of the European Union, Luxembourg. ISBN: 978-92-79-69283-3. https://doi.org/10.2760/096340.

Gaunand, A., Colinet, L., Joly, P.B., Matt, M., 2017. Counting what really counts? Assessing the political impact of science. The Journal of Technology Transfer 1–23.

Hill, S., 2016. Assessing (for) impact: future assessment of the societal impact of research. Palgrave Communications 2, 16073. https://doi.org/10.1057/palcomms.2016.73.

Joly, P.-B., Gaunand, A., Colinet, L., Laredo, P., Lemarie, S., Matt, M., 2015. ASIRPA: a comprehensive theory-based approach to assessing the societal impacts of a research organization. Research Evaluation 24 (4), 440–453.

Sarewitz, D., Pielke Jr., R.A., 2007. The neglected heart of science policy: reconciling supply of and demand for science. Environmental Science & Policy 10 (1), 5–16.

Sharpe, W.F., 1963. A simplified model for portfolio analysis. Management Science 9 (2), 277–293.

Topp, L., Mair, D., Smillie, L., Cairney, P., 2018. Knowledge management for policy impact: the case of the European Commission's Joint Research Centre. Palgrave Communications 4, 87.

Wallace, M.L., Rafols, I., 2015. Research portfolio analysis in science policy: moving from financial returns to societal benefits. Minerva 53 (2), 89–115.

Al Khudhairy, D., Schneiderbauer, S., Lotz-Iwen, H., 2009. The Security Dimension of GMES – Network of Excellence GMOSS: A European Think Tank for EO Technologies in Support of Security Issues. Springer Netherlands. ISBN: 978-1-4020-8483-6. https://doi.org/10.1007/978-1-4020-8484-3.

Allen, D., Coles, E., Kankaanranta, T., Mcmullan, C., Mobach, D., Norman, A., Perko, T., Pylvas, K., Wijngaards, N., 2017. Good practices and innovation in risk communication. EUR 28034 EN. In: Poljanšek, K., Marín Ferrer, M., De Groeve, T., Clark, I. (Eds.), Science for Disaster Risk Management 2017: Knowing Better and Losing Less. Publications Office of the European Union, Luxembourg. https://doi.org/10.2788/688605. Chapter 4.4.

Annunziato, A., 2005. Development and implementation of a tsunami wave propagation model at JRC. In: Proceedings of the International Symposium on Ocean Wave Measurement and Analysis JRC31442 http://publications.jrc.ec.europa.eu/repository/handle/JRC31442.

Annunziato, A., 2007. The tsunami assessment modelling system by the Joint Research Centre. Science of Tsunami Hazards: The International Journal of The Tsunami Society 26 (2), 70–92. JRC41955, ISSN: 8755-6839 http://tsunamisociety.org/STHVol26N2Y2007.pdf.

Boersma, F.K., Allen, D., Comes, T., Stanciugelu, I., Terpstra, T., 2017. Communicating disaster risk. In: Poljanšek, K., Marín Ferrer, M., De Groeve, T., Clark, I. (Eds.), Science for Disaster Risk Management 2017: Knowing Better and Losing Less. Publications Office of the European Union, Luxembourg. https://doi.org/10.2788/688605. EUR 28034 EN. Chapter 4.

Broglia, M., Corbane, C., Carrion, D., Lemoine, G., Pesaresi, M., 2010. Validation Protocol for Emergency Response Geo-Information Products. Publications Office of the European Union. https://doi.org/10.2788/63690. EUR 24496 EN.

Broglia, M., Louvrier, C., Lemoine, G., 2013. Copernicus-EMS Mapping Guidelines and Best Practice. Publications Office of the European Union. https://doi.org/10.2788/91765. EUR 26072 EN.

Clark, I., De Groeve, T., Marín Ferrer, M., Poljanšek, K., Faivre, N., Peter, D., Quevauviller, P., Boersma, F.K., Krausmann, E., Murray, V., Papadopoulos, G.A., Salamon, P., Simmons, D.C., Wilkinson, E., Casajus Valles, A., Doherty, B., Galliano, D., 2017. Future challenges of disaster risk management. In: Poljanšek, K., Marín Ferrer, M., De Groeve, T., Clark, I. (Eds.), Science for Disaster Risk Management 2017: Knowing Better and Losing Less. Publications Office of the European Union, Luxembourg. https://doi.org/10.2788/688605. EUR 28034 EN. Chapter 6.

Comes, T., Adrot, A., Rizza, C., 2017. Decision-making under uncertainty. In: Poljanšek, K., Marín Ferrer, M., De Groeve, T., Clark, I. (Eds.), Science for Disaster Risk Management 2017: Knowing Better and Losing Less. Publications Office of the European Union, Luxembourg. https://doi.org/10.2788/688605. EUR 28034 EN. Chapter 4.2.

Corban, C., Carrion, D., Lemoine, G., Broglia, M., 2011. Comparison of damage assessment maps derived from very high spatial resolution satellite and aerial imagery of the Haiti 2010 earthquake impact area. Earthquake Spectra 27 (S1), S199–S218. https://doi.org/10.1193/1.3630223.

De Groeve, T., Casajus Valles, A., 2015. Science Policy Interfaces in Disaster Risk Management in the EU. Mapping the Support provided by Science in the EU Civil Protection Mechanism. Publications Office of the European Union, Luxembourg. ISBN: 978-92-79-52740-1. https://doi.org/10.2788/023384.

De Groeve, T., Vernaccini, L., Annunziato, A., 2006. Modelling disaster impact for the global disaster alert and coordination system. In: Van de Walle, B., Turoff, M. (Eds.), Proceedings of the 3rd International ISCRAM Conference, pp. 409–417 Newark, NJ (USA), May 2006 http://idl.iscram.org/files/degroeve/2006/429_DeGroeve_etal2006.pdf. [Accessed 5 May 2020].

De Groeve, T., Thielen Del Pozo, J., Brakenridge, R.G., Adler, R., Alfieri, L., Kull, D., Lindsay, F., Imperiali, O., Pappenberger, F., Rudari, R., Salamon, P., Villars, N., Wyjad, K., 2015. Joining forces in a global flood partnership. Bulletin of the American Meteorological Society 96 (5), ES97–ES100. https://doi.org/10.1175/BAMS-D-14-00147.1. AMER METEOROLOGICAL SOC.

European Commission, 2018. Emergency Response Coordination Centre ECHO Factsheet. http://ec.europa.eu/echo/files/aid/countries/factsheets/thematic/ERC_en.pdf. [Accessed 5 May 2020].

Fonio, C., Annunziato, A., 2018. Network of European Facilities I: European Network of Crisis Management Laboratories (ENCML). Publications Office of the European Union. https://doi.org/10.2788/291111. EUR 28334 EN.

IFRC, 2005. Data or Dialogue? The Role of Information in Disasters. International Federation of Red Cross and Red Crescent Societies, Geneva. http://www.ifrc.org/en/publications-and-reports/world-disasters-report/wdr2005/. [Accessed 5 May 2020].

IWG-SEM, 2015. Emergency Mapping Guidelines. http://www.un-spider.org/sites/default/files/IWG_SEM_EmergencyMappingGuidelines_v1_Final.pdf. [Accessed 5 May 2020].

Marin Ferrer, M., Casajus Valles, A., Civiletti, G., 2016. Science Policy Interfaces in Disaster Risk Management in the EU: Requirements and Conditions for Efficient SPIs in Practice. Publications Office of the European Union. https://doi.org/10.2788/944382. EUR 28280 EN, ISBN: 978-92-79-64399-6, OP LB-NA-28280-EN-C (print).

Marin Ferrer, M., Vernaccini, L., Poljansek, K., 2017. INFORM Index for Risk Management: Concept and Methodology, Version 2017. Publications Office of the European Union. https://doi.org/10.2760/08037. EUR 28655 EN.

OCHA, 2012. Humanitarian and Country Icons 2012. https://reliefweb.int/report/world/world-humanitarian-and-country-icons-2012. [Accessed 5 May 2020].

Pesaresi, M., Syrris, V., Julea, A., 2016. A new method for Earth observation data analytics based on symbolic machine learning. Remote Sensing 8 (5), 399. https://doi.org/10.3390/rs8050399.

Probst, P., Annunziato, A., 2017. JRC Storm Surge System: New Developments. EUR 29079 EN.

Probst, P., Franchello, G., 2012. Global Storm Surge Forecast and Inundation Modelling. EUR 25233 EN.

Salamon, P., Kettner, A., Coughlan de Perez, E., Rudari, R., Trigg, M., Weerts, A., Cohen, S., Prados, A., Wu, H., Schumann, G., Ward, P., Neal, J., Bernhofen, M., Livesey, D., Alfieri, L., Bhardwaj, A., Prudhomme, C., Nelson, J., Ficchì, A., Bevington, J., Tavakoly, A., Brakenridge, R., Galantowicz, J., Matgen, P., Winsemius, H., Green, D., Glasscoe, M., Schultz, L., 2018. The Global Flood Partnership Annual Meeting 2018 – Bridging the Gap between Science and Users. European Commission, Ispra. ISBN: 978-92-79-93665-4. https://doi.org/10.2760/05644. PUBSY No. JRC113100.

San Miguel, J., 2017. Copernicus Emergency Management System – Global Wildfire Information System. Dataset. JRC107127 http://data.jrc.ec.europa.eu/collection/CEMS-GWIS.

UNISDR, 2015. The Sendai Framework for Disaster Risk Reduction 2015–2030, UNISDR/GE/2015 – ICLUX EN5000, first ed.

UNISDR, 2016. The Science and Technology Roadmap to Support the Implementation of the Sendai Framework for Disaster Risk Reduction 2015–2030. https://www.preventionweb.net/files/45270_unisdrscienceandtechnologyroadmap.pdf.

Vogt, J., Barbosa, P., Cammalleri, C., Saiote Carrao, H., Lavaysse, C., 2017. Drought Risk Management: Needs and Experiences in Europe. https://doi.org/10.1201/9781315265551-23. JRC106951.

Chapter 17

Cartwright, N., 2007. Are RCTs the gold standard? BioSocieties 2 (1), 11–20.

Codagnone, C., Bogliacino, F., Ivchenko, A., Veltri, G., Gaskell, G., 2014. Study on Online Gambling and Adequate Measures for the Protection of Consumers of Gambling Services. European Commission. Final Report.

Dessart, F., Barriero-Hurlé, J., van Bavel, R., 2019. Behavioural factors affecting the adoption of sustainable farming practices: a policy-oriented review. European Review of Agricultural Economics 46 (3), 417–471.

European Commission, 2014. Recommendation 2014/478/EU of the European Commission on principles for the protection of consumers and players of online gambling services and for the prevention of minors from gambling online. Official Journal of the European Union 214, 38–46.

European Union, 2014. Regulation (EU) 1286/2014 of the European Parliament and of the Council of 26 November 2014on key information documents for packaged retail and insurance-based investment products (PRIIPs). Official Journal of the European Union 352, 1–23.

European Union, 2017. Regulation (EU) 2017/1369 of the European Parliament and of the Council of 4 July 2017 setting a framework for energy labelling. Official Journal of the European Union 198, 1–23.

Fiske, S.T., Taylor, S.E., 2013. Social Cognition: From Brains to Culture. Sage, London.

GfK Consortium, 2018. Behavioural Study on Advertising and Marketing Practices in Online Social Media. European Commission. JUST/03/2015 85 01, Final Report.

Goldstein, N.J., Cialdini, R.B., Griskevicius, V., 2008. A room with a viewpoint: using social norms to motivate environmental conservation in hotels. Journal of Consumer Research 35 (3), 472–482.

Kahneman, D., Tversky, A., 1979. Prospect theory: an analysis of decision under risk. Econometrica 47 (2), 263–292.

Kahneman, D., 2011. Thinking, Fast and Slow. Penguin, London.

London Economics, 2014. Study on the Impact of the Energy Label – and Potential Changes to it – on Consumer Understanding and on Purhcase Decisions. European Commission. ENER/C3/2013-428, Final Report.

Lourenço, J.S., Ciriolo, E., Rafael Almeida, S., Troussard, X., 2016. Behavioural Insights Applied to Policy: European Report 2016 EUR 27726 EN. Publications Office of the European Union, Luxembourg.

Lunn, P., 2014. Regulatory Policy and Behavioural Economics. OECD Publishing, Paris.

OECD, 2017. Behavioural Insights and Public Policy: Lessons from Around the World. OECD Publishing, Paris.

Sunstein, C.R., 2014. Nudging: a very short guide. Journal of Consumer Policy 37 (4), 583–588.

Thaler, R., Sunstein, C., 2008. Nudge: Improving Decisions about Health, Wealth, and Happiness. Penguin, London.

Troussard, X., van Bavel, R., 2018. How can behavioural insights be used to improve EU policy? Intereconomics 53 (1), 8–12.

van Bavel, R., Hermann, B., Esposito, G., Proestakis, A., 2013. Applying Behavioural Sciences to EU Policy-Making. EUR 26033 EN. Publications Office of the European Union, Luxembourg.

Zaltman, G., 2003. How Customers Think: Essential Insights into the Mind of the Market. Harvard Business Press, Watertown, MA.

Arrow, K.J., Raynaud, H., 1986. Social Choice and Multicriterion Decision Making. M.I.T. Press, Cambridge.

Becker, W., Saisana, M., Paruolo, P., Vandecasteele, I., 2017. Weights and importance in composite indicators: closing the gap. Ecological Indicators 80, 12–22.

Benessia, A., Guimarães Pereira, Â., 2015. The Internet of Things: do we really need and want to be smart? In: Guimarães Pereira, Funtowicz (Eds.), Science, Philosophy and Sustainability: The End of the Cartesian Dream. Routledge, London.

Bratti, M., Ghirelli, C., Santangelo, G., 2018. Vocational training for unemployed youth in Latvia. Evidence from a Regression Discontinuity Design. IZA Discussion Paper No. 11870.

Cacuci Dan, G., Ionescu-Bujor, M., Navon, M., 2005. Sensitivity and Uncertainty Analysis: Applications to Large-Scale Systems. Chapman & Hall.

Card, D., Chetty, R., Feldstein, M., Saez, E., 2010. Expanding access to administrative data for research in the United States. In: Schultze, C.L., Newlon, D.H. (Eds.), Ten Years and beyond: Economists Answer NSF's Call for Long-Term Research Agendas. American Economic Association, Nashville.

Conti, M., Ferrara, A.R., Ferraresi, M., 2019. Did the EU Airport Charges Directive lead to lower aeronautical charges? Empirical evidence from a diff-in-diff research design. Economics of Transportation 17, 24–39. https://doi.org/10.1016/j.ecotra.2018.12.001. ISSN 2212-0122.

Crato, N., Paruolo, P. (Eds.), 2019. Data-driven Policy Impact Evaluation: How Access to Microdata Is Transforming Policy Design. Springer. Available at: https://www.springer.com/it/book/9783319784601.

Cucciniello, M., Porumbescu, G.A., Grimmelikhuijsen, S., 2017. 25 Years of Transparency Research: Evidence and Future Directions. Public Administration Review 77 (1), 32–44. https://doi.org/10.1111/puar.12685.

Dasgupta, P., 2001. Valuing objects and evaluating policies in imperfect economies. Economic Journal 111 (May), C1–C29.

Figueira, J., Greco, S., Ehrgott, M. (Eds.), 2016. Multiple-criteria Decision Analysis. State of the Art Surveys. Springer International Series in Operations Research and Management Science, New York.

Frame, B., O'Connor, M., 2011. Integrating valuation and deliberation: the purpose of sustainability assessment. Environmental Science & Policy 14, 1–10.

Funtowicz, S.O., Ravetz, J.R., 1990. Uncertainty and Quality in Science for Policy. Kluwer Academic Publishers, Dordrecht.

Funtowicz, S.O., Ravetz, J.R., 1991. A new scientific methodology for global environmental issues. In: Costanza, R. (Ed.), Ecological Economics. New York, Columbia, pp. 137–152.

Ghirelli, C., Havari, E., Santangelo, G., Scettri, M., 2019. Does on-the-job training help graduates find a job? Evidence from an Italian region. International Journal of Manpower 40 (3), 500–524. https://doi.org/10.1108/IJM-02-2018-0062.

Heckman, J.J., 2010. Building bridges between structural and program evaluation approaches to evaluating policy. Journal of Economic Literature 48 (2), 356–398.

Heckman, J.J., Vytlacil, E.J., 2007a. Econometric evaluation of social programs, Part 1: causal models, structural models, and econometric policy evaluation. In: Heckman, J.J., Leamer, E.E. (Eds.), Handbook of Econometrics 6B. North-Holland, Amsterdam, Netherlands, pp. 4779–4874.

Heckman, J.J., Vytlacil, E.J., 2007b. Econometric evaluation of social programs, Part II: using the marginal treatment effect to organize alternative econometric estimators to evaluate social programs, and to forecast their effects in new environments. In: Heckman, J.J., Leamer, E.E. (Eds.), Handbook of Econometrics 6B. North-Holland, Amsterdam, Netherlands, pp. 4875–5143.

Helton, J.C., Johnson, J.D., Salaberry, C.J., Storlie, C.B., 2006. Survey of sampling based methods for uncertainty and sensitivity analysis. Reliability Engineering & System Safety 91, 1175–1209.

Hoyland, B., Moene, K., 2012. The tyranny of international index rankings. Journal of Development Economics 1–14.

Imbens, G.W., Wooldridge, J.M., 2009. Recent developments in the econometrics of program evaluation. Journal of Economic Literature 47 (1), 5–86.

Imbens, G.W., Rubin, D.B., 2015. Causal Inference for Statistics, Social, and Biomedical Sciences: An Introduction. Cambridge University Press.

Ishizaka, A., Nemery, P., 2013. Multi-criteria Decision Analysis: Methods and Software. John Wiley & Sons.

Jerrim, J., de Vries, R., 2017. The limitations of quantitative social science for informing public policy. Evidence & Policy 13 (1), 117–133.

Keeney, R., Raiffa, H., 1976. Decision with Multiple Objectives: Preferences and Value Trade-Offs. Wiley, New York.

Kelley, J.G., Simmons, B.A., 2015. Politics by number: indicators as social pressure in international relations. American Journal of Political Science 59 (1), 55–70.

Martelli, S., Janssens-Maenhout, G., Paruolo, P., Bréchet, T., Strobl, E., Guizzardi, D., Cerutti, A.K., Iancu, A., 2018. Do voters support local commitments for climate change mitigation in Italy? Ecological Economics 144, 27–35. https://doi.org/10.1016/j.ecolecon.2017.06.035.

Munda, G., 2008. Social Multi-Criteria Evaluation for a Sustainable Economy. Springer, Heidelberg, New York.

Munda, G., 2016. Beyond welfare economics: some methodological issues. Journal of Economic Methodology 23 (Issue 2), 185–202.

OECD/EC JRC (Organisation for Economic Co-operation and Development/European Commission, Joint Research Centre), 2008. Handbook on Constructing Composite Indicators: Methodology and User Guide. OECD, Paris.

Ostlaender, N., Bailly-Salins, T., Hardy, M., Perego, A., Friis-Christensen, A., Dalla Costa, S., 2015. Describing models in context – A step towards enhanced transparency of scientific processes underpinning policy making. International Journal of Spatial Data Infrastructures Research 10, 27–54. https://doi.org/10.2902/1725-0463.2015.10.art2.

Pisoni, E., Albrecht, D., Mara, T.A., Rosati, R., Tarantola, S., Thunis, P., 2018. Application of Uncertainty and Sensitivity Analysis to the Air Quality SHERPA Modelling Tool, vol. 183. Elsevier - Atmospheric Environment, pp. 84–93. https://doi.org/10.1016/j.atmosenv.2018.04.006.

Poel, M., Schroeder, R., Treperman, J., Rubinstein, M., Meyer, E., Mahieu, B., Scholten, C., Svetachova, M., 2015. Data for Policy: A Study of Big Data and Other Innovative Data-Driven Approaches for Evidence-Informed Policymaking — Report about the State-of-the-Art. Technopolis Group, Oxford Internet Institute and Centre for European Policy Studies. https://ofti.org/wp-content/uploads/2015/05/dataforpolicy.pdf.

Roy, B., 1996. Multicriteria Methodology for Decision Analysis. Kluwer, Dordrecht.

Saisana, M., Saltelli, A., Tarantola, S., 2005. Uncertainty and sensitivity analysis techniques as tools for the analysis and validation of composite indicators. Journal of the Royal Statistical Society A 168 (2), 307–323.

Saltelli, A., Ratto, M., Andres, T., Campolongo, F., Cariboni, J., Gatelli, D., Saisana, M., Tarantola, S., 2008. Global Sensitivity Analysis. John Wiley & Sons, The Primer, England.

Saltelli, A., van der Sluijs, J., Guimarães Pereira, Â., Funtowiz, S.O., 2013. What do I make of your Latinorum? Sensitivity auditing of mathematical modelling. International Journal of Foresight and Innovation Policy 9 (2/3/4), 213–234.

Sen, A., 2009. The Idea of Justice. The Belknap Press of Harvard University Press, Cambridge, Massachusetts.

Silberzahn, R., et al., 2018. Many analysts, one data set: making transparent how variations in analytic choices affect results. Advances in Methods and Practices in Psychological Science 1 (3), 337–356.

Chapter 19

Agrawal, A., Cockburn, I., Galasso, A., Oettl, A., 2011. Why are Some Regions More Innovative than Others? The Role of Firm Size Diversity. NBER Working Paper, No. 17793.

Committee of the Regions, 2017a. Plenary Session XX of the Committee of the Regions. Markku Markkula's intervention, Brussels.

Committee of the Regions, 2017b. Next Steps for a Sustainable European Future – European Action for Sustainability. Brussels.

Committee of the Regions, 2018. Territorial Analysis of the Country-specific Recommendations for 2018. Brussels.

Department of Economy, Science and Innovation of Flanders, 2014. The Strategic Policy Framework for Smart Specialisation in Flanders. Policy Note. Rev. 12/2014.

European Commission, 2012. Guide to Research and Innovation Strategies for Smart Specialisation (RIS3). Brussels.

European Commission, 2015. Better Regulation Guidelines. SWD(2015) 111 final. Brussels.

European Commission, 2017a. Practical Handbook for Regional Authorities. Brussels.

European Commission, 2017b. RIS3 in Practice – Implementation Examples – Good Governance. http://s3platform.jrc.ec.europa.eu/documents/20182/173082/2-RIS3+In+practice-Good-Governance.pdf/1e07a48f-9214-4714-8aa3-219e8ec98065. [Accessed 5 May 2020].

European Commission, 2019. Reflection Paper towards a Sustainable Europe by 2030. COM/2019/22 final. Brussels.

Eurostat, 2017. Regions and Cities Illustrated (RCI). https://ec.europa.eu/eurostat/cache/RCI/#?vis=nuts2.scitech&lang=en. [Accessed 5 May 2020].

Eurostat website. Nomenclature of Territorial Units for Statistics – Background. http://ec.europa.eu/eurostat/web/nuts/background. [Accessed on 5 May 2020].

Foray, D., 2015. Smart Specialisation - Opportunities and Challenges for Regional Innovation Policy. Regional Studies Association, Routledge.

Fraunhofer, I.S.I., 2013. Smart Specialisation Approaches: A New Policy Paradigm on its Way from Concept to Practice. Karlsruhe.

Gianelle, C., Kyriakou, D., Cohen, C., Przeor, M., 2016. Implementing Smart Specialisation: A Handbook. European Commission, Brussels.

Hausmann, R., Rodrik, D., 2003. Economic development as self-discovery. Journal of Development Economics 72 (2 December), 603–633.

Henderson, R., Cockburn, I., 1996. Scale, scope and spillovers: the determinants of research productivity in drug discovery. The RAND Journal of Economics 27 (1), 32–59.

Martínez-López, D., Palazuelos Martínez, M., 2019. Breaking with the past in smart specialisation: a new model of selection of business stakeholders within the entrepreneurial process of discovery. Springer Journal of Knowledge Economy 10 (4), 1643–1656.

OECD, 2009. Regions Matter – Economic Recovery, Innovation and Sustainable Growth. Paris.

OECD, 2018. Multi-level Governance, Decentralisation, Subnational Finance and Investment. OECD Regional Development Policy Committee (2017–2018).

Periañez, I., Kyriakou, D., Palazuelos Martínez, M., 2015. Strengthening decision-making capacity through Stakeholder's engagement in smart specialisation. In: Jucevičius, R., Bruneckienė, J., von Carlsburg, G. (Eds.), International Practices in Smart Development. Peter Lang, Brussels, Oxford, pp. 42–60.

Rodríguez-Pose, A., 2018. The revenge of the places that don't matter (and what to do about it). Cambridge Journal of Regions, Economy and Society 11 (1), 189–209.

Rodrik, D., 2004. Industrial Policy for the Twenty-first Century. CEPR Discussion Paper Series, No. 4767.

Smart Specialisation Platform, 2018. Smart Stories. http://s3platform.jrc.ec.europa.eu/-/how-the-project-s3-4alpclusters-supports-the-implementation-of-s3-?inheritRedirect=true. [Accessed 5 May 2020].

Tomaney, J., 2010. Place-based Approaches to Regional Development: Global Trends and Australian Implications. Australian Business Foundation.

Trajtenberg, M., 2002. Government support for commercial R&D: lessons from the Israeli experience. In: Jaffe, A., Lerner, J., Stern, S. (Eds.), Innovation Policy and the Economy, vol. 2. NBER Books, National Bureau of Economic Research.

United Nations, Sustainable Development Knowledge Platform, 2018. Thematic Review: Implementing the SDGs: Lessons from the Regions.

Index